Politics of
Sino-Indian Confrontation

Books by the same author

Indian Communism: Split Within a Split (Vikas, 1969)
Maoism in India (Vikas, 1971)

POLITICS OF SINO-INDIAN CONFRONTATION

MOHAN RAM

WITHDRAWN

VIKAS PUBLISHING HOUSE PVT LTD
Delhi   Bombay   Bangalore
Kanpur   London

VIKAS PUBLISHING HOUSE PVT LTD
5 Daryaganj, Ansari Road, Delhi-110006
Savoy Chambers, 5 Wallace Street, Bombay-400001
10 First Main Road, Gandhi Nagar, Bangalore-560009
80 Canning Road, Kanpur-208001
17/19 High Street, Harlesden, London N W 10

© Mohan Ram, 1973

SBN 7069 0266 1

PRINTED IN INDIA
By Delhi Press, Jhandewalan Extension, Rani Jhansi Road,
New Delhi, 110055, and Published by Mrs Sharda Chawla,
Vikas Publishing House, 5 Daryaganj, Ansari Road, Delhi-110006

Preface

The Sino-Indian border dispute has been in the deep freeze and the two Asian neighbours in continuous confrontation since their border war in 1962.

China's diplomatic offensive, on the basis of its reactivated foreign policy after the Cultural Revolution, has made little difference to this confrontation which is largely a function of the wider Sino-Soviet ideological conflict that split the international communist movement wide open a decade ago.

India has been central to the ideological conflict because it had become the converging point of Soviet and United States interests with the decline of the cold war and the beginning of the detente. India was drawn into the vortex of the big power politics to contain China through an Asian confrontation. As a result, India lost its leverage vis-a-vis the big powers and its confrontation with China increased its dependence on them.

After what looked like signs of a coming thaw in Sino-Indian relations (in 1970), two developments would appear to have set the clock back: China's attitude to the Bangla Desh crisis, and the treaty India signed with Soviet Union in August 1971, amidst the crisis. Both these developments are directly relevant to the Sino-Soviet ideological conflict and to Sino-Indian relations.

Ideology, and India as a factor in the Sino-Soviet ideological conflict, and their interaction on Sino-Indian relations is the focus of this study, which by no means can claim to be complete or comprehensive. This study has little to do with the merits of the Sino-Indian border dispute. And it is least interested in establishing the proximate responsibility for the 1962 border war or for India's military debacle in it.

It does not claim to make any startling disclosures based on "inside dope" about the conduct of India's military operations in the war, or seek to find scapegoats or whitewash tarnished reputations. There are enough books obsessed with these pet themes but hardly any so far on the ideological origins of the conflict and the military confrontation that climaxed it.

Almost all the books on this subject by Indian authors have been content to end with the 1962 war. The decade of confrontation that followed the war, the distortion of India's priorities it caused, and the real price of 1962 have not been assessed.

This study, besides attempting an ideological interpretation of the confrontation, seeks to examine its impact on India's proclaimed policies which make it, in the Soviet view, the very model of a country engaged in peaceful transition to socialism via the national democratic state— a formulation of Khrushchevian revisionism Peking never accepted. It examines the role of the big powers in the border dispute and the conflict, beginning with the collapse of India's China policy in 1959 with the Lama revolt in Tibet.

Ten years after the border war, one hears less of the jingoistic rhetoric in India about fighting China to a finish to recover lost territory. The Indian public opinion has gradually shifted in favour of China which is the largest and the most powerful Third World country today. There is a growing demand for an end to the frustrating confrontation which has deprived India of its leverage in world affairs. The border dispute and the territorial claims are the least important factors in the situation now because for over ten years the status quo has continued on the border and any suggestion that China has territorial designs on India lacks credibility.

This book seeks to put some of the issues in the confrontation in perspective, ten years after the border war.

The author has no pretension to scholarship or access to exclusive sources, which is the "in" thing with the New Delhi press corps. Nevertheless, this is the work of a journalist who has reported and analysed the confrontation as part of his New Delhi beat.

With every book he writes, an author's debt to his publisher and his friends grows. So it does with this one.

May 1973

MOHAN RAM

Contents

1/ The Issue — 1
2/ Bandung Phase — 20
3/ Beyond Maps : Ideology — 50
4/ Compulsive Drift — 83
5/ The Road to 1962 — 108
6/ The Price of 1962 — 141
7/ Continuing Deadlock — 177
8/ Elusive Detente — 213
   Bibliography — 234
   Index — 237

1 / The Issue

The Sino-Indian border dispute escalated into a military conflict in 1962 and has remained frozen since. It imposed on the ground a boundary line most acceptable to China and the status quo has continued for a decade now. According to India, China was already in occupation of 12,000 square miles of Indian-claimed territory in the Aksai-chin area of the Ladakh sector before the 1962 war, and extended the occupation to another 2,500 square miles in the same sector as a result of the war. There is no Indian-claimed territory under Chinese occupation in the other sectors (the central and NEFA sectors) along the 2,500-mile border.

Whatever the Chinese objectives in the border dispute during its different stages and at various points of time, there was little doubt that they had a vital stake in the Aksai-chin area through which runs a strategic highway linking two of its provinces—Tibet and Sinkiang. Chinese claims to areas on India's northeastern border (the NEFA sector) where India had all along insisted that the McMahon Line was the indisputable border, were perhaps advanced to strengthen their bargaining position over Aksai-chin in the western sector. As late as July 1961, when the dispute appeared to have gone past the point of return, the Secretary-General of India's External Affairs Ministry who visited Peking gathered the impression that the Chinese were prepared to give up their larger claims and to accept India's sovereignty of Kashmir in return for India's acceptance of their sovereignty of Aksai-chin.[1] Under pressure from Parliament, however, Prime Minister Nehru insisted that the Chinese pull out from Aksai-chin as the condition for negotiations. The Chinese were not prepared to do this until India also withdrew from the territory claimed by them.[2]

The dispute was deadlocked even before it was really negotiated and both the sides stepped up military preparations and this escalation culminated in the 1962 border war. China has been a satisfied power since 1962 and has made no attempt to alter the status quo since its unilateral cease-fire to end the war. There have been several minor incidents and incursions and even exchange of fire on one occasion but the border dispsute itself has remained frozen, not one square inch of territory changing hands after the cease-fire.

What in origin was beyond doubt a border dispute has come to acquire an ideological dimension at a later stage when it let itself be drawn into the vortex of the Sino-Soviet ideological dispute. Relevant to the ideological dispute were the divergent attitudes of the two communist giants to India's ruling class alliance. Exacerbation of Sino-Indian relations and the resultant military conflict in 1962 were in essence the function of the larger ideological conflict. The failure of the two Asian giants to settle their border dispute is a symptom of the ideological conflict and not its cause.

The border dispute is today the least important factor in Sino-Indian relations, which have remained at the lowest level for over a decade now. Yet the border dispute has become relevant again, this time as a factor in the Indo-Pakistan dispute over Kashmir which has been the cause of a twenty-five-year confrontation, often frustrating and resulting in three war till 1971. The first war in 1947-48 and the second in 1965 were both over Kashmir. The third, in 1971, was primarily over Bangladesh, the erstwhile eastern wing of Pakistan which wanted to secede, and the secessionists had India's support. But Pakistan aimed its military operations on India's western border in an attempt to find a military solution to the Kashmir issue. With the emergence of an independent Bangladesh in December 1971, a new power balance emerged in the subcontinent.

India has linked durable peace with Pakistan to a package solution of all the outstanding bilateral problems and Kashmir is indisputably the most important of them. Pakistan has been in occupation of over a third of Jammu and Kashmir (Kashmir for short) since the 1947-48 war, though in the Indian view Kashmir's accession to the Indian Union in 1947 was final, irrevocable, and complete. There has been a tenuous cease-fire line running across Kashmir since 1949, supervised by United Nations military observers. At the India-Pakistan summit conference held in Simla in June-July 1972 to normalise relations between the two countries after the December 1971 war, India raised the question of a durable boundary with Pakistan. Pending a final solution of the Kashmir question, both sides agreed to honour the actual line of control in Kashmir as on 17 December 1971, the day India's unilateral cease-fire offer to end the war came into force. It was also agreed at Simla that along the rest of the Indo-Pakistan border, troops of either country would withdraw from each other's territory occupied during the war.

India has all along maintained that Kashmir is beyond dispute. It took the Kashmir issue to the United Nations during the 1947-48 war to vacate Kashmir of Pakistani troops. Later the idea of a plebiscite to decide the future of Kashmir governed the situation for some time. After the United States-Pakistan military aid pact in 1954, India stopped all discussions on the plebiscite proposal and began asserting that the issue was beyond dispute.

But Pakistani occupation of over 32,000 square miles of Kashmir area is a reality India cannot overlook. India may not be averse to converting the cease-fire line in Kashmir, with a few adjustments aimed at its rationalisation, into a durable international boundary. This is on he assumption that the issue has already been settled on the ground and only a few minor adjustments are called for. It would mean formalisation of the de facto situation in Kashmir vis-a-vis Pakistan to end the dispute.[3]

CHINA, THE THIRD PARTY

Whatever the shape of the Indo-Pakistan settlement on Kashmir, it cannot be a complete solution of the Kashmir problem because a part of the Kashmir dispute is to be settled by India and China. The Aksai-chin area is in Ladakh which is a part of

Kashmir. China was not a party to the Kashmir dispute when India took it to the United Nations. But now according to India, 14,500 square miles of the Aksai-chin area in Kashmir is under Chinese occupation.

Apart from the dispute over the Aksai-chin area, China is a party to the Kashmir dispute in another sense. In 1963, China and Pakistan signed a boundary agreement after negotiations on China's border with the "contiguous areas the defence of which is under the control of Pakistan". This related to the Kashmir area under Pakistani occupation as a result of the 1947-48 war with India. The agreement was a temporary one, for it provided that after the settlement of the Kashmir dispute between India and Pakistan, "the sovereign authorities concerned" would reopen negotiations with China regarding the boundary of Kashmir so that a formal boundary treaty could replace the provisional agreement. India protested against the negotiations which resulted in the 1963 agreement and later against the agreement itself. In its view there could be no Sino-Pakistan border or a border dispute between them because the area bordering China under Pakistani occupation did not belong to Pakistan but to India. While vesting the agreement with a tentative quality, the Chinese scored a point here. The Chinese have been maintaining that the Karakoram range is the boundary between Sinkiang and Kashmir and their claim to Aksai-chin derives from this argument. By securing Pakistani recognition of their claim line, the Chinese were seeking to justify their claim to the Aksai-chin area, a large part of which was already in their possession. Thus China became a third party to the Kashmir issue between India and Pakistan in 1963. Unless India and Pakistan agree to a settlement of the Kashmir issue on the basis of the de facto situation (which means Pakistan retaining the part of Kashmir it occupies) China will be a party to the dispute. Yet, India's dispute with China over Aksai-chin (also a part of Kashmir) would remain.

The Indo-Pakistan dispute over Kashmir relates to territory and not the border, while India's dispute with China over Aksai-chin, at present, relates to the border and not to territory. Both

Pakistan and India claim the whole of Kashmir (which includes the Aksai-chin area on China's border). Its contention that Kashmir was beyond dispute notwithstanding, India has been obliged to discuss the question with Pakistan, first in 1962-63 at six rounds of ministerial talks, and later at the Simla summit in 1972.[4]

Though India has held Pakistani occupation of the Kashmir area as outright aggression, it is prepared to negotiate a "final settlement of the Jammu and Kashmir" question without insisting on Pakistani vacation of the occupied area. In contrast, India had consistently refused to negotiate the border dispute with China until the Indian-claimed area in Ladakh was vacated first. This was despite the admission by Prime Minister Jawaharlal Nehru more than once that the border here had not been clearly demarcated and in any case was not so firm or clear as the border in the NEFA sector where the McMahon Line constituted the indisputable boundary.

India's readiness to seek a final solution of the Kashmir question with Pakistan could also imply a similar readiness to seek a solution of the border dispute with China which in effect relates to 14,500 square miles of the Aksai-chin area already under Chinese occupation. In the past (1962-63) India was not averse to seeking a solution of the Kashmir issue through negotiations but its leadership lacked the political strength to face belligerent domestic opinion with any formula that might give Pakistan any part of Kashmir. It could not negotiate the border dispute with China for much the same reason. With the 1962 military debacle in the war with China began the erosion of the ruling party's strength. A strong current of anti-Congressism asserted itself in a string of by-elections early in 1963, following the 1962 war. It was not until 1971 (after the 1969 split in the ruling Congress party) that one-party dominance, which seemed to decline in 1967, returned giving Prime Minister Indira Gandhi and her party a policy cushion even her father Jawaharlal Nehru lacked in his last days.

The divergent Indian approaches to the dispute with Pakistan and China is proof that the Sino-Indian border dispute has less to do with territory (14,500 square miles, almost uninhabited, through which a strategic Chinese highway passes) than with other factors. If India could agree with Pakistan to settle all bilateral issues including Kashmir by peaceful means and on the basis of a commitment to peaceful co-existence (the Simla Agreement provides this) there is no convincing reason it should not approach the border dispute with China along the same lines. Unlike Pakistan, India and China had subscribed to the now famous Five Principles of peaceful co-existence as early as 1954. Now, by implication, Pakistan subscribes to these principle because the Simla Agreement incorporates them. China has reiterated its faith in these principles as late as February 1972 through the Nixon-Chou En-lai communique. Later, after the Simla Agreement, the New China News Agency (*Hsinhua*) and Premier Chou En-lai reacted swiftly to the "principles" underlying the Agreement. On 5 July 1972 (three days after the Simla Agreement), the Chou En-lai-Sirimao Bandaranaike communique in Peking encouraged resolution of conflicts through peaceful negotiations, which contextually could only mean bilateral negotiations.

IDEOLOGICAL ROOTS

But something more than the border dispute is impeding restoration of normal Sino-Indian relations. The issue can be understood only in relation to the ideological roots of the border dispute and the totality of Sino-Indian relations since 1949.

The emergence of a united and free China in 1949 was a resounding defeat for the post-Secnd World War imperialism in general and a setback to United States' designs in Asia. But the early years of relations between communist China and formally non-aligned India (which became free in 1947) were cold and barren until after India's foreign policy began asserting its independence of the West in a cold war situation. Not reconciled to the reality of a united, free China, United States fought the war in Korea and later tried to humiliate China by undertaking to protect Taiwan and flinging the SEATO in its face. The

Nehru-Chou En-lai declaration of the Five Principles of peaceful co-existence (*Panch Shila* as the Indian called it) in 1954 was to be Asia's challenge to imperialism in the days of the Dullesian pactomania. These principles were also to become the basis of Chine's relations with all the Third World nations. The Afro-Asian conference at Bandung in 1955 affirmed these principles, defining a new form of neutralism designed to give the Third World countries freedom of action in a cold war world. The Five Principles and the Bandung conference marked a clear shift in the Chinese foreign policy. China had reappraised its dependence on the Soviet Union and begun to identify itself with the Third World, emerging as a non-aligned power and ceasing to be a member of the Soviet-led bloc in the cold war. China wanted to create a zone of peace at the height of the cold war but Taiwan remained for it an immediate zone of shame. Shortly thereafter United States intervened in the Vietnam war, menacing China's security.

China's peace offensive during the Bandung phase (1954-58) aimed at enlisting the non-aligned, newly free nations against imperialism. This implied recognition of the anti-imperialist potential of the national bourgeoisie in these countries. Sino-Indian relations recorded its peak during this phase. Soviet Union was alarmed at the Chinese peace offensive and launched a drive to influence the non-aligned world. It was seeking a detente with United States and in the process assigned a new role for the national bourgeoisie in countries of the peace zone. In the process it revised the fundamental of Marxism-Leninism and innovated the thesis of peaceful co-existence of two world systems. As a corollary to this thesis, it developed the theory of peaceful transition to socialism in the newly-free countries. Socialism was to be achieved through a transitional phase described as "national democracy" under the hegemony of the national bourgeoisie in these countries, which deserved socialist diplomatic and economic support. In the Soviet view, the alternative to peaceful co-existence was a nuclear war while to the Chinese it was just war. The Soviet leadership was not enthusiastic even about local wars and revolutionary wars lest they forced confrontation with United States. The premium was on a detente with United States. Khrushchev went to meet Eisenhower at Camp David and the logical culmination of this phase was the Soviet capitulation in the Cuban missile crisis in 1962.

By 1959 (after the Lama revolt in Tibet on India's borders) China was convinced that the national bourgeoisie of the newly-free countries was no longer capable of any useful anti-imperialist role. This reassessment followed the Tibet revolt, to which the Indian bourgeoisie's attitude was in the least bellicose. The new Chinese assessment held that since capitalism was weak in these newly-free countries, their national bourgeoisie was coming to terms with imperialism in their anxiety to get aid from both the world camps. Thus Sino-Soviet differences over the peaceful co-existence thesis, the peaceful transition to socialism theory, and the character of the national bourgeoisie in the newly-free countries found expression in their divergent attitudes to India. The Soviet leadership had made India the model of a peace zone country capable of peaceful transition to socialism. India began getting massive Soviet economic aid from 1955 on while aid to China was becoming sparse and niggardly. The attitude to India was becoming one of the issues in the Sino-Soviet ideological dispute. Sino-Indian relations deteriorated almost in proportion to the improvement in Soviet-Indian relations. This, indeed, had its impact on the Sino-Indian border dispute giving it an ideological dimension.

With Nikita Khrushchev's quest for a detente, Soviet and United States interests began converging on India in the last 1950s. Knowledge of Sino-Soviet differences (which had not reached the stage of open disputation yet) and of the super-power readiness to back India hardened Nehru's attitude to the border dispute. According to an authoritative account there were two schools of thought in India at this stage. One believed that a firm stand against China would have the support of both Soviet Union and United States, and China would not risk a war. The other thought China was quite capable of taking the risk at some future opportunity.[5] The Soviet attitude to the border dispute in turn complicated the larger Sino-Soviet ideological dispute. Thus after a point the Sino-Indian border dispute leading to a military conflict in 1962 and the Sino-Soviet border dispute which became public early in 1963, were the function of the ideological dispute.

The 1962 border war not only underlined the debacle of India's China policy but reduced its non-alignment into double alignment when it accepted military aid from both the camps. Neither camp had serious objection to India getting military aid from the other and this convergence was a highpoint of the super power detente. India's growing dependence on the super powers distorted its domestic priorities and diluted its basic policies.

With the detente (underlined by the Soviet capitulation on Cuba and the support of both super powers to India) the ideological dispute sharpened. The alternative general line for the world communist movement proposed by the Chinese party in 1963 escalated the dispute to a new level. It was a collision of two conflicting attitudes to the role of the national liberation movements when Vietnam had become the focal point of the contradictions of the new epoch. To Soviet Union, the contradiction between the socialist camp and the imperialist camp was about the only global contradiction while the Chinese identified the one between the oppressed nations and imperialism as the foremost contradiction.

Early in 1965, when United States escalated the Vietnam conflict, China was indeed worried about the chances of a direct war with United States or a wider Indo-China war that would necessitate direct involvement. The summer of 1965 witnessed the full development of China's approaches to the first intermediate zone of the Third World. Its aim was to have the Afro-Asian conference[6] convened without Soviet participation, around the theme of unity against United States imperialism. This was the beginning of the Chinese strategy for the Third World aimed against both the super powers.

On 17 April, Soviet Union offered China limited military co-operation for united action in Vietnam[7] but the Chinese rejected it on 14 July because they saw in it a ruse for a rapprochement on Soviet terms. In autumn 1965 China and United States were dangerously close to war because 50,000 Peoples Liberation Army regulars had gone to North Vietnam to proclaim the Chinese resolve to enter the war directly if United States escalated it beyond a point.

Amidst the intense foreign policy debate in Peking (on whether to opt for more militant action in Vietnam or to seek a rapprochement with United States), Lin Piao spelt out his famous strategy of People's War, based on guerilla tactics.[8] Lin's strategy was based on an application of the 1963 alternative Chinese general line to the Third World reality. The emphasis was on Third World support to the Vietnamese struggle to defeat United States. The main task was the elimination of all imperialism and colonialism and the completion of national liberation struggles. United States imperialism was described as the most ferocious enemy of the peoples of the Third World and the world as a whole. Soviet Union was its accomplice because it was striving to "undermine the solidarity and the revolutionary cause" of the Afro-Asian people and had placed itself in antagonism with them and the people of the world.

Before the Lin Piao line triumphed in the Peking foreign policy debate, the earlier Chinese Third World strategy was in shambles. The Algiers Afro-Asian conference was a non-starter and there were counter-revolutionary coups in other Afro-Asian countries, notably Indonesia, resulting in the massacre of its powerful communist party. United States had stepped up the Vietnam war inducting more and more ground forces. The Chinese thought the centre of gravity of United States global strategy had shifted to East Asia because its detente with Soviet Union made diversion of some of its forces to the East possible. Alongside, Soviet-Japanese relations were also warming up. The Chinese saw a qualitative change in the world revolutionary situation. Even United States, with Soviet help, was attempting an anti-China *cordon sanitaire* and to stamp out the Asian people's struggles, particularly in Vietnam, and to expand the conflict to the other Indo-China countries.

The Lin Piao line was implemented in June-July 1967 when

China called for armed revolutions in India, Burma and Indonesia and stepped up support to revolutionary movements in the Third World. By transferring the struggle against imperialism to the Third World, the Chinese were challenging anew, on a higher plane, the Soviet ideological positions on key issues like peaceful co-existence, peaceful competition and peaceful transition to socialism.

The Cultural Revolution phase (1966-68) found China's foreign policy at a low ebb. The Czechoslovak developments late in 1968 sharpened the Sino-Soviet ideological conflict further. China branded Soviet Union a social imperialist power. Then came the confrontation on the Sino-Soviet border climaxed by the Ussuri clashes early in 1969. The 9th congress of the Communist Party of China in April signalled the end of the cultural revolution, permitting the leadership to give serious thought to foreign policy matters after a three-year interregnum. Two major factors shaped the new thinking: the potential danger from "social imperialism" and the signs of readiness of several Western countries to have normal relations with China. China launched a peace offensive on the basis of the Five Principles. The Soviet leadership tried to counter this by offering a collective security system for Asia.

The Chinese peace offensive aimed at a new front of the Third World in a world of the two super powers. The results indeed were spectacular. Henry Kissinger's dramatic visit to Peking in July 1971 to solicit an invitation for President Nixon was a diplomatic coup for China and underlined the resounding defeat of United States plans to quarantine China. This triumph was followed by China entering the United Nations with the help of a massive Third World vote.

At this stage, Pakistan was facing disintegration as its eastern wing witnessed an upheaval on the secessionist demand of its Bengali-speaking people. United States discovered that Pakistan, which had been receiving military aid from it as part of a plan to contain communism in Asia, was China's closest non-communist ally. For quite some time Pakistan had been manoeuvring between China and United States amidst deterioration of Sino-

Soviet and Sino-Indian relations. The 1965 Sino-Pakistan war was the epitome of the Dullesian doctrine of getting Asians to fight Asians in action. When the war broke out United States decided to ban the sale of lethal military ware to both Pakistan and India. Pakistan turned to China for military aid and Soviet Union made this development the pretext for reviving the frozen arms race in the subcontinent. This was part of the new Soviet policy for South Asia.

INDIA'S WEAKNESS

India had been drawn into the super power game of containing China and in the bargain its non-alignment had lapsed into double alignment. In the early years India had countered United States pressures by seeking Soviet economic aid and later by using this aid as a lever to secure more Western aid. With permanent tension along its borders with Pakistan and China, India began depending on both the super powers, after the 1962 war with China. In the wake of the 1965 war with Pakistan, the distortion of India's priorities and basic policies became all the more grotesque. Economic dependence on both the camps increased. Foreign aid had accounted for a fifth of India's total investment in development during the first three Five Year Plans (1950-51 to 1965-66). Yet the Fourth Plan remained unimplemented for over four years due to aid uncertainty and serious economic crises.

The Soviet decision in mid-1968 to give Pakistan military hardware (when the 1965 United States embargo was still on) ignoring India's protests, and United States overtures to China for a rapprochement[9] underlined India's helplessness vis a-vis the super powers. India's continuing confrontation with China and Pakistan had increased its aid dependence and curtailed the manoeuvrability of its foreign policy. A chance of regaining the manoeuvrability lay in ending the confrontation with one of the neighbours.

Significantly, the first admission of the loss of India's foreign policy manoeuvrability came when Soviet arms aid to Pakistan became known and India's protests were ignored. In mid-1968, Prime Minister Indira Gandhi hinted at a more flexible foreign policy and on 1 January 1969 indicated readiness for a dialogue with China. India's relations with Soviet Union were running into rough weather over arms to Pakistan and inordinate delays in the delivery of equipment for some of the vital Indian industrial projects. The Sino-Soviet border was hotting up and this was the time the Soviet leadership wanted India's support most. So early in 1969 came a series of Soviet gestures to stabilise India as an ally to confront China. India was promised more military supplies and quicker deliveries of delayed equipment for the projects. A treaty of friendship[10] was also offered at this stage, even before Leonid Brezhnev announced his security plan for Asia in mid-1969. The Soviet effort succeeded. When there were clashes along the Sino-Soviet border, India supported Soviet border claims without so much as examining the issue on merits. Soviet Union managed to stabilise relations with India which had struck a bad patch. The arms race, revived by Soviet sales to Pakistan, continued. When Pakistan received some arms, India protested and as a result was given more arms. Pakistan in turn protested and received more arms. There seemed to be a tacit super power understanding on maintaining an arms balance in the subcontinent, because to offset any large scale Soviet arms delivery to India, United States abetted surreptitious third country sale of hardware to Pakistan.

The political crisis in India which began with the split in the ruling Congress party in mid-1969 deprived Indira Gandhi of her Parliament majority. This delayed her decision on the treaty with Soviet Union, proposed early in 1969. It was not until after March 1971 that she could re-establish her majority in Parliament through a snap election. Anti-Congressism, which began snowballing in the wake of the 1962 military debacle, reached formidable proportions at the 1967 general elections at which the Congress party lost about half the States and managed to retain power at the federal level with a slender majority in Parliament.

Indira Gandhi had barely won her massive mandate in March

1971, leading her party to a landslide victory, when the autonomy demand of the Bengali-speaking eastern wing of Pakistan turned into a movement for secession, and a civil war. A few million refugees swarmed across the border into India during the early months of the civil war as Pakistani forces cracked down on the secessionists. India's support to the secessionist cause made another Indo-Pakistan war imminent.

United States, which had lifted its 1965 embargo on arms to Pakistan, reimposed it after the Pakistani crackdown of the Bangladesh secessionists in March 1971 but was surreptitiously shipping military hardware despite India's protests. In July, Henry Kissinger visited New Delhi ostensibly to hear India's case, and the Indian government tried to explain to him the serious implications of any United States arms deliveries to Pakistan. Kissinger went to Pakistan from India and then to Peking on his James Bond like mission.

China's ping-pong diplomacy earlier in the year[11] and the Kissinger mission leading to plans for Nixon's visit to Peking (which took place in February 1972) was proof that the two countries wanted to normalise their relations. Soviet Union had achieved rough parity with United States in the thermonuclear field and had cut down its force commitments in Europe. A million Soviet troops were massed on the border with China. When China responded to United States overtures, it was a tactical manoeuvre within the framework of its foreign policy aims. China wanted to ensure that the Soviet-United States detente in Europe when translated into an entente did not redue its own position into one of subordination to the super powers. In Asia, China aimed at eliminating the United States presence, checking Soviet influence, and preventing the super powers from building up Japan as a military power. In the Chinese view, United States was a disengaging power in Asia, and Soviet Union an expanding power.

CHINA'S NEW WORLD VIEW

Tactically China wanted greater flexibility in foreign policy to deal with the immediate threat it saw from Soviet Union. It wanted to divide and weaken all its opponents by rallying the Third World into a formidable front against them. It had a vital interest in re-entering the world scene in a big way and appealing directly to people even outside the Third World.

The new situation opened up for India options it never had before. Here was an opportunity to regain its leverage vis-a-vis both the super powers by seeking normalisation of relations with China and ending the confrontation. The bona fides of India's claim to be a Third World country lay in its attitude to the super powers.

In the post-cultural revolution phase official and political assessments in New Delhi of China's intentions ruled out a military conflict while the military assessments pointed to the contrary. Besides, China had launched a peace offensive, reviving the Bandung spirit in a changed strategic environment, to keep the super power influence out of the Third World.

However, the Kissinger mission to Peking seemed to have unnerved New Delhi. While formally welcoming the steps for normal Sino-United States relations, New Delhi saw in them a threat to India's interests. The prospect of a war with Pakistan in the near future over the Bangladesh issue and the bogey of Chinese intervention in such a war pushed New Delhi into a frame of action that betrayed loss of nerve. India rushed into a twenty-year treaty of peace, friendship and co-operation on 9 August 1971 in a frantic effort to foresall a war with Pakistan. The treaty provides for mutual consultations, in the event of a threat of aggression to either country, for steps to eliminate such a threat. But the treaty did not prevent a war because before the year was out the two countries had fought decisively and Pakistan emerged a defeated, truncated entity having lost its eastern wing.

China's attitude to the Bangladesh struggle (which India had backed from the beginning) was one of the factors prompting India to rush into a treaty with Soviet Union. The treaty had been mooted early in 1969 when Indo-Soviet relations were not too cordial after Soviet arms supplies to Pakistan had become known.

According to Indira Gandhi, China's attitude to India was undergoing a change in the direction of normal relations until the Bangladesh issue cropped up.[12] But in retrospect it is difficult to assess to what extent the signing of the treaty hardened China's (which no doubt thinks it was aimed at it) attitude to the Bangladesh issue. In the initial stages, China looked at the Bangladesh crisis as an internal affair of Pakistan. Even Soviet Union held this view for a long time after the treaty had been signed. China had been assailing Indian and Soviet attempts at intervention in Pakistan's domestic affairs.

India's treaty with Soviet Union (which in retrospect has been justified by Indian opinion on the plea that it prevented China's intervention in the 1971 war with Pakistan) hardened China's attitude to India, Soviet Union and the Bangladesh issue. China saw in the treaty the first step towards a Soviet-sponsored anti-China alliance in Asia. The treaty linked a Third World country with Soviet Union which had been confrnoting China militarily. This development and the Bangladesh crisis together interacted on a complex situation hindering normalisation of Sino-Indian relations. Yet China made a significant gesture inviting an Indian table tennis team to Peking for an Afro-Asian tournament in October-November 1971. China was even reassessing its attitude to the Bangladesh issue, and early in November, when Z. A. Bhutto went to Peking as President Yahya Khan's emissary, there was a student demonstration there to protest against repression in East Pakistan. China was about to declare support to the Bangladesh cause when, in its view, it took on the character of a direct Indo-Pakistani issue and became part of Soviet designs in the subcontinent.

When the Indo-Pakistan war began on 3 December 1971, India assumed that China would not directly intervene on Pakistan's side. India's mountain divisions on the borders with China were diverted for operations against Pakistani forces. It was subsequently revealed that Soviet Union, bound by treaty, assured India that any Chinese attack would be countered with a thrust in the remote Sinkiang province, China's nuclear and rocket test area.[13] China's failure to open a front against India during the war should have disappointed the Soviet leadership if only because it denied them the opportunity to destroy the Chinese nuclear and rocket installations.

From the beginning of the Bangladesh crisis, China had seen Soviet designs behind it. So the Indo-Pakistan war was also seen as part of the same design.[14]

When Nixon visited Peking in February 1972, the Chinese position vis-a-vis the Bangladesh issue was roughly this: (a) the territorial unity of a state must be inviolable from outside; (b) India therefore committed aggression against Pakistan by sending its troops into the eastern wing; (c) Pakistan and Bangladesh should resolve their problems bilaterally; (d) Indian troops must withdraw from Bangladesh, and (e) Indian "aggression" in Pakistan must be vacated and the old cease-fire line restored. China also continued to support the right of self-determination for the people of Kashmir.

In March 1972 India entered a treaty with Bangladesh on the lines of its treaty with Soviet Union earlier. Thereby, Bangladesh and Soviet Union were linked through India's treaties with them. This development no doubt added to Chinese apprehensions about Soviet designs in the subcontinent.

Indian troops pulled out of Bangladesh eventually. The Simla Agreement of 2 July 1972 provided for the return of each other's occupied territory and legitimisation of the new cease-fire line in Kashmir. The Simla Agreement provided the basis for normal Indo-Pakistan relations by eliminating third party intervention and the use of force to settle the issue. China was quick to welcome the outcome of the Simla summit. Chou En-lai, on 5 July, hailed the "principles" underlying the agreement. In his communique with Mrs Sirimao Bandaranaike of Ceylon, he urged resolution of conflicts through peaceful negotiations which contextually could only mean bilateral negotiations on the lines of the Indo-Pakistan negotiations, in contrast to the Soviet-sponsored negotiations at Tashkent after their 1965 war.

By implication, China is not averse to a solution of its border dispute with India on the basis of the very principles underlying the Simla Agreement between India and Pakistan. Normalisation of the situation and durable peace in the restructured subcontinent entails the elimination of the basic cause of the Indo-Pakistan conflict (the Kashmir issue), and normal Pakistan-Bangladesh and Sino-Indian relations. Normalisation of Indo-Pakistan and Pakistan-Bangladesh relations would dialectically make for normal Sino-Indian, Sino-Bangladesh relations. But the elimination of the super powers from the affairs of the subcontinent is the prerequisite for such normalisation. It is essentially a matter of restructuring relations between the countries of the subcontinent, which is part of the Third World, and China, which is the most powerful Third World country today.

Notes

[1] R.K. Nehru, "Relations with China and Pakistan," *Times of India*, Independence Day Supplement, 15 August 1972.

[2] The zig-zag border between India and China as demarcated in the two conflicting sets of maps was over 2,500 miles. At some places the borders coincided and at others were in wide variance. The disputed territory added up to about 50,000 square miles.

[3] Prime Minister Indira Gandhi indicated such a possibility. At her press conference in New Delhi on 12 July 1972 (after the Simla summit), when asked whether an attempt was made at Simla to secure Pakistani agreement to the Kashmir cease-fire line being made the international boundary, she said, "I am sure you know me well enough by now and that you know our point of view on this matter. But all these things are under discussion and I do not think any useful purpose will be served by talking about them here."

Later, asked if it was India's stand that part of Kashmir held by Pakistan was part of India, she said: "We do regard it as such."

Still later, she said, "Well, we will consider it" when asked, "If it is guaranteed by a situation in which the cease-fire line in Kashmir was recognised as the international border to assure that the dispute was eventually resolved and the subcontinent assured of durable peace, would you accept it?"

[4] The Simla Agreement, while providing for another summit of the Indian and Pakistani leaders, wanted in the meantime, a meeting of the representatives of the two sides "to discuss further the modalities and arrangements for the establishment of durable peace and normalisation of relations" including the question of "a final settlement of Jammu and Kashmir."

[5] R.K. Nehru, *op. cit.*

[6] It was scheduled to be held in Algiers but did not take place because of a coup in Algeria on the eve of the conference.

[7] Shortly after the offer had been made, Prime Minister Lal Bahadur Shastri visited Moscow (in May). The Chinese regarded Shastri an "anti-China cavaliar" and "Washington's pet". Therefore the warm Soviet welcome to Shastri must have added to the doubts about the bona fides of the offer.

[8] "Long Live the Victory of People's War," 2 September 1965.

[9] Following the 1968 United States elections, China agreed to resume the Warsaw talks between the ambassadors of the two countries which had been suspended for a long time.

[10] The treaty was eventually signed on 9 August 1971.

[11] A United States table tennis team visited China, signifying steps towards a rapprochement.

[12] Press Conference, New Delhi, 12 July 1972.

[13] Jack Anderson, "Clashback on Indo-Pakistan War," *The Statesman*, New Delhi, 13 August 1972.

[14] Chinese delegate Chen Chu said in the United Nations Third Committee during the war that "India had launched large-scale aggression against Pakistan, with the aim, *with another super power*, of hegemony to the Indian Ocean and the subcontinent", *The Times of India*, Delhi, 12 December 1971.

2 / Bandung Phase

The early years of Sino-Indian relations were lukewarm and uneventful. When India became independent in 1947 it sought the total withdrawal of European colonialism from South-East Asia, and in the process tried to secure its own interests as the region's largest country. The new China that emerged in 1949 was a factor the rest of Asia could not overlook. From the beginning India looked at new China as an expansionist neighbour and this conditioned its China policy. As Prime Minister Jawaharlal Nehru was to recall later:

Ever since the Chinese Revolution we naturally had to think of what the new China was likely to be. We realized that this revolution was going to be a big factor in Asia, in the whole world, in regard to us. We realized—we knew that amount of history—that *a strong China is normally an expansionist China. Throughout history that has been the case.* And we felt that the great push towards industrialization of that country, plus the amazing pace of its population increase, would together lead to a most dangerous situation. *Taken also with the fact of China's somewhat inherent tendency to be expansive when she is strong, we realized the danger to India.*[1]

Nevertheless, United States attempts in the early 1950s to dominate Asia in the name of containing communism forced India and China closer on the basis of the famous Five Principles of peaceful co-existence (*Panch Shila*). Sino-Indian amity touched its peak at the Afro-Asian Conference in Bandung (April 1955), meant to warn imperialists old and new to keep off Asia. However, shortly after Bandung, Soviet Union launched a drive for closer relations with Asian countries and Sino-Indian relations began deteriorating alongside developments that were to result in a super power detente in 1961. The similarity of United States and Soviet responses to the Sino-Indian border conflict in 1962 underlines the convergence of their interests in India, made possible by a thaw in the cold war.

Though India became free in August 1947, the interim government of undivided India (formed about a year earlier), had established diplomatic relations with the major powers. The early years of India's relations with Soviet Union and United States were largely barren because India's non-alignment was suspect with both. When the People's Republic of China was formally proclaimed on 1 October 1949, India was the second Asian country to recognise it, on 30 December.[2]

The emergence of a strong, united China was of immense significance to India which has a 2,000-mile border with Tibet which is a part of China. Nehru realised this when he told the Indian Parliament on 17 March 1950:

> Very great revolutionary changes have taken place in that country. Some people may approve of them, others may not. It is not a question of approving or disapproving; it is a question of recognising a major event in history; of appreciating it and dealing with it. When it was quite clear, about three months ago, that the new Chinese government, now in possession of practically the entire mainland of China, was a stable government and there was no force which was likely to supplant it, we offered recognition to this new government and suggested that we exchange diplomatic relations.

Communism, Nehru and United States

When India desired diplomatic relations with China, the communist world was still confused in its understanding of the meaning of India's independence. The initial Soviet confusion leading to an unfriendly attitude to India was to last until Stalin's last days. It was reflected in the zig-zags of the Indian communist movement. In fact, the origins of the 1964 split in the Communist Party of India can be traced back to its confusion over the nature of the Mountbatten Award which divided India to create Pakistan and transfer power.[3] The Mountbatten Award of 3 June 1947 was denounced by the party's general secretary, P. C. Joshi, as a "diabolical plan" to "balkanise" India because it involved not only the division of the country into two but excluded the numerous princely states from the settlement.[4] Almost simultaneously, a Soviet authority described the award as a manoeuvre to perpetuate British control of the subcontinent. But there was no forthright condemnation of the leadership for its compromise—this was also the CPI's line—suggesting that a large section of the Congress party under Nehru's leadership was still a progressive force.[5] The CPI leadership had not read this article when it went into a huddle to produce a resolution pledging unqualified support to Nehru's leadership and calling for a national front.[6] This was patently a non-class approach, on the assumption that the new government was not an imperialist government or its satellite and was beset with problems and threatened by an imperialist conspiracy. It thus sanctioned a united front from above with the government and the section in the Congress party behind Nehru.

According to a latter-day account, the first ideological trend to emerge in the CPI after independence had found expression in this resolution. The ideological basis of the resolution was the assumption that though imperialism was forced to make "important concessions to the urgent demand of the national liberation movement", complete independence was not a reality yet. Since imperialism and feudalism continued to be well-entrenched, the anti-imperialist front the CPI was out to build called for "unity of all—from [Mahatma] Gandhi to communists".[7]

Moscow's assessment of the Mountbatten Award did not tally with the CPI's. A Soviet article in July heralded cold war on Nehru government when the CPI had just decided on unqualified support to it. The article charged the Congress leadership —in its view the representative of the big bourgeoisie—with capitulating to reaction and imperialism, and with being content with its deal for formal independence alongside continued economic and military ties with the old imperialism. So the CPI should forge an anti-imperialist front from below drawing the wavering sections of the bourgeoisie into it.[8]

In any case, the CPI's June line was to change soon, coinciding with the famous Zhdanov line laid down at the first meeting of the Cominform in September. The earlier Zhukov line while indicating Soviet cold war against Nehru was not clear whether the Indian bourgeoisie was to be fought or not. The Zhdanov line did not clarify this point either.

Zhdanov's two-camp theory (of the world being divided into two hostile formations—the socialist camp and the imperialist camp) was essentially Europe-centred. The CPI, at its second congress in 1948 interpreted it to mean that in every country outside the socialist camp, including the colonies, the bourgeoisie and its servitors were lining up with the Anglo-United States imperialists in the fight against the forces of democracy and socialism. "This new correlation of forces expressed itself in the formation of two camps, which face each other in irreconcilable conflict."[9] The CPI, which had become an appendage of the Congress immediately after independence, was now in open war with the government set up through "fake" independence.

One could at best surmise that Moscow had no clear line yet for the newly free Asian countries, more particularly India, and the CPI had read the Zhdanov line all wrong to arrive at incorrect formulations. The CPI swung from its "right reformism" to "left sectarianism" and settled for the Titoite theory of the intertwining of the two stages of revolution (democratic and socialist) in India, assuming that the country was already capitalist. Opposition to this came from the communists of the Andhra region in south-central India who were leading a peasant partisan war in the Telengana districts since 1946. They had invoked Mao Tse-tung's *New Democracy*[10] in justification of their strategy of a two-stage revolution based on a four-class alliance. In fact, the first recorded debate on the legitimacy of Mao's theories as part of Marxism-Leninism took place in India, between the CPI's central leadership and the "peasant communists" of the Andhra region.[11]

The Zhdanov line as understood and implemented in South-east Asia resulted in abortive insurrections in India, Burma, Malaya, Indonesia and the Philippines. It was not until after the Chinese revolution had recorded its complete triumph and cold war had replaced class struggle on the Soviet agenda that the Cominform abandoned the Zhdanov line and thought of a broad peace front against United States. The Cominform intervened in 1950 to get the CPI to accept a strategy of two-stage revolution based on a four-class alliance. Later in 1951, the Cominform intervened again to force the CPI to abandon armed struggle in Telengana, settle for peaceful constitutionalism and support the Nehru government.[12]

Soviet disapproval of armed struggle in India stemmed from an anxiety to win over Nehru as a non-aligned ally as part of the peace front. The CPI was required to launch a "peace offensive" through a broad front. The Nehru government had thus secured qualified support from Moscow because its foreign policy did not always promote Anglo-United States interests. R. Palme Dutt, the British party leader through whom the Cominform intervened in CPI affairs, also saw the possibility of a Sino-Indian conflict even at this stage. "India is a country bordering China and at least sections of the Indian bourgeoisie realise that a war with China might mean their doom. They are also conscious of the fact that China is rapidly emerging as the leader of Asia." While there was a trend in Indian big business (led by Sardar Patel, regarded a rightist by the CPI) leaning heavily on Anglo-United States imperialism, Nehru represented the interests of the monopolist big bourgeoisie. This differentiation of the bourgeoisie explained Nehru's vacillation and it was for the communists to exploit his anti-imperialist stand on Korea, the bomb, etc.[13] The Cominform line wanted the CPI to regard United State imperialism the main enemy, soft-pedal the fight against continued British domination of India, and line up behind Nehru. The accent was to be on building a broad-based peace front against United States and the tasks of India's democratic revolution were to take the back seat.

Nehru, who had taken the initiative to solve the Korean problem and demanded stoppage of hydrogen bomb tests, found himself moving away from the dead-centre of rigid non-alignment towards the Soviet camp when United States designs in the subcontinent became known.

India's non-alignment was responsible for the hesitant start to its relations with United States. During Nehru's United States visit in 1949, the two countries appeared to have achieved a degree of identity on world affairs but Nehru was not prepared to commit himself to United States plans to contain communism. He went ahead to recognise new China shortly after it came into being, and actively mediated in the Korean war. Nevertheless, United States gave India substantial food aid to tide over the near-famine situation in 1951. Though President Truman's Point Four programme had been announced in January 1949, the India-United States Technical Co-operation Programme reflecting the Four Point approach was organised only in 1951.

India's mediatory role in the Korean war and later in Indo-China affairs collided with the Dullesian strategy of ideological polarisation and massive military containment of communism. Stalin died in March 1953 but not the United States obsession with the containment of communism.

The Indian subcontinent was strategic to the containment plan which envisaged a series of defence pacts and military bases to encircle Soviet Union and China. It is not very widely known that Nehru was sounded in 1953 about a defence pact by at least two visiting United States dignitaries—Vice-President Richard Nixon and Secretary of State John F. Dulles.[14] United States initially wanted a pact covering both India and Pakistan. Only after Nehru's refusal to discuss such an agreement did United States turn to Pakistan for a bilateral pact.

Nehru denounced the plan weeks before it was officially announced on 24 February 1954 and formalised in May 1954. He raised three issues with Pakistan Prime Minister Mohomed Ali in this connection. He said the pact would bring cold war to India's door step, sharply alter the military balance between

Pakistan and India, and bring back foreign domination of the subcontinent in a disguised form. Nehru thought Pakistan was acquiring armed strength against India, and when he denounced United States policy and declared that "the countries of Asia and certainly India do not accept this policy and do not propose to be dominated by any country", Soviet Premier Georgi Melankov hailed India's "great contribution to the cause of peace".[15]

To India, the immediate threat was not from Soviet Union or from China. It was from Pakistan. The pact not only aggravated Indo-Pakistan tensions but opened a tenuous phase in Indo-United States relations which was to last until 1958. Soviet reaction to the pact was sharp because Pakistan had earlier signed a defence pact with Turkey at United States instance. Pakistan was later to join the Baghdad Pact (which became the CENTO) and the SEATO grouping.

Nehru had taken up the United States-Pakistan pact with President Eisenhower and was assured in a letter on 24 February 1954 that Pakistan would be required to promise that United States military aid would not be used against India, and that United States would be coming to India's aid if Pakistan did not keep the promise. But the assurance meant little to India. Nehru pointed out in Parliament that when aggression took place in Kashmir (1947-48) nothing was done to thwart it. United States had not yet condemned it and "we are asked not to press this point in the interest of peace".

Eisenhower had offered similar arms aid to India. This left Nehru cold. "In making this suggestion the President has done less than justice to us or to himself. If we object to military aid being given to Pakistan, we would be hypocrites and unprincipled opportunists to accept such aid ourselves." Nehru referred to a statement by Walter Roberts, United States Under-Secretary of State ("the United States must dominate Asia for an indefinite period and pose a military threat to Communist China until it broke up internally"[16]) India's policy towards China was different from that of United States and "wholly opposed to each other", Nehru said.[17]

India's relations with Soviet Union warmed up even before

the United States-Pakistan pact was signed. The pact helped the dominant leadership of the CPI to hustle the following into supporting Nehru because Soviet foreign policy interests reuqired such support, especially after Pakistan's entry into the Baghdad and SEATO alliances. India also realised the need for closer relations with China, albeit in response to United States machinations.

Communists proclaimed the People's Republic of China on 1 October 1949 (Chiang Kai-shek fled to Taiwan on 7 December) and claimed restoration of China's complete independence and territorial integrity. It meant re-establishment of the Peking regime's authority over Tibet and Taiwan. But the unforeseen Korean war broke out on 25 June 1950 and brought down in three days President Truman's interdiction against any Chinese attack on Taiwan. Thus Taiwan became the immediate zone of shame for the regime in Peking. United States moved its Seventh Fleet into Taiwan straits pushing China into a tight corner.

When the war broke out, Soviet Union was boycotting the Security Council proceedings following the predictable defeat of its resolution on 13 January to secure China's admission to the United Nations. On 13 July India proposed a formula to save Soviet face: Soviet Union should return to the Council and the People's Republic of China admitted to it in the place of Taiwan as the best means of reaching a settlement on Korea. China showed little interest in the proposal and the Korean problem because it was more worried about United States decision to protect Taiwan. Soviet Union did return to the Council on 1 August though Taiwan continued as member. China took about three months to decide to induct volunteers in Korea. The Korean war introduced a new factor in India's relations with China. According to K. M. Panikkar, ambassador to Peking, India's major policy aim at this point was "to check the drift to war all over the world".[18] In autumn 1950, Panikkar's endeavour in Peking was to prevent a war between China and United States.

The Tibet Issue

When the Chinese decided to move troops into Tibet (in August 1950), India came face to face with a new reality—of having to give up its special interests and extra-territorial rights of the early twentieth century inherited from British rulers. India's ruling elite was not reconciled to China establishing its authority over Tibet or to India giving up its special interests. Nehru, however, thought that the British policy of claiming special interests in Tibet could not be maintained by India.[19] Nevertheless, India's response to the situation was far from clear, though Panikkar in an aide memoire on 26 August underscored to the Chinese government the desirability of a peaceful solution to the Tibet problem. He was assured that while China regarded Tibet its integral part it had no intention of using force to settle the issue. It wanted a negotiated settlement with Tibet's representatives.[20] When Chinese troops entered Tibet, India deplored the timing of the action (on the eve of the United Nations General Assembly decision on China's admission) because it would give "powerful support" to those who opposed China's entry into United Nations and its Security Council. Besides

> the international situation is so delicate, any move that is likely to be interpreted as a disturbance of peace may prejudice the position of China in the eyes of the world.[21]

India's interest, it was contended, was only to ensure China's entry into United Nations without avoidable delay and further "that if possible, a peaceful soltuion" to the Tibet issue, because military action might cause "unrest and disturbance on her own borders".[22]

However, New Delhi's note five days later must have raised doubts in Peking about India's bona fides. It expressed surprise and regret that China should have ordered the advance of its troops into Tibet especially when a Tibetan delegation had decided to proceed to Peking immediately for negotiations. There had been some delay in the departure of the delegation, partly

...owing to lack of knowledge on the part of the Tibetan delegation in dealing with *other countries* ...[23]

Further:

> Now that the *invasion* of Tibet has been ordered by the Chinese Government, peaceful negotiations can hardly be synchronized with it and there will naturally be fear on the part of the Tibetans that negotiations will be under duress.[24]

Reference to China in relation to Tibet as some "other" country and description of the Chinese troop advance into Tibet as "invasion" hardly squared with the Indian stand proclaimed in the earlier communication. These references in the note amounted to questioning China's sovereignty over Tibet. No wonder it invited a strong rebuff from Peking. On 30 October, China made clear that Tibet was part of China and therefore entirely a domestic problem brooking no foreign interference, that the Chinese army had to enter Tibet to "liberate the Tibetan people and *defend the frontiers of China*", and that the Tibetan delegation was delaying departure *"under outside instigation"*. It also assailed India's attempt to link up the Tibet issue with that of China's United Nations entry and alleged that India had been "affected by foreign influences hostile to China in Tibet" when it deplored the presence of Chinese troops in Tibet.[25]

India's reply, though strongly worded, bristled with contradictions. It was "amazed" at the insinuation that India was "affected by foreign influences" regarding its own stance and with regard to the Tibetan delegation and assured China that it had "no desire to interfere or to gain any advantage" and that it had sought peaceful settlement of the Tibet issue "adjusting the legitimate Tibetan claim to autonomy within the framework of Chinese suzerainty". Every step India had taken was to "check the drift to war", an effort often "misunderstood and criticised". India had persisted in this endeavour "regardless of the displeasure of great nations". India had no territorial ambitions in Tibet and did not seek any novel, privileged position for itself or its nationals. The note made these specific points:

(a) Tibet's autonomy was a fact "which the Chinese government were themselves willing to recognise and foster". An "adjustment" and "reconciliation" of the "legitimate Tibetan claim to autonomy within the framework of Chinese suzerainty should, therefore, be obtained by "peaceful means".

(b) India's concern was not an "unwarranted interference" in China's internal affairs but well-meant advice of a neighbour interested in solving a problem that concerned it.

(c) It was true India had "advised" the Tibetan government but since there was no justification for military operations or for imposing a solution, it was "no longer in a position to advise the Tibetan delegation to proceed to Peking unless the Chinese government think it fit to order their troops to halt their advance into Tibet".

(d) "At the same time *certain rights have grown out of usage and agreements* which are natural among neighbours with close cultural and commercial relations." These had found expression in the presence of the Indian government's agent in Lhasa, existence of trade agencies in Gynatse and Yatung, and maintenance of post and telegraph services on the route and "small military escort" to protect this trade route "sanctioned for over 40 years". India was "anxious that these establishments, which are to the mutual interest of India and Tibet, and do not detract in any way from Chinese suzerainty over Tibet", should continue.

(e) India favoured peaceful settlement of international disputes and the recent developments in Tibet had affected "our friendly relations".[26]

Thus India recognised Tibet as part of China but harped on extra-territorial rights which amounted to abridging China's suzerainty over Tibet. By admitting that it had advised the Tibetan government, India laid itself open to the charge that it had interfered in China's internal affairs. India and China had different concepts of "autonomy" just as they had different concepts of "suzerainty". To India suzerainty meant a little less than sovereignty; to China the two terms were synonyms.

China's reply on 16 November welcomed India's "renewed

declaration" that it had no political or territorial ambitions in "China's Tibet", just ignored India's claim to "certain rights" but hoped the "problems relating to Sino-Indian diplomatic, commercial and cultural relations with respect to Tibet may be solved properly through normal diplomatic channels". China had a point here. India was making China's domestic problem "an international dispute calculated to increase world tension". In an aide memoire on 26 August India had conceded Chinese sovereignty over Tibet, but now, when China actually exercised its sovereign rights, India was attempting to influence and obstruct the operation.

Thus Sino-Indian differences over Tibet flowed from divergent approaches to Tibet's autonomy. When the Indian Parliament debated the Tibet issue (6-7 December), Nehru gave no indication of these differences and merely said that he had insisted on Tibetan autonomy within Chinese suzerainty which he explained was not the same as sovereignty. Sino-Indian correspondence on China broke off with this. Two members of the Tibetan delegation on their way to Peking met officials of India's External Affairs Ministry in New Delhi. Ten days before the Sino-Tibetan agreement was signed in Peking in April 1951, Nehru told newsmen in New Delhi that "the Chinese attitude for the past quarter of a century or more had been that Tibet was an integral part of China". He implied that India was reconciled to the situation and would accept China's claim without reservation.

Nevertheless, this was not the whole story, as a latter-day account of what happened inside Nehru's government would reveal. B. N. Mullik, who retired as India's intelligence chief, has disclosed that some in the government seriously wanted a war with China over Tibet in 1950. At a meeting called by the Foreign Secretary (ambassador Panikkar and army chief K. M. Cariappa were present) the question as to what should be done to prevent the Chinese from pressing their claim to sovereignty by armed invasion was discussed.

Mullik who was also present at the meeting, records the discussion:

On the question of India sending troops to stop the Chinese, Panikkar explained that legally India's action would be indefensible. However, when the question was put to General Cariappa, he quite categorically said that he could not spare any troops or could spare no more than a battalion.... What the General said at that time was indeed very discouraging and disappointing because I had also favoured military intervention in Tibet to save it from China. But the General gave the correct and realistic position, the sum total of which was that India was in no position whatsoever at that time to intervene militarily in Tibet to prevent Chinese aggression.[27]

Impracticability of armed intervention rather than a desire for a peaceful solution of the Tibet issue seems to have deterred the belligerent sections of the Indian government from sending troops to a territory on which India declared it had no designs. Given adequate military strength, India might have embarked on a military campaign in Tibet in 1950. To this day, the same belligerency persists over Tibet, and India's elite circles have not ceased mourning the loss of a "buffer" between "democratic" India and communist China. Nehru was to be lambasted for recognising China without a quid pro quo, namely Chinese guarantee of Tibet's autonomy. These elites have not forgotten the rebuff the Nehru government invited on itself by proffering advice against Chinese troop movement into Tibet.[28]

With the Sino-Tibetan agreement in Peking in May 1951 began a new phase in Sino-Indian relations. The question of India's rights in Tibet remained. India's note of 31 October 1950 had referred to these rights but China's reply on 16 November had ignored them, merely saying "the problems relating to Sino-Indian dipomatic, commercial and cultural relations with respect to Tibet may be solved properly and to our mutual benefit through normal diplomatic channels". In February 1952, Panikkar raised this question and expressed India's readiness to arrive at a satisfactory settlement. Prime Minister Chou En-lai replied that there was "no difficulty in safeguarding the economic and cultural interests of India and Tibet". It was not until after 29

April 1954 (when the Sino-Indian "trade and intercourse" agreement on Tibet was signed in Peking) that the issue was settled.

Prelude to Panch Shila

Once Chinese sovereignty over Tibet became a reality India appeared to be making a conscious effort, within the framework of its non-aligned foreign policy, at developing an approach of amity with China. By mid-1950s, India had begun asserting independence of the Western camp and its foreign policy had acquired a few distinctive features: it was one of dynamic neutrality between the two blocs; friendship with all nations (especially Britain which had its contradictions with United States) and China; continued links with the British Commonwealth; an effort to extend the non-aligned zone, and general support to all struggles of colonial people for independence.

Despite the estrangement with China over Tibet, India was trying to avert a war between United States and China over Korea and was pleading for China's admission to United Nations and for withdrawal of United States protection to Taiwan.[29] Chinese volunteers entered Korea in mid-October and after initial successes, suffered heavy losses. But China rejected the United Nations truce proposal of 17 January 1951 and repeated its demand for withdrawal of all foreign troops from Korea, an end to United States protection to Taiwan, a rightful place for itself in United Nations, and an immediate conference of seven nations to work out a settlement for Korea. India was among the seven proposed by China, others besides itself being Soviet Union, Britain, United States, France and Egypt. United States, opposed to these demands, tried to get United Nations to brand China aggressor. India and Burma were the only non-communist countries which opposed the motion when the General Assembly voted it on 1 February.[30] Over two years later, when the Neutral Nations Repatriation Commission for Korean war prisoners was constituted in June 1953, India agreed to serve on it. India's relations with China had improved considerably. An unofficial goodwill delegation led by Pandit Sunderlal had visited China in 1951, followed by an official delegation led by Mrs Vijyalakshmi Pandit the next year. In May 1952, a rice agreement was signed between the two countries.

In December 1953, India initiated talks with China on its inteterests in Tibet. An eight-year agreement was signed four months later "to facilitate pilgrimage and travel" and to "promote trade and cultural intercourse between Tibet region of China and India". The agreement implied full recognition by India of China's sovereignty over Tibet. But opposition to this recognition came from the extreme right and the anti-communist social democrats of the country. Critics who saw a complete Indian surrender to China were not wanting in Parliament and outside. The pro-Jana Sangh weekly, *Organiser*, commenting on the Parliament debate (in the course of which Nehru had pleaded that they should accept an existing situation in Tibet) wondered "how the annexation of Tibet—over which Nehru had been unhappy to one stage ('Whom are they liberating? And from whom?')—has now been accepted by him as only the 'old position'." It charged the government was acquiescing to Chinese "aggression" which made it "the murder of the actual independence of Tibet".[31] Representatives of the social-democratic Praja Socialist Party which later was to spearhead a vicious anti-China campaign, called the recognition of China's authority over Tibet a "folly" and called the agreement the first international document to set a seal on the abolition of Tibetan autonomy.[32]

Nehru defending the agreement blasted the jingoist rhetoric of his critics in Parliament who had referred to the "melancholy chapter of Tibet". "What did any honourable member of this House expect us to do in regard to Tibet any time?" he asked, advising them to read the history of Tibet, China and British India. "Where do we come into the picture unless we want to assume the aggressive role of interfering with other countries?" he asked and provided the answer: "We do not go like Don Quixote with lance in hand against everything we dislike; we put up with these things because we would be, without making any difference, only getting into trouble."[33]

Nehru was reconciled to the new situation but not his critics who were to resume the attack five years later. He had to be more forthright in 1959:

> All kinds of extra-territorial privileges were imposed on Tibet because Tibet was weak and there was the British empire. With some variations, we inherited these when India became independent. Regardless of what happened in Tibet or China or anywhere, we could not according to our own policy, maintain our forces in a foreign country, even if there had been no change in Tibet.... Apparently, some people seem to imagine that we have surrendered some privileges in Tibet. The privileges we surrendered were privileges we do not seek to have in any other country in the world, Tibet or any other.[34]

And again:

> They were sitting in Tibet. Our telling them that we did not recognize it would mean nothing.... The result would have been that they would have achieved their dominance over Tibet completely and the only thing is that we should have quarelled with them and we would have come near breaking point with them....[35]

The Sino-Indian agreement on Tibet ended the second phase in the relations between the two neighbours. With it began what later came to be known as the Bandung phase. This was the direct result of the new elan Nehru's non-alignment had discovered for itself, the direct Indian response to United States attempt to dominate Asia. Even as the Korean war was on, United States had decided on an aggressive defence line, to stretch from Western Europe to Japan, to contain communism. United States first tried to organise local bilateral military arrangements to supplement the NATO. Later it decided to knock together multilateral military pacts that linked weak Asian nations with strong western powers and provided bases in the Asian mainland against the Eurasian heartland. The Indian subcontinent was strategic to the defence perimeter but India had rejected alignment with either of the power blocs and ruled out military alliances. Dulles could not countenance this. Early in 1953, United States had begun talks with Pakistan for a bilateral military alliance. Before this alliance was formalised in 1954, Pakistan had entered a military pact with Turkey persuaded by United States. Thus Turkey, Iran and Pakistan had become militarily interlinked. Finally, Pakistan was to provide the crucial link between the Baghdad pact (which became the CENTO) aimed against Soviet Union and SEATO (aimed against China).

United States involvement in Pakistan added to the tensions in the Indian subcontinent. Though Nehru continued to bracket imperialism and communism as threats of the same kind, India, trying to enlarge the non-aligned peace zone, moved closer to Soviet Union and China. Soviet Union was anxious to stabilise India as a non-aligned ally against United States. China, smarting under the humiliation of its inability to liberate Taiwan, found itself encircled menacingly by United States. This was the situation when the Geneva conference on Korea and Indo-China was convened. Chou's visit to New Delhi on his way back from Geneva in June 1954 launched the famous *Panch Shila* (Five Principles) as Asia's answer to United States designs in Asia. These principles were nothing new: they had already been listed in the Sino-Indian agreement on Tibet a few weeks earlier but had not yet been christened *Panch Shila*.[36] They were: mutual respect for each other's territorial integrity and sovereignty; mutual non-aggression; mutual non-interference in each other's affairs; equality and mutual benefit; and peaceful co-existence.

Shorn of the verbiage, the *Panch Shila* was little more than a reiteration of the principles of non-interference and peaceful co-existence. According to India, it was restatement in more specific terms of the principles embodied in the United Nations Charter. The third and fifth principles had appeared as early as October 1949 in a communique of the Central People's Government of the Republic of China and were subsequently described by a Chinese writer as a "guiding principle" of his country's foreign policy consistently pursued since October 1949. Not until after the Five Principles were reaffirmed by Nehru and Chou did they acquire any significance. In essence, it was a formula through which all nations could co-exist peacefully. As Chou told newsmen in New Delhi after signing the declaration:

> The rights of the people of each nation to national independence and self-determination must be respected. The people of each nation should have the right to choose their own state system and way of life, without interference from other nations. Revolution cannot be exported; at the same time, outside interference with the common will expressed by the people of any nation would not be permitted.

This was how China looked at *Panch Shila* in a tense world situation: the Korean armistice had been achieved by 1953 end and fighting in Indo-China had not been signed yet. China was still sought to be quarantined through the deployment of United States troops in Japan, Korea and Taiwan and the stationing of the Seventh Fleet in the Pacific. China had to break this encirclement by befriending one of the principal Asian countries which had shown an independent policy through its role in Geneva, especially its six point plan for an Indo-China settlement. Thus to China, *Panch Shila* was part of the diplomatic offensive it had launched at Geneva. Chou had talked of Asian unity at Geneva on 28 April 1954.

After the Nehru-Chou declaration in 1954, Indian used *Panch Shila* in declarations it made with several countries. So much so, on the eve of the Bandung conference, when Nehru tried to equate communism and anti-communism, an Indian communist leader joined issue with him pointing out that the essence of *Panch Shila* could be traced back to the 1949 World Peace Conference in Paris, and the fact that non-communist countries like India, Burma and Indonesia had accepted the same *Panch Shila* "is a triumph of the ideas for which the communist movement the world over has always fought".[37]

India's support to the Five Principles was motivated by a different set of considerations. The formula of peaceful co-existence originated in the context of India's strained relations with China over Tibet. A powerful China on the north was viewed with misgiving and apprehension by India. Minor military precautions were taken when Chinese forces moved into Tibet in 1950. But the prospect of a Sino-Indian military confrontation was forbidding to Nehru. India just could not afford to antagonise China though it could not support China in everything. This lesson was well learnt after the rebuff over Tibet. According to an Indian analyst, the five principles were meant "to soothe China's fears, allay her economic suspicions and convince her that in India she had a friend. On the other hand, it might draw China out of her embattled isolation, and by pledging her to non-interference and non-aggression, pin her down to a policy, and commit her, through her own solemn undertakings, to staying with her own boundaries".[38]

Nevertheless, the Five Principles were to become Asia's counter-thrust to the Dullesian doctrine of making Asians fight Asians. These principles were to help enlarge the non-aligned zone and counter alignments and military groupings. Both India and China wanted colonialism eliminated from South-East Asia and the return of Western domination of the region forestalled. India was opposing the SEATO and openly challenging the Western view that communist China was a threat to the region. China, on its part, responded to India's role by pledging not to export revolution and not interfere in the affairs of other countries. At the end of his Rangoon visit in June 1954, Chou declared in a joint communique with U Nu:

> ... the people of each nation should have the right to choose his own state system and way of life without interference from other nations. Revolution cannot be exported; at the same time outside interference with the common will expressed by the people of any nation should not be permitted.[39]

The Five Principles were relevant to Asia in another sense. United States flung the SEATO in Asia's face in angry response to the Geneva agreement on Indo-China which formalised the existence of North Vietnam as a communist state. United States refused to be a party to it. India thought CENTO and SEATO threatened it to the extent Pakistan was a member of these alliances. The CENTO was directly aimed against Soviet Union and the SEATO against China. At this juncture, China was closer to India than Soviet Union was and therefore the SEATO was more obnoxious to India than the CENTO. The pacts divided Asia into aligned and non-aligned countries and the Five Principles became the rallying cry of anti-imperialist Asia.

BANDUNG: CHALLENGE TO UNITED STATES

To India, with the declaration of the Five Principles in June 1954 began a new awareness of the significance of friendly relations with China. Nehru saw "a certain historic change in the relationships of forces in Asia" and proclaimed India's readiness for similar declarations with other countries. His response to those who doubted the earnestness of such declarations was simple: even if they were not sincerely meant

> the result would be to create a force in favour of peace and non-interference...peace as well as security can best be maintained by efforts at collective peace and avoidance of war. If this cannot be done in the world as a whole, then an attempt should be made to have areas where such peace can be maintained. Gradually that area will spread....[40]

In the months that followed, Nehru's effort was in the direction of widening the area of non-alignment through an Asian pattern of collective peace as India's alternative to the collective security proposals of the West. When agreement on Indo-China was reached in July at Geneva, Nehru saw for it a "memorable place in history" because it provided "the alternative, or the deterrent, to what threatened to lead to World War III". The French were crediting Nehru with influencing Chou who in turn was believed to have softened Ho Chi-minh. To Nehru it perhaps meant widening of the peace area because the SEATO could not now be extended easily to cover the Indo-China countries though it was premature to say that because of the Geneva agreement these would not align with any group. If nothing else, the Geneva conference proved that communist and non-communist countries could negotiate to ease world tensions. An Indian journalist, Dr K. S. Shelvankar, reported from Geneva that "the conference was considered to have shown conclusively that China is not a puppet but a genuinely independent power, conscious of her strength and at the same time determined to work in closest harmony with the Soviet Union and other communist countries". More important:

> One factor that is emphasised in all comments is the close collaboration that has developed between India and China. This is taken as possibly marking a new stage in the evolution of relations between Europe and Asia.[41]

The next highpoint in Sino-Indian relations was Nehru's visit to China in October, preceded by the signing of a two-year trade agreement between the two countries. The Chinese party paper, *People's Daily*, hailed the visit as "a major event in the relations of Asian nations",[42] and Indian correspondents covering the tour reported the biggest welcome ever extended to a visiting leader.

There was speculation in New Delhi that Nehru had gone to Peking to obtain some guarantee or assurance of good behaviour by China and that doubts had arisen about the sincerity of China's professions. On return Nehru set all speculation to rest and gave his own assessment of the visit. One major difficulty in the world was "the prevalance of fear and reactions to that all-pervading fear" which created mounting tensions. Chinese leaders had assured him that they were "anxious" that "everything should be done to remove this fear and apprehension from men's minds". He recalled that there had been many crises "even during the year—in March and September—when war on a big scale appeared near" but fortunately they "passed without disaster".

The Geneva conference marked a turning point in post-war history. Unfortunately the Manila [SEATO] treaty came somewhat in the way of that new atmosphere which Geneva had started. Nevertheless there have been many indications in recent months of this improved world atmosphere for which credit must go to all the great powers.[43]

His visit had not only resulted in deeper understanding between India and China but probably had

> ... helped a little in easing the existing tensions in Indo-China and in South-east Asia. As such, it helped in the larger and vital problems of world peace.[44]

This was the strategic environment in which preparations began for the Afro-Asian conference in April 1955. The idea of this conference can be traced back to the April 1954 Colombo conference of five Asian powers.[45]

A few weeks before the Colombo meet, the French rout had begun in Dien Bien Phu inviting the threat of United States nuclear intervention. To ward this off Britain had to pay the price of agreeing in principle to the creation of SEATO. The Geneva conference began two days before the Colombo meeting, and seventeen days after it Pakistan and United States entered a military pact. Even as the Dullesian pactomania was gripping the region, India and China signed the agreement on Tibet the day after the Colombo meet.

In an intensely cold war situation, the Colombo conference could not achieve much. Anti-colonialism came into conflict with anti-communism. The five Prime Ministers met next in Bongor (Indonesia) in December to arrange the Bandung conference, largely on Indonesian initiative.

The months preceding the Bandung conference were an eventful period in Asia. The SEATO pact was formally signed in Manila in September 1954 and the Chinese resumed shelling the off-shore Quemoy and Matsu islands garrisoned by Taiwanese troops. United States retaliated by entering a mutual defence pact with Taiwan on 2 December. The crisis was escalating in early 1955 and Indonesia tried to call a meeting of the Colombo Five. But Soviet Union suggested that the matter be handled by the Five together with United States, United Kingdom, China and itself. This proposal achieved little but the situation eased for other reasons. In West Asia, Iraq and Turkey signed a military pact on 24 February and four days later Israeli troops raided the Gaza strip forcing Egypt closer to Soviet Union and to India. (Cold-shouldered by the West, President Nasser entered a massive arms deal with Soviet Union in September, provoking United States to withdraw aid to the Aswan Dam project. Nasser hit back nationalising the Suez Canal and this led to the Anglo-French-United States war against Egypt in October 1956).[46]

About this time, a major change was coming over Soviet policy towards India. On 8 February (when Melankov was ousted as Prime Minister) Foreign Minister Molotov announced his government's acceptance of the Five Principles, claimed that Soviet foreign policy had always been based on it and urged other countries to accept it.

In such a situation, the Bandung idea, mooted at Bongor, should have appealed to the Chinese. Only a temporary stability had been achieved with regard to the three major crisis areas on its periphery—an armistic agreement in Korea, truce in Indo-China, and a stalemate in Quemoy-Matsu.[47] It was in China's interest to utilise the lull to improve relations with Afro-Asian neutral countries.

In India, Nehru set the tone for Bandung with a policy speech in Parliament on 31 March. Countries meeting at Bandung had "different outlooks and differing approaches" but would discuss matters "in the context of co-existence". This was the spirit of *Panch Shila*, which was a challenge to the world, to which "each country will have to give a direct answer". Nehru was equating communism and anti-communism, both of which "interfered in other people's internal affairs". They were more concerned with racialism and colonialism. Military pacts like the SEATO and the Turkey-Pakistan alliance had a bearing on the new Indian policy.[48]

People's Daily welcomed Nehru's statement as "agreeing with the aspirations of the Asian peoples and peace-lovers in the rest of the world.... It was perfectly possible to strengthen solidarity and co-operation among the Asian and African peoples if they could carry into practice the Five Principles of co-existence without foreign intervention" and the conference "offers favourable opportunity for carrying forward this possibility".[49]

But the Indian communists, closer to Moscow than to Peking, seemed to have reservations about Nehru's approach because it had an anti-communist slant. Though Nehru's statement was hailed as a "great" speech which "obviously denounced the war moves of the imperialists" and rightly presented the *Panch Shila* as the challenge to the world, Nehru had struck a jarring note, the party journal wrote. Nehru had "just in passing fired a shot in the air and said, 'The charge is made—rightly, I say, sometimes—about communist interference in other countries'. This sentence has no relevance at all..." Editor Ramamurti entered a case-by-case argument to prove that interference came from "imperialist countries and not from communist countries". Rallying Asia against this bloc was an historic task for India. "Will Nehru concentrate on this historic task and cease raising nonexistent myths about communist interference?" he asked.[50]

Indian and Chinese policies were converging on *Panch Shila* (Five Principles) which was in the air during the seventeen days between Nehru's speech and the opening of the Bandung conference. Prince Nordom Sihanouk of Cambodia and Foreign Minister Pham Van Dong of North Vietnam who visited India affirmed faith in the Five Principles in their joint statements with the Indian side. But the question whether communist countries like China would strictly adhere to the principles of non-interference was being raised in several non-aligned capitals. The prospect of China participating in the Bandung conference could not have enthused them.

Before the conference began formally on 18 April, there was speculation that Nehru had gone prepared with certain suggestions on Taiwan (believed to have been discussed earlier in London by Krishna Menon and Sir Anthony Eden), that Menon, who was associated with the Geneva agreement, was holding preliminary discussions with representatives of Laos, Cambodia and North Vietnam, and that Menon in his three-hour meeting with Chou discussed the fears of the countries bordering China.

As soon as the conference began, anti-colonialism of the non-aligned participants collided with the anti-communism of the countries which had entered military blocs or agreements. Pakistan's Mohomed Ali joined issue on behalf of the aligned, countering the Nehru-Chou doctrine of the Five Principles of co-existence with his own seven principles which among other things attempted to justify Pakistan's membership of SEATO by demanding the right of collective or individual self-defence for all nations.

Chou's 19 April speech reaffirmed China's allegiance to the Five Principles and underlined his endeavour to "seek common ground and not create divergence". He was no doubt conciliatory and constructive. Despite Chou's moderation and reasonableness, the conference was running aground on the fifth day, sharp differences developing over issues of colonialism and world peace. The draft resolution on colonialism was deadlocked when some participants insisted that communism should be denounced as a new form of colonialism. The debate on world peace divided along predictable lines: some defending collective security and others favouring co-existence based on the Five Principles. An impassioned speech by Nehru deprecated the approach of the pro-West participants. Ceylon's Sir John Kotelawala tried to draw a red herring across the trail. He wanted from China two conditions before the question of co-existence could be discussed: China should ask all local communist parties in Asia and Africa to disband, and China should use the influence with Soviet Union to get the Cominform dissolved.

On the sixth day (23 April), the Nehru-Chou tandem seemed to have emerged as a force to be reckoned with. Both the leaders reiterated the need for co-existence and the futility of the arms race and military alliances. Nehru, however, equated communism and anti-communism (and the Cominform and the SEATO) once again. "Both are dangerous," and if co-existence was to be real, the Cominform and other similar organisations "which did not fit in with the pattern of peaceful approach must wind up". But a few hours later, Chou made a sensational announcement—China's willingness to negotiate with United States and to discuss relaxation of tension in the Far East "and especially in the Formosa [Taiwan] area". This overshadowed all the other developments of the day.

The conference ended on 24 April amidst jubilation and with a lengthy communique and a 10-point declaration which reflected a compromise between countries ideologically as far removed as China and Turkey. The declaration endorsed the Five Principles but added five new principles. In sum, at least two of the ten points were contradictory or almost contradictory. The additions were significant, and obviously to accommodate the aligned countries which had entered pacts or defence arrangements. The right of each nation to defend itself singly or collectively was conceded but subject to provisos: it should be in conformity with the United Nations Charter; the arrangements should not be used to serve Big Power interests, and the countries should abstain from acts or threats of aggression or use of force against territorial integrity or political independence of any country.

The final communique condemned colonialism in all its manifestations.[51]

Krishna Menon was to note several years later that Bandung was successful in the sense that it presented a front of Asian unity. It brought important gains for China: it could enter the Asian-African mainstream despite United States attempts to isolate it. Though a communist country (and the lone one at Bandung), it could secure acceptance as a non-aligned Asian power independent of Soviet Union. There were three groups of countries at Bandung: Turkey, Iraq, Pakistan, Thailand and the Philippines which were anti-communist (and by extension, anti-China); India, Burma and Indonesia which believed in peaceful co-existence with China because their main opposition was to racialism and colonialism and they were not belligerent in their anti-communism; and the third group of countries which were not clear about their position.

At Bandung Chou could sign with the Indonesian Prime Minister a treaty providing for overseas Chinese in Indonesia to give up their dual citizenship.[52] Chou could make contacts with Egypt's Nasser. Egypt recognised China the next year and Cairo became China's political beach-head to Middle East and Africa. Chou also made contacts with Pakistan's Mohomed Ali. Like other Asian countries which had entered United States-sponsored military blocs and pacts, Pakistan had no objective reason to be anti-China. Pakistan looked at its military alliance with United States as one aimed against India. Chou was quick to note this differentiation.

Bandung prevented an immediate war between China and United States over Taiwan. Partly as a result of Chou's offer of talks with United States, the tension over Taiwan was to ease soon and talks between representatives of the two countries began in Geneva. (At Bandung, Chou had also invited Menon to Peking to negotiate the release of United States pilots held prisoner in China.)

At Bandung China could demonstrate that it had developed diplomatic independence of Soviet Union. Between November 1955 and February 1956, Chou could visit eight Asian countries (North Vietnam, Cambodia, India, Burma, Pakistan, Afghanistan, Nepal and Ceylon) and launch a diplomatic offensive in the "Bandung spirit".

To India and Nehru, Bandung meant the enlargement of the Afro-Asian area of peace which included China which was not regarded a member of one of the cold war blocs but an independent, non-aligned Asian power. India thought it had succeeded in dissuading Cambodia and Laos from getting close to the SEATO and prevented the United States from winning them over. India also thought it had succeeded in containing Chinese and Vietnamese political influence in Indo-China. In the Indian view, Bandung was a vindication of the Five Principles and a rebuff to United States machinations in the region. Indian public opinion was encouraged to believe that Nehru was the real spirit at Bandung while in fact Chou had made a tremendous impression on all and had projected for himself the image of a most affable and reasonable man. The Indian press even paid left-handed compliments to Chou attributing his success at Bandung to Nehru's role in building Chou's image among the participants and chaperoning his debut in the international arena.

For nearly two years after the conference, the Bandung spirit permeated the foreign policies of India and China as well as their bilateral relations. A peace offensive was China's answer to the United States designs in Asia and India had a role in the broad Asian-African peace front against United States, which Soviet Union wanted to. The post-Bandung period witnessed the peak of Sino-Indian amity but this was to be a short-lived phase.

Notes

[1] *India's Foreign Policy: Selected Speeches of Prime Minister Jawaharlal Nehru, September 1946-April 1961*, New Delhi, Ministry of Information and Broadcasting, 1961, p. 369. Italics supplied.

[2] Soviet Union was the first country to recognise the new republic the day after its formal proclamation. Burma was the first Asian country to accord it recognition. By 1954, only six Asian countries—Burma, India, Indonesia, Pakistan, Ceylon and Afghanistan—had recognised China.

[3] For a detailed analysis see Mohan Ram, *Indian Communism: Split Within A Split*, New Delhi, Vikas, 1969, pp. 8-24.

[4] P. C. Joshi, "The Mountbatten Award," *People's Age*, 8 June 1947.

[5] A. Dyakov, "The New British Plan for India," *New Times*, Moscow, 13 June 1947.

[6] Central Committee of the CPI, "Statement of Policy," *People's Age*, 29 June 1947.

[7] E.M.S. Namboodiripad, *Note for the Programme of the CPI*, New Delhi, 1964.

[8] E.M. Zhukov, "The Indian Situation," Russian original in 1947; *On Colonial Question*, Bombay, People's Publishing House, 1948.

[9] *Political Thesis of the CPI*, Bombay 1948, pp. 75-76.

[10] Cf. Mohan Ram, *op.cit.*, pp. 24-25.

[11] *Ibid.*, pp. 24-32.

[12] This change came after a delegation of the CPI leaders visited Moscow clandestinely for consultations with Soviet leadership. It is possible that the Indian government connived at this visit because it knew that Soviet attitude

to India was changing and the CPI leadership might be persuaded in Moscow to give up armed struggle.

[13] "Palme Dutt Answers Questions on India," *Crossroads* weekly, Bombay, 19 January 1951.

[14] Russel Brines, *Indo-Pakistani Conflict*, London, Pall Mall, 1968, p. 120.

[15] *The Hindu*, 2 March 1954.

[16] Roberts said this before a sub-committee of the United States Congress on 26 January 1954.

[17] Lok Sabha, 1 March 1954.

[18] K.M. Panikkar, *In Two Chinas: Momoirs of a Diplomat*, London, Allen and Unwin, 1955, p. 102.

[19] *Ibid.*, p. 102.

[20] Narendra Goyal, *Prelude to India*, New Delhi, Cambridge Book and Stationery Store, 1964, p. 6.

[21] Memorandum from the Indian Ambassador, 21 October 1950.

[22] *Ibid.*

[23] Note from the Government of India to the Foreign Ministry of China, 26 October 1950, italics supplied.

[24] *Ibid.*, italics supplied.

[25] Reply of the People's Republic of China to the Memorandum and Note of the Government of India, 31 October 1950, italics supplied.

[26] Note from Government of India to the Foreign Minister of China, 31 October 1950, (all italics supplied). The Chinese source, in publishing the document, consistently used the term "sovereignty" wherever the Indian original had used "suzerainty".

[27] B.N. Mullik, *My Years With Nehru: the Chinese Betrayal*, New Delhi, Allied, 1971, pp. 80-81.

[28] In 1959, when the Lama revolt broke out in Tibet, the Indian press recalled the 1950 "rebuff". *Eg.*, *The Statesman*, 22 March 1959.

[29] On 2 October 1950, Chou En-lai in an interview to Panikkar thanked Nehru for his peace efforts and disclosed that China would intervene in the Korean war if Americans crossed 38th parallel.

[30] Nine neutral nations abstained from voting.

[31] *Organiser*, 24 May 1954.

[32] *Thought*, 29 May 1954.

[33] Lok Sabha, 30 September 1954.

[34] Lok Sabha, 30 March 1959.

[35] Rajya Sabha, 9 December 1959.

[36] T.N. Kaul, India's ambassador in Peking, is credited with formulating them.

[37] P. Ramamurti, "Will Panch Shila Be Asia's Challenge to Imperialists From Bandung Conference?" *New Age* weekly, 10 April 1955.

[38] G.H. Jansen, *Afro-Asia and Non-Alignment*, London, Faber and Faber, 1966, p. 131.

[39] *People's China* 16 July 1954.

[40] Nehru said this in a circular letter to Presidents of Pradesh Congress Committees annotating the Five Principles.

[41] *The Hindu*, 23 July 1954.
[42] Editorial on 19 October, 1954.
[43] Statement in Parliament, 22 November 1954.
[44] *Ibid.*
[45] Ceylon took the initiative. Others were: India, Pakistan, Burma and Indonesia.
[46] Nasser was introduced to Chou by Nehru at Bandung. Nasser sought Chou's help to get Soviet arms which were delivered through Czechoslovakia. This has been confirmed by Nasser's biographer. Cf. Mohomed Heikal, "Nasser: the Inside Story—2," *Blitz*, 8 January 1972.
[47] On 8 March, United States Secretary of State, Dulles, had threatened to use tactical nuclear weapons in the event of "open armed aggression" on these islands, and Soviet Union, preoccupied with Europe and busy negotiating the Warsaw pact, did not extend open support to China against the threat.
[48] Nehru's ministerial aid, Syed Mohmoud, spoke in Parliament the next day about the disruptive nature of such pacts. But for the SEATO, China would not have to prepare for war and would have been in a better position to pursue policies of peace and co-operation, he said.
[49] 5 April 1955.
[50] P. Ramamurti, "Will Panch Shila Be Asia's Challenge to Imperialists from Bandung Conference," *New Age* weekly, 10 April 1955.
[51] Krishna Menon has disclosed that he had suggested this phrase as a compromise. Cf. Michael Brecher, *India and World Politics: Krishna Menon's View of the World*, London, Oxford University Press, 1968, p. 53.
[52] The agreement as drawn was to Indonesia's advantage because it aimed at keeping the number of Chinese opting for Indonesian citizenship at the lowest. It was, however, not implemented for other reasons.

3/ Beyond Maps: Ideology

China's effort towards closer relations with India and other non-aligned countries during the Bandung phase was to compel Soviet Union to recognise a new reality. In a cold war situation, the national bourgeoisie of these countries, albe it out of sheer opportunism, were prepared to join a broad front against United States. China had no illusion about the fundamental character of the national bourgeoisie of these countries but realised the need for tactical unity between the socialist camp and the non-aligned world led by this class. The Chinese were the first to appreciate the potentialities of a front against United States machinations in Asia in the name of containing communism. Soviet Union launched a diplomatic offensive in the non-aligned world after Bandung, close on the heels of the Chinese breakthrough. A "peace zone" of non-aligned countries, with India as the leader, was the objective of the Soviet leadership which was developing the theory of peaceful co-existence of the two camps and had embarked on the road to a detente with United States when India's Jawaharlal Nehru was appealing for an end to the cold war.

The new-fangled thesis of peaceful co-existence together with its two corollaries—the theory of peaceful transition to socialism and the theory of national democracy, designed to woo the national bourgeoisie of the developing countries, was the starting point of Sino-Soviet ideological differences that were to force an open split in the world communist movement a few years later. The Soviet leaders identified India as the leader of the peace zone and the best example of a country capable of peaceful transition to socialism via national democracy. Thus, the attitude to India became one of the issues in the Sino-Soviet ideological conflict because the Chinese leadership did not share the Soviet enchantment with the ability of the national bourgeoisie in the "peace zone" countries to hasten transition to socialism by peaceful means.

The Soviet attitude to India and other non-aligned countries changed decisively after Bandung. In Indonesia, the Communist Party pledged support to the government's foreign policy within a month of the Bandung conference. Some three months later, the Communist Party of India declared support to Nehru's foreign policy, in keeping with the Soviet attitude. When Nehru and Chou En-lai launched the *Panch Shila* (Five Principles) in June 1954, *Pravda* was quick to welcome it.[1] A few weeks later, in September, Soviet leaders N. S. Khrushchev and N. A. Bulganin led a high-level delegation to Peking and their joint communique with the Chinese leaders endorsed their commitment to the Five Principles in their relation with "the countries of Asia and the Pacific and also with other states".[2] This was about the time the SEATO had formally come into being. India's opposition to the SEATO and refusal of non-aligned countries like Indonesia, Burma and Ceylon to join it impressed the Soviet leadership. On 8 February 1955, the Supreme Soviet adopted an important declaration commending the Five Principles to the rest of the world. Foreign Minister V. M. Molotov told the session:

> It is a fact of great historic importance that colonial India is no more, and there is an Indian Republic instead. This important transformation is characteristic of post-war developments in Asia. India's international prestige as a new and important factor of peace and friendship among nations is steadily rising.[3]

Molotov also appealed to governments and parliaments of all countries to accept the Five Principles as the "general platform for preserving and consolidating peace of all nations". Barely five weeks after the Bandung conference, Nehru had visited Soviet Union for the first time as Prime Minister. The Nehru-Bulganin communique reaffirmed faith in the Five Principles.

The Geneva conference of the Big Four met a month after Nehru's Soviet trip. Reporting to the Supreme Soviet, Prime Minister Bulganin said his government attached great value to Indo-Soviet co-operation "as an important factor in the struggle for peace in Asia—and not only in Asia—considers it indispensable to maintain this co-operation in future on the basis of the principles set out in the Indo-Soviet declaration and widely supported by peace-loving states".[4]

Soviet Union and India took the same positions on urgent Asian problems and this was of great importance in solving Asian and Far Eastern problems and in easing international tensions, Bulganin also said.[5] Thus Soviet Union was consciously promoting India as the leader of the peace zone and the Indian bourgeoisie in turn realised that it could pass on to Soviet Union and the socialist camp a part of the cost of industrialising the country. As it was to be claimed later, Soviet relations with India became the very epitome of the peaceful co-existence concept:

> Relations between Soviet Union and India have become synonymous with friendship and co-operation and eloquently proved the viability of peaceful co-existence between states having different socio-economic systems. Soviet-Indian co-operation is significant beyond the bounds of national frontiers; it became an important factor in world politics.[6]

Bulganin and Khrushchev visited India in November-December 1955 to a tumultuous welcome. Soviet Union had lost its terror for India's ruling elite and at the end of the safari, the Soviet leaders agreed to provide assistance to India's oil exploration effort and hydro-electric projects programme. More, they supported India on Kashmir (against Pakistan) and Goa, still a Portuguese colony. Pakistan was a member of the dreaded SEATO and CENTO, and Portugal of the NATO.

For the Communist Party of India it was a tortuous process adjusting to the new situation. Soviet Union had endorsed Nehru's foreign policy and even some of his domestic policies blighting the party's electoral chances. India became independent in August 1947 and the Cominform was founded a month after that. Zhadanov laid down his famous line at the first meeting of the Cominform and in the wake of this development, the CPI swung from its right reformism (tailing Nehru) to left sectarianism (total opposition to Nehru) and believed in a Titoite intertwining of the two stages of India's revolution, assuming that the country was already capitalist. In 1950, on the Cominform's intervention, it abandoned its 1948 left-sectarian line and switched to the Maoist strategy of a four-class alliance for a two-stage revolution. Another intervention, directly by Soviet leadership this time, forced the party to shelve if not abandon armed struggle as a tactic and settle for peaceful constitutionalism in 1951 and participate in the country's first adult franchise elections. In 1953, the main controversy in the party related to identification of the main enemy—British imperialism which still dominated the Indian economy or United States imperialism which was the enemy of communist parties the world over. The desired shift was achieved through British columnists.

The fight against British domination was compromised to suit Soviet cold war needs and the CPI equivocated calling for simultaneous struggles against both the imperialisms. In practice, the party lined up behind Nehru, whom the Soviet leadership was placating.[7] Soviet priority was for a world-wide peace front and the CPI was expected to exert pressure on Nehru to bring him into it. Already absorbed in the parliamentary system, the party made a "government of democratic unity" the main slogan at its third congress at Madurai in 1953-54. Left unity was to be the precondition for democratic unity because the party's immediate objective was an anti-United States peace front. General Secretary Ajoy Ghosh noted two conflicting trends at the congress. One saw in United States the only enemy to be fought, both for peace and national liberation though the two struggles were not identical or co-existensive. The other wanted to fight the British imperialism which abridged India's freedom. Ghosh argued that all those who wanted completion of India's independence had to join the peace front but all those fighting for peace did not have to join the struggle for freedom. Logically the emphasis was to be on a broad peace front, the struggle for full freedom taking the backseat.[8]

The CPI found itself supporting Nehru's foreign policy and on the eve of the Bandung meet staged an Asian conference in New Delhi attended among others by Soviet and Chinese delegates. With Soviet and Chinese support to Nehru's foreign policy, some CPI leaders, under the cover of fighting "imperialist machinations" in Asia tried to commit the party's support to Nehru's domestic policies as well. International intervention to strengthen the pro-Nehru wing in the CPI came in the form of an article by the Briitsh party leader R. Palme Dutt who wanted the struggles for freedom and peace telescoped into one.[9] His veiled directive was reinforced with direct Soviet advice through Ghosh who pleaded for "support to the peaceful aspects of Nehru's foreign policy" but regarded his domestic policies reactionary.

From now on it was a fierce struggle between two groups in the CPI over the party's attitude to the Nehru government and the ruling Congress party. The centrists led by Ghosh tried to hold the balance between the two groups. The fight for a new programme (to replace the 1951 programme) and a new tactical line culminated in an open split and formation of a second communist party in 1964.

Amidst the CPI controversy, Nehru launched a drive for closer relations with socialist countries. He visited China in 1954 and Soviet Union in 1955. Marshal Tito of Yugoslavia visited India in January 1955. Soviet leaders Bulganin and Khrushchev visited India later in the year. Indo-Soviet economic co-operation got into stride with Soviet aid for the Bhilai steel plant. Nehru's Congress party mounted an ideological offensive against the left opposition, setting itself the goal of a "socialist pattern of society" in January 1955. Moscow began seeing progressive features not only in Nehru's foreign policies but also in his domestic policies. A *Pravda* editorial to mark India's Republic Day, 1955, heralded the new Soviet attitude to Nehru. India was to become the pivot of the Soviet policy for Asia, particularly the countries of the peace zone. *Pravda's* praise for Nehru's foreign and domestic policies brought the CPI disaster in Andhra State where it was campaigning in the mid-term elections to the legislature, making an ambitious bid for power. Its electoral debacle in Andhra State was partly due to the shift in Soviet attitude to Nehru.

The left veneer of the Congress, and more particularly the Second Five Year Plan which embodied its economic policies, demanded reassessment of the situation. The result was a compromise in the CPI between the two groups demanding total opposition to Nehru's party and coalition with it. In June 1955, the CPI backed Nehru's foreign policies but extended qualified support to domestic policies in which it saw a "progressive orientation". The ultimate goal of a people's democratic government at the federal level (to make for peaceful transition to socialism) remained. The immediate objective, however, was a government of democratic unity in the States, conditions for which were to be created through mass struggles both supporting and opposing Nehru's policies. These struggles were to snowball into a nationwide movement affecting even the federal government. The CPI rejected direct co-operation with the government but did not rule out united action with the Congress party from below.

One group in the CPI attributed the left orientation in Nehru's policies to a split in the national bourgeoisie, one section seeking collaboration with imperialism and feudalism. Nehru's government, which sought socialist aid as a lever for more aid from the West, was seen as representing the progressive section of big business. The government had abandoned collaboration with imperialism and taken to peaceful co-existence and co-operation with the socialist camp. The drive for industrialisation aimed at liquidating colonialism, leading to economic independence, and Nehru had to move nearer the camp of peace and anti-imperialism. The need for a united national front as the prelude to a "government of national unity" meant a coalition with the Congress party, an emergency alliance to resist the "pro-imperialist" and "pro-feudal offensive". Another group, more explicit on this point, advanced the slogan of national democratic government. The third reiterated the formulations of the 1951 programme, namely, India was a semi-colonial and dependent country under a big bourgeois-landlord government collaborating with British imperialism.

In December 1955, Ghosh rejected the plan for a coalition with the Congress and in February 1956 (on the eve of the 20th Soviet party Congress) outlined the alternative programme of uniting with and struggling against the Congress to build a national democratic front. The Congress as a whole was not to be brought to the front because building it involved a struggle against some of its policies. Thus the CPI had settled for a strategy of "peaceful transition" and had anticipated the peaceful transition thesis of the 20th Soviet party Congress which was only formalising and legitimising what was already being practised under its guidance in India. By its support to the Nehru government, the Soviet leadership had brought the CPI round to backing Nehru's policies and striving for a national democratic front.

India and the form of its transition to socialism in particular has been an issue of Sino-Soviet ideological differences which can be traced back to the 20th Soviet party Congress in February 1956. Khrushchev's denigration of Stalin at the Congress invited sharp Chinese reaction not so much because it aimed at restoring capitalist relations in Soviet Union but because it was the beginning of a policy of detente with United States. Nehru hailed the trend revealed by the congress as "a step towards creation of conditions favourable to the pursuit of a policy of peaceful co-existence .. important for us as well as others'"[10] Nehru believed de-Stalinisation would help ease international tensions and his initiative at the Commonwealth prime ministers conference in July 1956 produced a joint statement indicating the willingness of member countries to facilitate increased contacts with Soviet Union. The Suez crisis in October found India a close ally of Soviet Union.

Khrushchev's peaceful transition thesis expounded at the 20th Soviet party Congress was in fact a corollary to his declaration that "peaceful co-existence" was the general line of the Soviet foreign policy. The peaceful transition thesis was based on an integrated strategy. In the changed world environment, the powerful socialist camp could provide the support base of world revolution and interacting on the local progressive forces, bring about a new correlation to make peaceful transition possible in newly-free countries. The features of the new environment—the emergence of a vast peace zone in Asia and the degree of economic and diplomatic support the socialist camp could give these countries to prevent their rapproachement with the West were crucial to the strategy. The transition as outlined by the Soviet leadership involved three stages. The working class, by rallying itself and other forces was in a position to defeat the forces opposed to popular interest, to capture a majority in parliament, and transform it into a genuine instrument of people's will.

The winning of a stable parliamentary majority backed by a mass revolutionary movement of the proletariat and of all the working people could create for the working class of a number of capitalist and former colonial countries the conditions needed to secure fundamental social change.
In countries where capitalism is still strong and has a huge military and police apparatus at its disposal, the reactionary forces will of course inevitably offer serious resistance. There the transition to socialism will be attended by sharp, revolutionary struggle.[11]

Parliamentarism was the broad basis of the new Soviet thesis. Countries which could strive for peaceful transition were not specified. Peaceful transition was assumed to be the role and non-peaceful transition ("sharp class, revolutionary struggles") the exception. The concept of peaceful co-existence among nations with different political systems was revised to cover peaceful co-existence among classes within a country.
To the Chinese this amounted to a "clear revision of Marxist-Leninist teachings on the state and revolution and a clear denial of the universal significance of the October Revolution". Peaceful co-existence as advocated by Khrushchev amounted, accord-

ing to the Chinese party, to "excluding from the general line of the foreign policy of socialist countries their mutual assistance and co-operation as well as assistance by them to the revolutionary struggles of the oppressed peoples and nations, or to subordinating all this to the policy of so-called 'peaceful co-existence' ".[12]

The form of transition to socialism and attitude to revolutionary struggles of the Third World have been among the issues of the Sino-Soviet ideological dispute, one phase of which culminated in the alternative general line in the international communist movement.[13]

While the Soviet Party claims that the Chinese had accepted the peaceful transition thesis but later made a "180-degree turn" in their evaluation of the 20th Soviet party Congress,[14] the CPC maintains that it had always differed in "its views of the 20th congress" and that "leading comrades of the CPSU are aware of it".[15] It is on record that the Chinese raised this issue once again with the CPSU at the 1957 meeting of the communist and workers parties in Moscow. Peaceful transition was the main issue between the two big parties and the original draft declaration proposed by the CPSU was silent on non-peaceful transition and had mentioned only peaceful transition. Besides, it had described peaceful transition as "securing majority in parliament" and transforming it "from an instrument of the bourgeois dictatorship into an instrument of genuine people's state power". The CPC opposed this and expressed reservations on two successive drafts of the CPSU. A revised draft from the CPC provided the basis of discussion between the delegations of the two parties before their joint declaration was circulated among other delegations. The declaration in its final form (on 16 November 1957) made two major changes on the question of transition from capitalism to socialism compared to the first draft proposed by the CPSU. Firstly, the declaration, besides indicating the possibility of peaceful transition, referred to non-peaceful transition and asserted that "Leninism teaches, and experience confirms, that the ruling classes never relinquish power voluntarily". Secondly, in connection with securing "a firm majority in parliament" the declaration stressed "extra-parliamentary mass struggle" to smash the resistance and to create "the necessary conditions for peaceful realisation of socialist revolution". Though the CPC was not satisfied with this draft, it "conceded the point" because leaders of the CPSU had pleaded that the formulation should have some connection with that of their 20th Congress.[16]

Briefly, the CPC's position was: it would be more flexible to refer to both the forms of transition because that would leave the political initiative with the communists but referring only to peaceful transition would tie their hands; it might be tactically advantageous to refer to peaceful transition but would be inappropriate to over-emphasise its possibility; to the best of their knowledge there was still "not a country where this possibility is of any practical significance"; should such a possibility arise, communists could always take advantage of it; to obtain majority in parliament was not the same as smashing the old state machinery and establishing a new state machinery; peaceful transition to socialism should not be interpreted in such a way that it solely means "transition through parliamentary majority".[17]

Though neither the 20th Congress nor the 1957 Moscow declaration had specified the countries holding out the possibility of peaceful transition, there was little doubt the Soviet leadership saw greatest chances of such a transition in India. One of the postulates of Soviet strategy (economic and diplomatic support to the countries of the peace zone in Asia to prevent their alignment with the West) had been tried with some success in India and was already part of the Soviet experience. The CPI had been persuaded to accept the path of peaceful transition and initiate action for it. This was the background to the Sino-Indian border dispute when it began to build up.

The Border Dispute

The two countries had not discussed their border until Nehru raised the issue in Peking in 1954. In the north-eastern sector (the NEFA sector) India had taken the McMahon Line drawn by the British rulers in 1914 as the border, while China maintained that it had never recognised the McMahon Line. In the north-western sector (the Ladakh sector), the dispute related to conflicting claims by the two countries. While both the sides broadly accepted the traditional frontier as the boundary, the controversy was over the alignment of the boundary.

After its independence in 1947, India has been publishing maps which conformed to its idea of the border with China and the People's Republic of China established in 1949 had been publishing maps which did not differ from the Kuomintang government's. Late in 1950, Nehru rejected the Chinese claims implied in their maps and declared that "map or no map" the McMahon Line was India's "firm" frontier in the north-eastern sector. He wanted the Chinese to understand that there could be no transgression across the Himalayas and that India's frontiers were clear in its maps, clear in its statements and "clear to the world, and clear to China and clear to our own people...."[18]

China refrained from raising the issue. In autumn 1952, Girija Shankar Bajpai, a former Secretary-General of the External Affairs Ministry, wanted Nehru to secure a Chinese commitment recognising the McMahon Line. Ambassador K. M. Panikkar, however, dissuaded Nehru from raising the issue because he thought India had already stated its position clearly.[19] The border dispute was not mentioned by either side at the Sino-Indian talks in 1954 when Chou visited New Delhi. India was later to claim that the Chinese did not raise the issue because the "boundary was well-known and beyond dispute and there could be no question regarding it.... The Indian delegation throughout took the line that all questions at issue between the two countries were being considered and once the settlement was concluded, no question remained".[20] Nehru hailed the April 1954 Sino-Indian agreement on Tibet as "a new starting point in our relations with China and Tibet" and said the border was "firm and defined" and "not open to discussion with anybody". He is believed to have wanted a system of checkposts spread along the entire frontier. "More especially, we should have checkposts in such places as might be considered disputed areas."[21] To India, the border issue did not exist the moment Nehru and Chou had affirmed faith in the Five Principles (in June 1954). However, a United States scholar points out that no Indian map published before 1954 (Nehru was to raise the border issue with Chou in October 1954) showed the entire Indian border with China without reservation. According to him, a map dated 1948 (available in the U.S. Library of Congress) shows the McMahon Line but with the same symbols as used for the border between India and Pakistan labelled as "not demarcated as international boundary.... No line at all is shown for the outer border of Kashmir, which is labelled as 'Boundary Undefined'. No border is shown in the area just to the south-east of Kashmir and down to Nepal, between Uttar Pradesh and Tibet. A map published in 1950 shows the outer border of Kashmir and the rest of the border down to Nepal as a colour wash, without a line, and also labels it as 'Boundary Undefined'."[22]

Thus, while India seemed to be sure about the border in the NEFA sector it was not very clear about the border in the Ladakh sector in the early stages.

When Nehru visited Peking in 1954, he drew Chou's attention to certain Chinese maps which he deemed objectionable. Chou is believed to have said that these maps were really reproduction of other maps drawn before 1945 and his government had not had the time to revise them. Later at the Bandung conference in April 1955, Chou referred to China's border problems with some of its neighbours. China had not yet

> finally fixed our border line, and we are ready to do this. But before doing so we are willing to maintain the present situation by acknowledging that those parts of our border are parts which are undetermined. We are ready to restrain our government and people from crossing even one step across our border.... As to the determination of common borders which we are going to undertake with our neighbouring countries, we shall use only peaceful means and we shall not permit

any other kind or method.

In 1956, when Chou visited India, Nehru raised the border issue, and specifically the McMahon Line. Chou is believed to have said that whatever happened in the past, he would accept the McMahon Line as the border with India. Though China had not accepted this line

> because it was an accomplished fact, and because of the friendly relations which existed between China and the countries concerned, namely India and Burma, the Chinese government was of the opinion that they should give recognition to this McMahon Line. They had, however, not consulted the Tibetan authorities about it yet. They proposed to do so.[23]

India reopened the dispute in 1958, protesting against the Chinese maps on 21 August 1958 after *China Pictorial* had printed a map showing four of the five divisions of NEFA, areas of north Uttar Pradesh, and large areas of eastern Ladakh as Chinese. China's reply on 2 November said that "a new way" of drawing China's boundary would be determined "after surveys and consultations with neighbouring countries". Meantime, on 18 October India informally protested about the Chinese road across Aksai-chin in Ladakh linking Tibet with West Sinkiang.[24]

Nehru's letter to Chou on 14 December admitted that "certain very minor border problems" awaited settlement but India cannot and would not entertain any unreasonable claims. Significantly, he dealt with the maps but not with the Aksai-chin road. Chou's reply on 23 January 1959 said that "historically" no agreement had been concluded on the Sino-Indian boundary which had never been "formally delimited", that the Aksai-chin highway ran solely across Chinese territory, that the border troubles of the preceding years were the consequences of the lack of an agreement. Chinese maps had been consistent for decades. The McMahon Line was a "product of the British policy of aggression against the Tibet region of China" and this "illegal" line had never been recognised by his Government. He, however, implied that China would refrain from crossing the line for the time being and would not make a major issue of it. As for the boundary question as a whole, "as a provisional measure, the two sides should temporarily maintain the status quo". Chou was for a negotiated settlement but his government could not alter its version of the boundary "without having made surveys and without having consulted the countries concerned".

Chou's insistence on formal delineation of the border in consultation with other countries suggested a major territorial dispute over Aksai-chin as also a willingness to negotiate the entire boundary including the McMahon Line and he obviously referred to Burma, Sikkim, Bhutan, and Pakistan. Nehru's 22 March reply skirted the main issues but implied rejection of the suggestion that status quo should continue. Nehru insisted on what he regarded as the status quo ante. In other words, he wanted the Chinese to vacate the Aksai-chin area and restore the 1956 position when the road had not been built.

> I agree that the position as it was before the recent disputes should be respected by both the sides and that neither side should try to take unilateral action in exercise of what it conceives to be right. Further, if any possession has been secured recently, the position should be rectified.[25]

This shift in Nehru's stand indicated a new degree of inflexibility, the discussion shifting from the political to the legal plane.

This was the situation on the eve of the Tibet revolt (March-April 1959). The dispute had predated the revolt and was independent of it in origin but the revolt was among the factors straining relations between the two neighbours. Overall, on the eve of the revolt both admitted to some degree the existence of a dispute in the sense that some parts of the boundary were not finally delineated. China might have been willing to accept the McMahon Line as the existing reality and conferred de jure recognition on it but after negotiations, as it did with Burma.

But India regarded the matter closed, insisting that the McMahon Line was everything on the north-eastern border. China seemed to be insisting on a negotiated settlement even if it meant the eventual recognition of the McMahon Line. It was overlooking a vital fact: China's recognition of the line in the case of Burma (in 1957) was the *result* of negotiations and not the *basis* of negotiations.

As for the north-western (Ladakh) sector, India was talking of a firm, settled border and had ordered measures to defend it. But Nehru had admitted as late as 1959 that the border had not been clearly defined here, in contrast to his clear position that the border in the north-eastern (NffFA) sector and the middle sector. He said:

> It is a complicated thing, but we have always looked upon the Ladakh area as a different area ... vaguer area so far as the frontier is concerned because the exact alignment of the frontier is not at all clear as in the case of the McMahon Line.[26]

And:

> It is a matter of argument as to what of it [Ladakh] belongs to us and what part of it belongs to somebody else. It is not a dead clear matter. However I have to be frank to the House. It is not clear. I cannot go about doing things in a matter which has been challenged not today but for a hundred years. It has been challenged to the ownership of the territory [sic]. That has nothing to do with the McMahon Line.[27]

China wanted the status quo to continue but there was heavy domestic pressure on Nehru for recovery of the "lost" territory. Chou's 23 January letter was in line with his declaration in Bandung about his country's border problems. For India, however, the issue was beyond negotiation when the Tibet revolt added to the complications.

Revolt in Tibet

In 1955, there was a minor revolt in Tibet, engineered and led by serf-owners and involving the Khampa tribesmen. The Dalai Lama was in sympathy with it. When he visited India in 1956-57 he sought political asylum but eventually returned on the persuasion of Nehru and Chou (who visited India). In 1958, the revolt as well as the military action to contain it had assumed serious proportions. Following heavy fighting in Lhasa, the Dalai Lama fled to India crossing the border on 31 March. He arrived at Tezpur on 18 April. He said that the 1951 Lhasa agreement under which China recognised Tibet's suzerainty over Tibet was entered into because Tibet had "no options" left.

The Dalai Lama's statement was the signal for a fierce anti-China campaign by the rightist political forces (who had emerged in strength in Nehru's Congress party and outside) and the anti-communist left. Even Nehru seemed to have succumbed to the pressure of the campaign. On 27 April, he described the Tibet uprising as a "national revolt" and indirectly supported the charge that China was oppressing the Tibetan "nation". Part of the anti-China crusade in India aimed at proving that China had violated the Five Principles but questions of propriety were involved in India's conduct here, the fact that thousands of Tibetans had fled across the border and had been accepted as refugees by India notwithstanding. If the 1951 Sino-Tibet agreement was valid in India's view, Tibet was part of China and was therefore an internal matter of China. Yet the Indian Parliament debated the Tibet developments and several Indian quarters proffered advice to China about handling the problem without the use of force, etc. The CPI General Secretary Ajoy Ghosh could not help raising a few questions, despite his admiration for Nehru's socialism:

> He seems to think that India's conduct during the whole Tibetan episode has been unimpeachable and fully in conformity with *Panch Shila* while all the blame lies with China..

But at no time were the Chinese press and leaders so sharply critical of India as they are now.

Why? Because at no time in the past did the *Indian government* as distinct from private individuals, political parties and Press adopt such an attitude towards an internal matter of the Chinese People's Republic. Even the statements which Shri Nehru as the head of the Indian Government has made in recent period, cannot but be heavily biased in favour of the rebels. He does not even now seem to realise this.[28]

On 1 May *Hsinhua* reported that *People's Daily* had carried Nehru's 27 April statement together with an editorial, "Let us Study Nehru's Statement" commending it for a thorough discussion by all. China's reply to Nehru came in the form of a subsequent editorial in *People's Daily* on 6 May entitled "Revolution in Tibet and Nehru's Philosophy". It said that India had interfered in China's affairs over Tibet in 1950 through diplomatic channels and again on 13 April 1959 when Nehru said that China had not kept its assurances and agreements on Tibet and that armed intervention was taking place. Nehru was also assailed for his 14 April statement ("I do earnestly hope that the Tibetan people will be able to enjoy their autonomy and not be oppressed and suppressed by others"). The editorial took exception to the welcome given to the Dalai Lama and the statements of Congress party leaders including Mrs Indira Gandhi (who was its president) describing Tibet as a "country" and to the formation of a "People's Committee In Support of Tibet" by some political parties and anti-China campaign in the Indian press. All this, the editorial said, was quite understandable because the head of the Indian government had never pursued a "clear-cut hands-off policy".

The editorial was not charging India with the desire to occupy Tibet "or to make Tibet formally independent". But it suggested that India, through its interference was striving to prevent China from "exercising full sovereignty over its territory of Tibet". It refrained from attacking Nehru because he was

... different from many other persons who obviously bear ill-will towards China. He disagrees somewhat with us on the Tibet question. But in general he advocates Sino-Indian friendship. Of this we have no doubts whatsoever.

Nehru's sentiments ("it would be a great tragedy if two great countries of Asia—India and China—which have been peaceful neighbours for ages past should develop feelings of hostility for each other") were welcome because

Our basic interests are the same and our main enemy is also the same. We will certainly not forget our common interests and fall into the trap of the common man.... Once the Indian side stops its words and deeds of interference in Tibet the present argument would end.

China was thus reaffirming the Five Principles by insisting on "non-interference" by India in China's internal affairs. The sustained hysteria inside Nehru's party and outside appeared to have worried China to the point of reckoning the possibility of an Indian military adventure in Tibet taking advantage of the disturbed situation there. Those who moaned the loss of a "buffer" between India and China in 1950 and thought that *Panch Shila* was born in sin would have loved to see the buffer restored through Indian liberation of Tibet if only as a solution to the Sino-Indian border problem. (The entire border between the two countries relates to Tibet.)

On 16 May, China's ambassador in New Delhi, P'an Tzu-li, gave expression to his government's apprehension when he made a statement to India's Foreign Secretary. Tibet was an "inalienable part of China's territory" and no foreign power had the right to "make Tibet semi-independent or even to turn it into a sphere of influence of a foreign country or a buffer zone". He alleged Indian intervention in China's internal affairs and suggested Indian involvement in the Dalai Lama's escape to India. He was, all the same, pleading that India should not intervene further and was assuring India that his country had no intention of antagonising it or even those countries which unlike India had lined up behind United States. China still wanted a broad front against United States.

> The enemy of the Chinese peoples lies in the East.... Although the Philippines, Thailand and Pakistan have joined the SEATO which is designed to oppose China, we have not treated those three countries as our principal enemy; our principal enemy is U.S. imperialism. India has not taken part in the South-East Asian treaty; it is not an opponent but a friend to our country. China will not be so foolish as to antagonise India in the West. The putting down of the rebellion and the carrying out of democratic reforms in Tibet will not in the least endanger India.... We cannot have two centres of attention, nor can take friend for foe.... You will be agreeing to our thinking regarding the view that China can only concentrate its main attention eastward of China, but not southwestward of China, nor is it necessary for it to do so.... *It seems that you too cannot have two fronts.*[29]

China was trying to convince India that just as it could not afford an adventure in the south-west where its principal fight was against United States, India could not afford a diversion when there was a real threat from Pakistan in the west.

India's response to the Tibet revolt was largely conditioned by the border disputes with China, which was seen as a greater threat to India's security than Pakistan. Significantly, China did not try to link the Tibet revolt with the border dispute. The 6 May *People's Daily* editorial did not mention any territorial claim or refer to the border dispute. It did not charge India with any territorial designs on Tibet or to make it "formally independent". It merely wanted an end to "words and deeds of interference in Tibet".

On 18 April, Chou's annual report to National People's Congress indicated a moderate line on the border issue. He referred to the progress in resolving the boundary differences with Burma and laid down the general policy. Mischief makers had exploited the undetermined boundary lines between China and some of its South-East Asian neighbours as "propaganda material". But these undetermined boundary lines were the "results of many historical causes, first and foremost, prolonged imperialist aggression". It was in the interest of both the parties "to maintain the status quo and not let the imperialists succeed in their scheme of discord between us".

Chou said in another context that "Tibetan reactionaries and certain foreign reactionaries" used areas on the Sino-Indian border for activities "designed to disrupt unity of our country and Sino-Indian friendship". Chou was not prepared to blame only India for the revolt. Chou was possibly answering the Indian charge of 22 March that Chinese troops had intruded into border areas like Khinzamane and Longju in the NEFA sector. Possibly, the Chinese had moved in to seal off the border with disturbed Tibet because they thought Indian territory was being used by rebels and "foreign reactionaries". There is ample evidence suggesting such use of Indian territory by interested parties to promote the Tibet revolt. Col. Fletcher Prouty, who helped organise United States Special Operations Force, has said:

... we knew the Chinese were eventually going to come up to Tibet. So we started recruiting a resistance force among the natives. Up to 42,000 Tibetans were put under arms. We flew groups of tribesmen from Tibet to Spain and from there to the Rocky Mountains in Colarado, where the atmosphere is similar to the Himalayas, for combat training. In six weeks they are back in Tibet, and a fairly good ground force was built up.[30]

Another disclosure lends substance to the Chinese charge here:

Since 1949, the U.S. ... at one time or the other has used Indian, Burmese, Laotian, Thai and perhaps Nepalese and Pakistani territory as staging areas for clandestine operations against China....

According to knowledgeable sources, the Central Intelligence Agency provided logistic support for the Dalai Lama's escape from Tibet, using STOL (short take-off and landing) aircraft based in India and also supported tribal revolts in Tibet...[31]

United States aircraft overflying Indian territory ferried arms for the Khampa rebels. As early as 1955, the rebels were supported by air drops arranged by radio links between Kuomintang forces in Tibet and Taiwan.[32] Covert airdrops continued even after the Tibet revolt in 1959 as Sino-Indian diplomatic exchanges concerning overflight of disputed borders would suggest. In 1960, India's Defence Minister Krishna Menon protested to Peking against repeated flights of Chinese planes over NEFA.[33] Chou told Nehru in private that investigations showed that the aircraft belonged to United States. An Indian protest was publicly rejected by China asserting that the aircraft

> ... took off from Bangkok, passed over Burma or China and crossed the Chinese-Indian border or penetrate deep into China's interior where they parachuted weapons, supplies and wireless sets to secret agents and then flew back to Bangkok...[34]

Chou was so certain that Chinese aircraft were not involved that he told the Burmese government that it could shoot any unidentified aircraft down or force them to land. The Burmese did shoot down a Kuomintang China bomber which crash landed in Thailand. Chiang Kai-shek apologised to the Thai government but such flights continued.[35]

THE LONGJU CLASH

After the Tibet revolt both the sides were advancing towards their claim lines to narrow down the no-man's land. In the NEFA sector, where considerable Chinese troop movement was reported, India began setting up posts along the McMahon Line.

There was a minor clash at Kinzamane on 7 August and a serious clash at Longju nearby on 25 August. Since 1954 India has been alleging Chinese incursions, squatting and pinpricks including detention of its police patrols in 1958. Besides, the construction of the Aksai-chin road had taken place. But the Longju clash climaxed the incidents in the wake of the Tibet revolt and underlined the seriousness of the border problem. Significantly, the Longju clash and not the Tibet revolt four months earlier marked the beginning of the Sino-Indian confrontation on the border.

Belligerent Indian opinion had linked the border issue with the Tibet revolt (there were even demands for the liberation of Tibet). But the Chinese approach tried to delink the two issues and Tibet could not have been the sole reason for their changed attitude towards India. Certain developments between the Tibet revolt and the Longju clash cannot be overlooked. The Soviets "unilaterally" scrapped the 1957 agreement on nuclear aid to China and this extended the Sino-Soviet ideological dispute to state-level relations. In May, Khrushchev had failed to carry out his ultimatum on Berlin and was anxious for a detente with United States. On 3 August came the announcement that Khrushchev would be visiting United States for the Camp David summit with President Eisenhower. Meantime in India Nehru had dismissed the 28-month-old communist ministry in Kerala State in July. (Ironically, the first communist ministry in the country which won power through the ballot box was toppled through an extra-constitutional agitation blessed by Indira Gandhi when her Congress party found that the government could not be defeated on the floor of the legislature.)

Whatever was behind the Longju clash, it served the Chinese a purpose. The Soviet reaction to the clash revealed for the first time its differences with China over the Sino-Indian border dispute. The Soviets had reservations about supporting China against non-communist India. The Soviet leadership allowed itself to be guided by the Communist Party of India, rather than the Chinese leadership, on the border issue. Thus the CPI acquired a role in the border dispute.

The CPI was to admit later that the "first breach in India-China friendship was created in the attitude and acts of the Indian government" towards the Tibet revolt and aid given to it and to the Dalai Lama to conduct his anti-China campaign in India.[36] But the party did not endorse even as early as May 1959 the Chinese charge that Kalimpong was the command centre of the rebels or that the Dalai Lama had made his 18 April statement in Tezpur under duress. It did not like the loose use by Chinese of the term "expansionist" in relation to India. This explains the absence of any reference in the Central Executive Committee's May 1959 statement to Kalimpong. The earlier resolution of the party's secretariat in March had endorsed the charge about the use of Kalimpong.

The CPI's private efforts to restrain the Chinese leadership on the Tibet issue dates back to this period. In a letter to the Chinese party on 3 May and another on 5 May, the CPI, while extending full support to the stand taken by "the Chinese comrades" deplored some of their statements regarding Kalimpong, "Indian expansionism", the Dalai Lama being used as "hostage" to blackmail China and his statements being made under duress. Disclosing this at the Moscow conference of communist parties in November 1960, the CPI general secretary pointed out that his party did not utter a single word in public to betray its differences with the Chinese party. Even if Nehru had made a few anti-Chinese statements, distinction should have been made between the "reactionaries" who were striving to change India's basic foreign policy and Nehru. His party's two letters to the Chinese had suggested a Nehru-Chou meeting to restore good relations between the two countries. The Chinese reply was curt and short. The CPI was told that its suggestion for a meeting of the two Prime Ministers was not proper. There was no response to any of the specific points raised in the two letters. Instead they were asked to study the *People's Daily* editorial, "The Revolution in Tibet and Nehru's Philosophy" for answers to all the questions.[37]

The uproar over Tibet had died down but the CPI had to go through a period of embarrassment when Nehru dismissed the government run by it in Kerala through a constitutional coup. Significantly, the Nehru government could sign two big Soviet credits (for Rs 3,000 million) even as it was planning to oust the communists from power in Kerala. The Nehru government's disregard even for buorgeois constitutional norms strengthened the left group in the CPI which was restive at the reformist moratorium on class struggle that accompanied the party's support to Nehru. The left group resented Soviet backing of Nehru's domestic and foreign policies because such support blunted the party's edge against the rightist forces in the country. The Kerala coup unnerved the CPI leadership and to add to its problems came a spate of reports of ill-treatment of Indian nationals in Tibet, of incidents on the Sino-Indian border and of worsening Sino-Indian relations. The CPI expected a big "reactionary offensive" in the wake of the coup in Kerala. The rightists had got a party of their own in the Swatantra Party in addition to the Hindu nationalist Jana Sangh. One of the main weapons of the "reaction", the CPI thought, was the strained Sino-Indian relations. On 20 August the CPI conveyed its apprehensions to the Chinese and implored them to be restrained. The CPI pleaded that the "continuation and accentuation of the present [Sino-Indian] differences would gravely endanger India's foreign policy, help the right wing to take India towards America and would help the drive against the Communist Party of India".[38]

The Communist Party of China was in no mood to help the CPI out of its predicament. The tension on the border continued and resulted in the Longju incident on 25 August. General Secretary Ajoy Ghosh was in Moscow, and at the urgent request of his secretariat he addressed another letter to the CPC on 3 September, pleading for Sino-Soviet government level negotiations and exchange of views on the border issue because delay would only help "the very forces that seek to create hostility against China and pull India towards the Anglo-American camp". The CPC ignored this letter. Worse, no less than eight notes had been exchanged between Peking and New Delhi during the 23 June-28 August 1959 interregnum but the CPC had not taken the CPI into confidence about them.

Pravda announced on 8 September that Ghosh was in Moscow and the following day *Tass* issued an official statement deploring the Longju clash. The statement quoted "Soviet leading circles" as hoping that the Chinese and Indian governments "would not allow the incident to further the aims of those circles who want the international situation to worsen" and that "both governments will settle the misunderstanding". It also noted that "this incident has been caught up by those circles in the Western countries, in the United States especially, who are seeking to prevent relaxation of international tension and aggravate the situation" on the eve of the proposed exchange of visits by Khrushchev and Eisenhower.

The Chinese account of the developments leading to the *Tass* statement throws new light on the episode. According to the Chinese, the Longju clash was provoked by Indians. On 6 September, a Chinese leader had told the Soviet Charge d'Affaires in Peking about the incident and China's policy of avoiding hostilities. On 9 September, the Soviet Charge informed the Chinese of his government's desire to issue a statement on 10 September deploring the incident. The same afternoon, the Chinese government gave him a copy of Chou's letter to Nehru proposing "friendly settlement of the border dispute". In the evening, the Charge d'Affaires was told by the Chinese that they had already published Chou's letter to Nehru and taking these developments into account there was no need for the proposed Soviet statement. Ignoring the Chinese plea, the Soviet government issued a statement a day ahead of its own schedule.[39]

SINO-SOVIET DIFFERENCES

China was to denounce this statement later as a "diplomatic rocket" against it and as the first overt disclosure of Sino-Soviet differences over India. The statement was no doubt in response to Ghosh's appeal to the Soviet leadership. By giving up its neutral stand in the Sino-Indian dispute, the Soviet leadership was serving notice on the Chinese that its support for China in the dispute cannot be taken for granted. Thereby it was helping the CPI out of its predicament and relieving pressure on it. The similarity between the *Tass* statement and the CPI secretariat's statement of 30 August was striking. The operative part of the former hoped that "both the governments will settle their misunderstanding, taking into account their mutual interests, in the spirit of traditional friendship between the peoples of China and India. The CPI had 'fervently" hoped "that immediate steps will be taken by both governments concerned to settle controversies with regard to the border dispute by mutual consultations".[40]

The Soviet leadership was equating a socialist country with a non-socialist country and was making known to the world that it was not supporting China against India which it regarded a country of the peace zone. At least this was the CPI's interpretation of the Soviet stand. Defending the *Tass* statement, Ghosh said later that neither India nor China was planning aggression against the other and that the statement was "entirely correct, wise and timely".[41] The Chinese saw in it open condemnation of their position and suggested that it was issued to please Eisenhower and that it had affected the interests of the peace camp and helped imperialists and Indian reactionaries.[42] The principal Sino-Soviet issue here was whether Soviet Union was right in equating India with a socialist country without examining the question of right and wrong. As the Chinese were to say later, "internal differences" among two fraternal parties were brought into the open for the first time through the 9 September statement and for the first time in history a socialist country had condemned another.[43]

Sino-Soviet ideological differences which date back to 1956 were the subject of strictly bilateral discussions in the first stage (1956-57). Formal disputation began towards the end of 1957 and other parties came to know about the differences which flowed from three vital factors: the divergent experiments of the Soviet and Chinese revolutions, their impact on the communist camp, and their interaction on the non-communist world. Soviet Union, aspiring for the status of a super power, was underlining peaceful competition of the two world systems and peaceful co-existence with United States. In the Chinese view, the concept of peaceful co-existence among countries with different systems was being stretched to cover peaceful transition to socialism. To the Chinese the best method of competing with United States lay in strengthening the world revolution. Soviet Union had attained nuclear capability and it had differences with China on the consequences of this achievement for the socialist camp and revolution in general. While Soviet Union saw in its nuclear capability the best chance of a detente with United States, the Chinese raised an important question: did the benefits of the achievement belong to the entire socialist camp, and would its nuclear strategy be executed under Soviet control or by the entire socialist camp, and in what form? The question was simply whether China would also be helped to attain nuclear capability. Soviet attitude to developing countries in the matter of economic aid was also becoming an issue. The Chinese wanted priority to the developing socialist camp while the Soviet premium was on countries ruled by the national bourgeoisie, like India, ostensibly to promote peaceful transition to socialism but in effect propping the national bourgeoisie. Exaggerating the danger of war (by posing a thermo-nuclear war as the alternative to peaceful co-existence), the Soviet leadership was abandoning revolution and seeking accommodation with imperialism, according to the Chinese.

These issues no doubt resulted in the gradual worsening of Sino-Soviet state-level relations. The Middle East crisis in 1958 posed a serious threat to world peace in the Soviet view. On 28 July Khrushchev suggested to United States, Britain and France a summit meeting with Soviet Union and India was to be invited to it. China did not like India being invited to the summit to its exclusion. On 31 July, Khrushchev made an unplanned, secret visit to Peking and on his return (3 August) abruptly announced withdrawal of the suggestion for a summit. On 23 August, the Chinese launched heavy artillery attacks on Quemoy following their declaration exactly a month earlier to "liberate" Taiwan "at any moment". In mid-August *Red Flag* had predicted the inevitable victory of the Chinese people against imperialism. It is possible that Khrushchev accompanied by Defence Minister Rodin Malinovsky had rushed to Peking to dissuade the Chinese from forcing the Taiwan issue. The crisis died down on 6 September when Chou offered to resume ambassador-level talks with United States which accepted the offer. When the danger of a Sino-United States war had passed, Khrushchev, on 7 September, told Eisenhower, among other things, that "an attack on the People's Republic of China ... is an attack on the Soviet Union". On 17 September he rejected the United States suggestion that he restrain China, charged the United States with interfering in Chinese affairs and threatened retaliation in the event of a nuclear attack on China.

The Taiwan crisis, however, revealed to the world the total lack of Sino-Soviet co-ordination in foreign policy matters. The Soviet leadership was to claim later that it pulled the chestnuts out of the fire for the Chinese. In 1959 Khrushchev stepped up his efforts for a Soviet-United States detente. On 3 August he announced a summit meeting with Eisenhower from 15-18 September at Camp David. The Longju incident on the Sino-Indian border took place barely three weeks before the summit.

The Soviet leadership was to allege later that the Taiwan crisis was meant to block the detente with United States, and the Longju clash to torpedo the Camp David talks. The Chinese, however, contended that the Soviet statement on the Longju clash was timed to please Eisenhower on the eve of the Camp David summit. There was little doubt the Soviet leadership feared that the Longju incident would prejudice the Camp David outcome.

The CPI Dilemma

India had become a subject of Sino-Soviet differences. Through its support to Nehru, the Soviet leadership had brought the Communist Party of India round to supporting his policies and striving for a national democratic front. General Secretary Ghosh, who had attended the 20th Soviet party congress, tried to push this line further. He told his party's fourth congress in

April 1956 that peaceful transition to socialism advocated by the Soviet leadership was a distinct possibility and "every Communist party in every country must try to turn the possibility into a reality". The Chinese had not yet raised the issue of nonpeaceful transition. The documents of the fourth CPI congress were an application of the peaceful transition thesis to India. The long-term objective of the government of a people's democracy remained but the immediate aim was "to progressively dislodge the bourgeoisie from its dominant position in the national government".

The tactics worked out by these documents required support to every government measure "against imperialism and feudalism" but resistance to policies which helped imperialism, feudalism and monopolies drawing the mass of Congressmen into it. There was to be no "general united front" with the Congress but the democratic front did not mean an anti-Congress front either. In sum, the documents initiated action for peaceful transition by seeking to rally the leftist forces around the CPI, mobilise the masses, sharpening class struggle, and use the Congress left to force a leftward shift in its policies. The CPI rightists were not reconciled to their defeat and sought to reopen the issue on the basis of a Soviet article which said the Nehru government had embarked on a non-capitalist path of development, that is, towards socialism through a growing role for the state sector.[14] The Soviet leadership was trying to bring the CPI closer to Nehru. But the CPI rejected the understanding behind the article and the rightist move collapsed.

The CPI entered the 1957 election battle on the basis of its fourth congress line. The peaceful transition approach seemed to have paid off in the Kerala State where the party won independent power. The ministry there, led by the CPI, became an important factor in the country's bourgeois parliamentary politics. The Congress had lost heavily in the general election in the country as a whole but the right and not the left was the beneficiary, the CPI success in Kerala notwithstanding.

Shortly thereafter, a CPI delegation led by Ghosh participated in the Moscow conference of communist and workers parties in

November 1957, where the Chinese attacked the Soviet peaceful transition thesis and forced its modification. The CPI which had anticipated the Soviet line and came in for severe Chinese criticism, especially for its decision to form a ministry in Kerala to function within the framework of India's bourgeois constitution. A latter-day Chinese commentary was to denounce the ministry as "the infamous model of peaceful transition and 'parliamentary road' which had won praise from the U.S. imperialists and modern revisionists".[45]

The CPI held an extraordinary congress in 1958 to assess the changed situation. The growing strength of the right inside and outside the Congress worried it most. The Congress was in crisis and the government's economic policies and planning had also run into a crisis. United States pressure on India was mounting. So the extreme right had to be fought, the CPI thought. The reactionaries outside the Congress who were out to scuttle the Second Five Year Plan had no popular mass base but drew their strength from like-minded elements inside the Congress and from some of the government policies. So it had to be a simultaneous battle against right reaction and the anti-people's policies of the government. The rightists in the CPI wanted a Congress-Communist coalition to counter the reactionary trends and the mounting United States pressures on the government. But Congress attempts to dislodge the Kerala ministry inhibited the CPI rightists from campaigning for their line of coalition with the Congress. The most significant achievement of the extraordinary party congress was the formal proclamation of its resolve to achieve a transition to socialism by peaceful means. This was incorporated in the party constitution and it was to be an unqualified commitment and not a mere tactic.

Chinese attitude to India was hardening as Nehru's Congress party stepped up its efforts in 1958 to topple the Kerala ministry, duly elected and enjoying majority in the legislature. Soviet Union, however, continued to support Nehru and expected the CPI to do likewise. The Kerala coup in July 1959 might have strengthened the belief of the Chinese leaders that as stated in

6 May *People's Daily* editorial, Nehru was making increasing concessions to the Indian "big bourgeoisie" and to "imperialism". About the time the Nehru government pulled off the coup in Kerala it also clinched two massive Soviet credits totalling 350 million roubles (Rs 3,000 million). CPI leftists resented Soviet support to Nehru because that blunted the edge of the party's struggle against the rightist forces in the country.

Thus, by September 1959, Sino-Soviet relations had deteriorated seriously and their differences over India had become public. The Sino-Indian border dispute was being drawn into the vortex of ideology.

Notes

[1] 1 July 1954.
[2] *New Times*, supplement to No. 42, 1954, p. 3.
[3] *New Times*, supplement to no. 7, 1955, p. 13.
[4] *Pravda*, 5 August 1955.
[5] *Ibid*.
[6] Pavlovsky, "Soviet-Indian Co-operation," *International Affairs* (Moscow), January 1970, p. 46.
[7] For a detailed account of these developments, cf. Gene D. Overstreet and Marshal Windmiller, *Communism in India*, California University, 1959; John H. Kautsky, *Moscow and the Communist Party of India*, New York and Cambridge, Wiley and MIT, 1956, and Mohan Ram, *Indian Communism: Split Within a Split*, Delhi, Vikas, 1969.
[8] Cf. Ajoy Ghosh, "On the Work of the Third Party Congress," *New Age* weekly, 24 January 1954.
[9] R. Palme Dutt, "New Features in the National Liberation Struggle of Colonial and Dependent People," *For a Lasting Peace, for a People's Democracy*, 8 October 1964.
[10] Lok Sabha, 20 March 1966.
[11] N.S. Khrushchev, *Report of the Central Committee of the Communist Party of Soviet Union to the XX Party Congress*, 14 February 1956, Moscow, 1956, pp. 42-46.
[12] Editorial Departments of *People's Daily* and *Red Flag*, "The Origin and Development of Differences Between the Leadership of the CPSU and Ourselves: Comment on the Open Letter of the Central Committee of CPSU—1," *Peking Review*, 13 September 1963.
[13] *A Proposal Concerning the General Line of the International Communist Movement*, Central Committee of the Communist Party of China, 14 June 1963.

[14] CPSU Central Committee, "Open Letter to Its Party Organizations at All Levels and to All Its Party Members," *Soviet News*, 16 July 1963.
[15] Editorial Departments of *People's Daily* and *Red Flag*, "The Origin and Development...," loc. cit.
[16] *Ibid.*
[17] Appendix to *ibid.*
[18] Rajya Sabha, 9 December 1959.
[19] Neville Maxwell, "China and India: The Un-negotiated Dispute," *China Quarterly*, no. 43, July-September 1970, p. 50.
[20] India, *White Paper III*, p. 91.
[21] Neville Maxwell, loc. cit., quotes this from a transcript of the original made available by D.R. Mankekar.
[22] Harold C. Hinton, *Communist China in World Politics*, Boston, Houghton Mifflin, 1966, p. 280. He also points out that none of these maps appear in the atlas on the border dispute published by India in 1960.
[23] This is quoted in a letter from the Communist Party of India to "fraternal parties" on 20 November 1962. But the quotation is not sourced in the letter.
[24] Completion of the road was announced by the Chinese in September 1958. Chou told Neville Maxwell that they had been building the road but Nehru knew about it from a pictorial magazine (*China Pictorial?*). Cf. *Sunday Times*, London, 5 December 1971.
[25] *White Paper I*, p. 5.
[26] Prime Minister on Sino-Indian Relations, New Delhi, Government of India 1961, *I*, p. 134.
[27] *Ibid.*, pp. 148-9.
[28] Ajoy Ghosh, "India-China Friendship—Repair the Damage," *New Age* weekly, 10 May 1959.
[29] India, *White Paper II*, pp. 12
[30] Quoted in Premen Addy, "New Delhi and the Bandung Spirit: A Reappraisal," *Frontier*, 27 November 1971.
[31] T.D. Allman in *The Guardian*, 4 October 1971, quoted in *ibid.*
[32] George Patterson, *Tragic Destiny*, New York, Praeger, 1959, pp. 136-8.
[33] *New York Times*, 7 April, 1960.
[34] NCNA, 7 September 1960.
[35] Allen Whiting, "What Nixon Must Do to Make Friends in Peking," *New York Review*, 9 October 1971.
[36] "On Certain Questions Before the International Communist Movement," Resolution of the Central Executive Committee of the CPI, 4-7 September 1960.
[37] Speech by Ajoy Ghosh at the World Conference of Communist and Workers Parties, November 1960.
[38] *Ibid.*
[39] "The Truth About How the Leaders of the CPSU Have Allied Themselves with India Against China," *People's Daily*, 2 November 1963.

[40] *The India-China Border Dispute and the Communist Party of India* (for party members only), New Delhi, 1963, p. 7.

[41] *Ibid.*, pp. 48-9.

[42] "The Truth About How...", *loc. cit.*

[43] "Whence the Differences—A Reply to Comrade Thorez and Other Comrades," *People's Daily*, 27 February 1963.

[44] Modeste Rubinstein, "A Non-capitalist Path for Underdeveloped Countries," *New Times*, 5 July 1956 and 2 August 1956.

[45] "Parliamentary Road in India—A Fiasco," *Peking Review*, 31 January 1969.

4/ Compulsive Drift

India's China policy collapsed with the Tibet revolt in March 1959 and the two border clashes that followed it—at Longju in the NEFA sector in August and a more serious one at Kong-ka pass in Ladakh in October. It was a slow drift towards a confrontation which came in 1962, largely a function of the escalating Sino-Soviet ideological dispute.

Prime Minister Jawaharlal Nehru, in a letter to Prime Minister Chou En-lai on 22 March, had suggested that both sides should respect the positions as they were before the dispute and neither side should attempt unilateral action "in exercise of what it conceives to be right". The Longju clash occurred after this. Chou, in his belated reply on 8 September, affirmed that his government "absolutely" did not recognise the "so-called McMahon Line" but Chinese troops had not crossed it. The border dispute as a whole was a "complicated question left over by history" and created by Britain which had carried out "extensive territorial expansion into China's Tibet region, and even the Sinkiang region". Chinese troop movements near the border were merely for "preventing remnant armed Tibetan rebels from crossing the border back and forth..." but the corresponding Indian moves were "unnecessary and provocative".[1]

To Nehru, this might have appeared a clear repudiation of the McMahon Line as the border on the eastern (NEFA) sector. Nevertheless, his sentiments favouring a negotiated settlement (22 March) were echoed by the Standing Committee of the Second National People's Congress of China on 13 September

> as a provisional measure, the two sides should maintain the long-existing status quo and not seek to change it by unila-

teral action, still less by force; as for some of the disputes, provisional agreements concerning individual places could be reached through negotiations to ensure the tranquillity of the border areas and uphold the friendship of the countries.

If Nehru's 22 March appeal for a status quo pending solution of the problem was constructive, so was the Chinese declaration of 13 September. Replying to the 8 September letter, Nehru on 26 September rejected any negotiation with China unless the territory claimed by it including the Aksai-chin area was vacated and further "threats and intimidations" ceased.[2]

Within a few days, the Sino-Indian border dispute was to be seriously discussed in Peking among Chinese, Soviet and Indian communist leaders. A delegation of the Communist Party of India, headed by General Secretary Ajoy Ghosh went to Peking for the tenth anniversary celebrations of the People's Republic of China on 1 October. On his way back from the Camp David summit with President Eisenhower, Soviet Premier Nikita Khrushchev went to Peking and harangued the Chinese leaders in public not to "test by force the stability of the capitalist system". Ghosh is believed to have prevailed upon the Soviet leaders present there to influence the Chinese leaders into a more conciliatory attitude to the border dispute with India. Despite what the CPI regarded an incorrect Chinese assessment of the Indian situation and the Nehru government's shift to rightist policies revealed in the discussions, Ghosh gained the impression that it was possible to solve the Sino-Indian border dispute through negotiations. He claimed a change in the Chinese attitude reflected in their stoppage of offensive expressions against India in their press, their participation in the World Agricultural Fair in New Delhi, their steps to contact the Indian government on the border dispute, and their initiative for a Nehru-Chou meeting.[3]

But before all this could materialise there was another clash on 21 October at Kong-ka which according to the Chinese had always been part of their territory. Disturbed about the implications of the clash, the CPI suggested to the Chinese party that the damage could still be repaired if the Chinese government immediately expressed regret over the clash, without blaming India for the happening and proclaimed a desire for negotiations to settle all disputes between the two countries.

This suggestion could not have impressed the Chinese leadership. On 26 September Nehru had rejected negotiations with the Chinese unless they pulled out of the Chinese-claimed territory including the Aksai-chin area. Yet Chou responded to the CPI appeal and wrote to Nehru on 7 November expressing regret over the Kong-ka pass clash. To avoid such incidents and to secure an "amicably peaceful settlement" he proposed that neither side should seek to alter the status quo in any manner. To creae a "favourable atmosphere for friendly settlement" each side should withdraw 20 kilometres at once from the McMahon Line in the NEFA sector and 20 kilometres from the line of each side's actual control in the Ladakh sector, and the two sides should refrain from sending armed personnel again to this zone. Thus Chou was proposing a demilitarised zone.[4] In effect it would have left the Chinese in possession of the road through Aksai-chin in Ladakh while the Indians would have given up their posts along the McMahon Line in the NEFA sector.

Nehru, on 16 November, rejected Chou's proposals for withdrawal all along the border but wanted it limited to the western sector—not a common distance but behind each other's claim line to ease the tension. He made three suggestions: (*i*) In Ladakh, China would withdraw to the boundary shown in the Indian maps, and India to the boundary shown in the Chinese maps leaving the vacated area unadministered. (*ii*) Along the rest of the frontier neither side should send out patrols from its checkposts. (*iii*) The Chinese should withdraw from the Longju post but Indians should not reoccupy it.

Nehru's "alternative proposals" would have entitled Chinese withdrawal from the entire Aksai-chin area through which their strategic road runs, and also the Cheng Chen-mo valley up to the Kong-ka pass (about 20,000 square miles in all) in the Ladakh sector. Against this it would have entailed the Indian withdrawal from the Damchok area in south-eastern Ladakh. In the NEFA sector, it would have required the Chinese pull-out from the Longju area. In effect it would have neutralised the disputed areas in Chinese occupation.

Nehru followed this up with an attack on Chinese "expansionism". He told the Lok Sabha on 27 November that China was in an "abnormal" state and that generally followed any major revolution. History showed that China had exhibited expansionist tendencies whenever it was strong. Now the combination of growing strength as a result of rapid industrialisation in China with the fact of a rapidly growing population created a "dangerous" and "explosive" situation.

Chou's reply on 17 December assured Nehru that the Chinese had stopped patrolling and proposed a meeting with him in any place in China or in Rangoon to reach "some agreement on principles as a guidance to concrete discussions of the boundary question by the two sides". Chou's letter implied rejection of Nehru's 16 November proposals. He was ready for a "partial solution" applying Nehru's Longju proposals to other areas as well and named ten such disputed places, all in Indian territory. He welcomed Nehru's proposal for stopping patrols from checkposts but this should apply not only to NEFA and the central sector but to Ladakh also.

Chou rejected Nehru's proposals on four grounds: (*i*) There was no reason to treat Ladakh as a special case as China was in actual control of the whole of the area shown in their 1956 maps except for one place occupied by India. (*ii*) It represented "a big step backward" from the principle agreed upon to maintain the status quo. (*iii*) It was unfair because "even the most anti-Chinese part of the Indian Press had pointed out India's concession as only theoretical" and India had no personnel there to withdraw while China had to withdraw from a 33,000 kilometre area. (*iv*) The area had long been under Chinese jurisdiction. Chou claimed that the road through Aksai-chin had been in existence since the Ching dynasty days and was used by the People's Liberation Army in 1950 to enter Tibet and that between March 1956 and October 1957 they had built through it a motorable highway 1,200 kilometres long without any challenge from India.

Chou suggested that if India should still insist that its claim to the Ladakh area was proper, then the principle it wanted applied here should apply to NEFA also. This would entail withdrawal of Indian armed and other personnel to the boundary shown in the Chinese maps, that is, nearly 35,000 square miles of territory in Indian possession.

Confronted with the proposal for talks, Nehru told Chou on 21 December that while he was always ready for a meeting, he did not see "how we can reach agreement on principles when there is such a complete disagreement about facts." He did not, however, reject the proposal for a meeting. Chou had wanted a meeting on 26 December and Nehru was unable to make it at such a short notice. Nehru did not propose an alternative date.

INDIA'S STAND HARDENS

By the end of 1959, India's stand on the dispute hardened and its manoeuvrability vastly reduced. It was not until September that India chose to publish up-to-date its exchanges with China. Thereafter, the exchanges were published as they took place. It was far from clear why Nehru chose to publish the accumulated exchanges in the form of a White Paper in September 1959 and not earlier. The result of the publication was a belligerent outburst of public opinion against China and the Indian government's handling of the issue. Nehru's detractors lost no time in making the charge that the fact of Chinese occupation of Indian-claimed territory had been withheld from the nation and this amounted to acquiescence to aggression. Nehru was wrong if he published the exchanges in the hope he would enlist public opinion for his firm stand on the border issue. The publication of the first *White Paper* only resulted in a backlash. Nehru could not resile from his public position that talks could take place only after China had vacated Indian-claimed territory. There was a fierce political campaign against any negotiations with China and even the proposed Chou-Nehru meeting was opposed as appeasement.

The hardening of India's stand can be attributed directly to two significant developments: Nehru's insight into the Sino-Soviet differences over India, and United States attitude to the Sino-Indian border dispute. By the end of 1959, Nehru was certain that Soviet and United States attitudes were converging on India and this would give him adequate leverage with China on the border issue, and a hard line would eventually pay off.

As early as 1950, Nehru had written to Sir Benegal Narsing Rau, India's representative at the United Nations:

> I have a strong feeling that the future of Asia is rather tied up with the relations between India and China. I see that both the USA and the UK on the one hand and the USSR on the other, for entirely different reasons are not anxious that India and China should be friendly towards each other. That itself is a significant fact which has to be borne in mind.[6]

Thus even since the birth of communist China Nehru was acting on the assumption that Soviet Union would not like India and China being friendly. By mid-1959, Nehru knew of the deteriorating Sino-Soviet relations. Immediately after the Tibet revolt and the first breach in Sino-Indian relations caused by it, Soviet Union extended massive economic aid to India. A latter-day account disclosed that Khrushchev promised Soviet support to India against China in May 1959. R. K. Karanjia, editor of the pro-Soviet Bombay weekly, *Blitz*, claims that when be told Khrushchev in the course of an interview of India's deteriorating relations with Pakistan and China and asked if Soviet Union would help India in the event of an attack from either of them, the reply was:

> All you have to do is to shout across the Himalayas and we shall rush to your rescue.[7]

Karanjia also learnt from Khrushchev that the Chinese were objecting to Soviet economic aid to non-aligned countries and this had stood in the way of Soviet help for the Aswan dam. This was the first disclosure of Sino-Soviet differences and on a crucial issue, and "a prophetic piece of news which I lost no time in passing on to Jawaharlal Nehru".[8]

The 9 September 1959 *Tass* statement on the Longju incident which made public the Sino-Soviet differences on India might have surprised the world but not Nehru. A few days after the Longju clash, when another clash took place at the Kong-ka pass, Khrushchev, returning from Camp David had talks with Mao Tse-tung in Peking to persuade the Chinese to settle the dispute with India. After the Kong-ka clash, Nehru sent an important personal message to Khrushchev through a ranking Soviet visitor, N. A. Mukhditonov, two days after that.

Khrushchev began queering the pitch for the Chinese when he reiterated his neutral stand in the Sino-Indian border dispute and called for a negotiated settlement. Reporting to the Supreme Soviet on 31 October, he deplored the incidents on the frontier between "two states friendly to us—the Chinese People's Republic to which we are bound by unbreakable bonds of brotherly friendship, and the Republic of India, with whom we have been successfully developing friendly relations". He was especially sorry about the incidents because there had been casualties on both sides. "We would have been happy if there were no more incidents on the Sino-Indian frontier, if the existing frontier disputes were settled by way of friendly negotiations to the mutual satisfaction of both sides."[9]

A week later, Khrushchev was to restate this, more outspokenly this time in an interview to the Moscow correspondent of the CPI weekly *New Age*. It was a "sad and stupid story". Nobody knew where the border was. He agreed with the correspondent that practically nobody lived there. Soviet Union had settled the differences over its border with Iran. "We gave up more than we gained" and "what were a few square miles to a country like the Soviet Union?"[10]

Khrushchev's pronouncements were meant to support India against China and also to provide the divided CPI leadership an alibi for its unqualified support to Nehru. When the party's

National Council met in Meerut amidst the renewed anti-China hysteria in the country and tension on the border, one section wanted the party to line up behind Nehru while another opposed it, pointing out that Nehru was yielding to rightist pressures, however feebly. The third thought Nehru was fighting the pressures single-handed. On the border dispute, one section thought the Indian government was primarily responsible for it because it had engineered tension between the two countries to cover up its retreat from progressive policies. Another blamed the Indian reactionaries for working up hysteria to oust Nehru. China had not committed aggression but its attitude to maps, etc., had strengthened the reactionaries. So the CPI sought to persuade the Chinese to be conciliatory. The 7 November letter from Chou indicated that the Chinese had responded to the CPI's appeal. The third section thought the Chinese had wrongly taken Nehru to be the spokesman of the Indian reaction and had crossed the border to make him see reason. But the result had been just the opposite. Nehru continued to oppose reaction at home and so deserved qualified support. The party should back the Indian government on Ladakh and ask the Chinese to vacate aggression.[11]

Nehru's policies backed by Khrushchev were central to the CPI differences. The right group tried to dissociate Nehru from the "reactionary" policies of his government and wanted to strengthen him against rightist pressure. The result was a compromise—support to the government's stand on the McMahon Line and equivocation on the western border (Ladakh sector). But there was a dispute as to what constituted the western border and about its delineation and this needed a friendly discussion between the two governments. The council wanted negotiations without either side insisting on the acceptance of its stand as the precondition. Meantime, clashes should be avoided. The council welcomed Chou's "constructive approach" to the dispute, and balanced this with its appreciation for Nehru's determination to pursue his "independent foreign policy" despite "terrific pressure" from "reactionary forces". Nehru had firmly rejected military alliances and stressed negotiations and settlement and warned against war psychosis.[12]

This compromise resolution might have fallen short of Khrushchev's expectations but strengthened Nehru nevertheless. Nehru was moving closer to Soviet thinking in favour of an East-West detente, which the Chinese could not have liked. As early as 21 October, he had drawn the line between the Soviet and Chinese brands of communism and Khrushchev was "eager and anxious" for an East-West understanding but the same desire did not exist in Peking. Soviet Union was a satisfied power but "China had not gotten over the first flush of its revolutionary mentality".[13]

Later, Nehru told the Lok Sabha on 27 November that no country cared more for peace than the Soviet Union and none cared less than China. He was hailing the Camp David spirit. In December, General Dwight Eisenhower, United States President, came to India and stressed the identity of the basic goals of the two countres.[14] He had earlier offered United States arms aid to India in 1959 when the border clashes took place[15] but Nehru had plainly turned it down. The offer had been conveyed discretely through his sister, Mrs Vijayalakshmi Pandit. India-United States relations which had deteriorated in 1954 and had remained at the lowest level since, began to improve in 1957-58 as the cold war thawed. The steady improvement in these relations was highlighted by the growth of a strong pro-India group in the United States Congress and Administration. The establishment in August 1958 of the World Bank consortium for India and Pakistan was an achievement of this group. United States anger over India's opposition to military pacts and blocs was gone. India's system of government suited the long term interests of United States. The Mutual Security Bill of 1959 contained a resolution, inserted by the Senators Edward Kennedy and Sherman Cooper, specifically mentioning the importance of India's development plans to U.S. security and the need for substantial and continuing aid.[16]

By 1959, both the big powers were stepping up economic aid to India. Soviet credit deals in 1959 totalled 350 million roubles (after 122 million roubles in 1955 and 113 million roubles in

1957). In the same year, the ruling Congress party decided on co-operative farming and radical land reforms and the rightists in the party walked out to form the Swatantra Party to protect private property and free enterprise. Instead of initiating radical land reforms and organising farmers to raise food production, the Indian government negotiated massive PL-480 foodgrain imports. These imports gave the government cushion for administrative and policy complacency until India accounted for almost a quarter of all the concessional food sales by United States. Land reforms were thus effectively sabotaged.

To Soviet Union, India was leader of the peace zone and therefore of strategic importance in its efforts towards a detente with United States. To United States India was of long-term strategic importance.[17] On 18 August 1960, referring to the stake of the two big powers in India's development effort, Nehru told the Lok Sabha:

> ...it is a remarkable thing and it is worth considering how these tremendous protagonists of the cold war can yet have this friendly feeling for India.

However, about the same time, Soviet Union was pulling out its technicians from China and thousands of Sino-Soviet agreements on economic co-operation were being scrapped.

CHINA PROPOSES TALKS

The Chinese, in a note on 2 January 1960 revived the suggestion for a Nehru-Chou meeting pointing out "the most basic fact" that the entire 2,500 mile boundary had never been delimited and "is, therefore, yet to be settled by negotiations". Pending formal delineation, the Chinese wanted the border demilitarised with no forward patrolling in disputed areas. The note was moderate in tone and the concluding paragraphs harped on the theme of Sino-Indian friendship in the interest of Asia and world peace. There was no alternative to peace because both the countries needed to concentrate on economic development.

It made two other points. It rejected as "sheer nonsense" the allegation that the Chinese wished to encroach on Sikkim and Bhutan. It admitted that the Sikkim-Tibet border had been formally delimited and there was no dispute about this sector, but a claim was made to north-eastern Bhutan.

In the Indian government's assessment, two aspects of the note were significant. One, it had stressed more clearly than ever before the importance of the Aksai-chin highway as the sole possible line of communication between Tibet and western Sinkiang. This was the crux of the Sino-Indian border problem. The other was the reiteration of readiness for an "overall settlement" on the basis of "historical background and the present actual situations". The reality was that China was already in occupation of all but a small area in Damchok claimed by it in the Ladakh area. In NEFA, India was in occupation of almost the entire area claimed by China.

All this amounted to the suggestion that China might be willing to give up its claims in NEFA if India agreed to formalise the existing reality in Ladakh. It was quite possible that the Chinese had pressed their claims in the NEFA sector to be able to secure recognition of the reality in Ladakh. The fact remained that India did not know about the Aksai-chin highway until after it had been completed by the Chinese.[18]

The renewed Chinese proposal for talks found Nehru in a dilemma. He had ruled out negotiations unless the Chinese vacated the Indian-claimed territory and negotiations could only relate to minor adjustments. He had also held that no agreement on principles was possible when there was complete disagreement on facts. The political challenge to Nehru's leadership was growing within his party and outside and for the first time the consensus on his foreign policy had fractured over the Tibet issue and his non-alignment was under attack. Yet despite his reservations about its utility, he could not rule out a meeting with Chou. At his press conference in New Delhi on 8 January he could not say precisely when and on what conditions he could meet Chou, "but I cannot rule it out. It may well take place, but as I said, there is no talk about it at the present moment and there is no proposal to that effect, that is, specific proposal". Nehru was not against talks but opposed negotiations. Thus, his invitation to Chou on 5 February 1960 (through Ambassador G. Parthasarathy) to visit New Delhi made clear that there would be no negotiations but merely talks.

On 24 February Nehru told the New Delhi press corps that Chou's inviting him to meet him had put him in a position where he would have to refuse to meet him "under certain circumstances as I thought might be done". But the point was "in the balance. After much thought we thought it was desirable to have a chance of meeting instead of merely taking up this negative attitude even though it was by no means certain that any positive good might result from the meeting".

A heated anti-China campaign by political groups opposed to Nehru and the press was already on in India. Even a meeting of the two Prime Ministers was regarded as capitulation on India's part. Nehru's sharp reaction to questions at a press conference would bear this out.

Correspondent: What is your hunch about it Do you think he will accept the invitation...?
Another Correspondent: After the outbursts of opposition groups...
Nehru: Why not, I add, the Press. I must say it has not enhanced the great reputation of some newspapers in India...

Certain developments between Chou's proposal for a meeting (made in December 1959) and Nehru's decision to invite Chou cannot be overlooked. The Chinese had pressured the Soviet leadership to change their attitude to the Sino-Indian border dispute. Between 10 December 1959 and 30 January 1960, Chinese leaders had six rounds of talks about this with the Soviet ambassador in Peking. They pointed out that it was wrong for Soviet Union to have maintained "strict neutrality" and far from being neutral Soviet statements had in fact censured China and favoured India. The Chinese were to claim later that on 6 February the Soviet party central committee had told its Chinese counterpart that "one cannot possibly seriously think that a State such as India, which is militarily and economically immeasurably weaker than China, would really launch a military attack on China and commit aggression against it"; that China's handling of the question was "an expression of narrow nationalist attitude"; and that "when shooting was heard on the eve of N. S. Khrushchev's trip to the United States, the whole world considered this to be an event that could hamper peace-loving activity of the Soviet Union".[19]

Soviet President Voroshilov had in the meantime visited India with a high-level entourage in January and the dates for Khrushchev's visit to India in February had been agreed upon. When Chou promptly accepted the invitation to visit New Delhi in April, he had little doubt about where the Soviet sympathies lay. Before Chou's visit took place, the Sino-Soviet ideological dispute had transcended the stage of inter-party exchanges. It exploded in the open in April when the Chinese challenged Khrushchev through the *Red Flag* article "Long Live Leninism!" which was the first comprehensive theoretical attack on Soviet ideological positions.

On the eve of Chou's visit, the overall picture was complex. The CPI, whose ministry in Kerala had been toppled through a constitutional coup, had been routed by an anti-communist alliance. The rightist forces had gained strength and were campaigning for a shift in Nehru's foreign policy. Yet Khrushchev had visited India after the CPI rout in Kerala, thereby demonstrating his approval of Nehru's policies. Earlier in January, Burma and China had reached an accord on their border and signed a treaty of friendship. Nepal's Prime Minister B. P. Koirala had visited Peking in March and concluded an agreement with the Chinese on the border. An Indian government brochure on 22 December 1959 had said it was willing to explore the possibilities of a peaceful settlement but only on the basis of "existing borders and such minor rectifications of the frontier as may be considered necessary by agreement". Other points in the brochure were: (*i*) India's traditional frontier with China was well-known, being based on treaty, agreement and custom.

Till recently no Chinese government had ever challenged it. (*ii*) The present controversies over the frontiers arose because the Chinese government, for the first time, had laid claim to extensive areas of Indian territory (through its 8 September 1959 letter). (*iii*) The tension on the border in the last few months had increased because China was pushing forward to assert claims and this led to clashes.

Aksai-chin—The Issue

To China, the road across Aksai-chin, linking Tibet with west Sinkiang was a vital line of communication. It was already in possession of the area and wanted to formalise an existing reality. At one stage Nehru had admitted that the Ladakh border had not been formally demarcated and had been challenged for a long time. He had said on 10 September 1959 in the Rajya Sabha:

> It is a complicated thing, but we have always looked upon the Ladakh area as a different area ... a vaguer area so far as the frontier is concerned because the exact alignment of the frontier is not at all clear as in the case of the McMahon Line.[20]

Again, on 12 September 1959, he told the Lok Sabha:

> ... it is a matter of argument as to what part of it [Aksai-chin] belongs to us and what part of it belongs to somebody else. It is not a dead clear matter. However, I have to be frank to the House. It is not clear. I cannot go about doing things in a matter which has been challenged not today but for a hundred years. It has been challenged to the ownership of this strip of territory. That has nothing to do with the McMahon Line. ... It has been in challenge all the time.[21]

The substance of Nehru's statement on Ladakh was: it was a disputed area and he was less certain about India's claim to it than about the area on this side of the McMahon Line. This could have given the Chinese the impression that India might be prepared for settlement on Ladakh in return for their acceptance of the McMahon Line. But now Nehru was asserting that no dispute existed over Ladakh and that it had always been clearly demarcated.

India's position had gradually hardened, from the admission that the position with regard to Aksai-chin was qualitatively different from that of the McMahon Line (about which it was very sanguine), to the assertion that India's "traditional border was well-known".

The Chinese, on their part, had all along contended that the border had never been delimited. They might have challenged the McMahon Line so that they could bargain better over Aksai-chin to formalise an existing reality. Chou's 7 November 1959 proposal for a 20-kilometre withdrawal by either side from positions of actual control aimed at this. Willingness to recognise the McMahon Line was implied in the offer and it was to be reiterated on 2 January 1960 through a note.

During Chou's talks in New Delhi it was clear that this willingness flowed from the Chinese position in Ladakh—they were equating the "present actualities" with the concept of "traditional customary line" which approximated their position in Ladakh. The "traditional customary line" was not be "mechanically defined or predetermined by any geographic principle" but was "bound to undergo changes owing to political, economic and other reasons". To the Chinese, the McMahon Line was the "traditional customary line" in the NEFA sector, and they were willing to recognise it as such *after* the formality of negotiations (as they had done in the case of Burma). A quid pro quo was involved here: Indian recognition of the Chinese claim line in Ladakh on the basis of the actual situation. It was not a question of maps or the application of the watershed principle to draw the line but one of a political settlement affecting China's vital logistic interests in Aksai-chin.

India's Defence Minister V. K. Krishna Menon realised this and proposed a formula. In return for a long-term lease of the area China needed in Aksai-chin (and was already in possession of) it should give India an equal area in the Chumbi valley, the dagger dividing Sikkim and Bhutan. The valley was of immense strategic value to India's border defence in the central sector where there was no dispute. Nehru was in favour of this formula which was mooted when Chou came to New Delhi. Perhaps anticipating hostile domestic reaction to such a deal, Nehru wanted to play safe when he tried to carry two of his most conservative Cabinet colleagues—the late Govind Vallabh Pant and Morarji Desai—with him. Pant threatened to quit if Nehru accepted the formula[22] and Desai pontificated to Chou until the latter walked out of the room in anger. So the formula could not be mooted with Chou at the New Delhi talks.

In retrospect, it would seem the Menon formula for a "political" deal was about the closest India and China came to solving their border problem before it escalated into an armed conflict in late 1962. Nehru could not carry his colleagues with him on the formula under which China would have exchanged the Chumbi valley for the Aksai-chin area and recognised the McMahon Line with a few minor adjustments. From now on Nehru began yielding to domestic pressures inch by inch until the issue was past the point of no return. Nehru was reluctant to risk a confrontation with his detractors over the Menon formula possibly because he did no visualise an end to the border problem even if the formula appealed to him. He had already assumed that China was expansionist and a long conflict lay ahead.

Briefing officials on the eve of Chou's visit, Nehru said the combination of China's growing strength and its industrialisation and its vast population made it an explosive, dominant, and dangerous problem not only for India but for the world in the next twenty years. Even Soviet Union was worried and feared China. India would not break with China immediately though the old friendship and understanding between the two were no longer there. The border had become live and dangerous though he did not visualise an immediate war. Besides India's dislike for war, the terrain and the weather were to India's disadvantage and so in their enthusiasm and anger they could not allow themselves to be trapped in an extricable situation in the high mountains. The frontier, nevertheless, would remain dangerous unless China broke up, which could not happen so easily.[23]

During the Chou-Nehru talks, assisted by officials, it was found that the entire disputed area could not be considered one piece. Claims and counter-claims over different parts of the boundary made the picture complicated. Chou suggested that by way of mutual acommodation and friendly give and take, the entire disputed territory in Indian occupation together with unoccupied disputed territory might be considered Indian territory in future. Similarly the disputed territory in Chinese occupation should be considered Chinese territory. This formula would have given about three-fourths of the entire disputed territory (about 50,000 square miles) to India. It would have ensured China the possession of the Aksai-chin area. Chou is believed to have pointed out that Aksai-chin was of strategic value to China because United States had military bases very near west Aksai-chin.[24]

Nehru could not have agreed to the formula because his critics would have charged him with appeasement and sought his ouster. There was no issue other than the border with China on which they could have rallied forces against Nehru. He is reported to have told Chou: "We have to satisfy our people," and Chou replied, "But Mr Prime Minister, we too have to satisfy our people."[25]

The Chou-Nehru talks were a failure. The joint communique on 25 April revealed that the only agreement between the two sides was on joint team of officials to examine, check and study all documents, maps and other material on which each side relied in support of its stand, and to report to the two governments to help further consideration of the question. Chou told a midnight press conference that (i) there existed a dispute on the boundary. (ii) There existed between the two countries a line of actual control up to which each side exercised administrative jurisdiction. (iii) While determining the boundary between the two countries, certain geographical principles, such as watershed, river valleys and mountain passes would be applicable equally to all sectors of the boundary. (iv) A settlement of the boundary question between the two countries should take into account the national feelings of the peoples of the Himalayas and the Karakoram mountains respectively. (v) Pending a settlement of the question through discussions, both sides should keep to the line of actual control and should not advance any territorial claims as preconditions, but individual adjustments may be made. (vi) To ensure tranquillity on the border to facilitate discussions, both sides should continue to refrain from patrolling along all sectors of the boundary.[26]

Chou's plea for recognition of actual realities and the appointment of a boundary commission were rejected by Nehru. The suggestion about refraining from patrolling the border was also rejected.

Shortly after the Chou-Nehru talks, Pandit Sunderlal, who had met Chou in New Delhi, wrote to Soviet Premier Khrushchev about the internal and external pulls on the Indian government over the border dispute. Sunderlal said the only solution would be complete surrender by China of all the disputed territory in the interest of Sino-Indian friendship. He appealed to Khrushchev to use his influence with the Chinese in the matter. There was no formal reply from the Soviet Premier but it was orally conveyed to Sunderlal that he should find out from Nehru the Indian government's reaction to a formula: China was to retain 12,500 square miles of territory in its occupation in the Aksai-chin region and India was to get 37,000 square miles or so of the disputed territory. In lieu of what China retained, India was to get an equal area somewhere else but contiguous to the border line.[27] In effect this was the same as Krishna Menon's under which India was to get an equal area in the Chumbi valley.[28]

The Chinese were serious about Aksai-chin and everything else was unimportant to them. Sunderlal immediately sounded Nehru. Nehru pondered for a while and said in Hindustani the equivalent of this: "I do not know where they will give us the territory in exchange of Aksai-chin. I do not know what the people will think of it. I do not know what to do. I cannot decide easily or quickly."

SINO-SOVIET DISPUTE

Even as the teams of officials got down to work with a four-month deadline, the boundary dispute was being drawn into the vortex of the new phase of the Sino-Soviet ideological dispute. Following the Chinese attack on Soviet ideological positions ("Long Live Leninism !" in *Red Flag*) the Soviet party circulated a "Letter of Information" on 21 June 1960, on the eve of the Rumanian party congress, to all participating parties, including the Chinese. It attacked the Chinese positions on ideological issues. At the congress proper, Khrushchev launched his offensive charging the Chinese with planning to set off a third world war and with being "purely nationalist" on their border dispute with India and of employing Trotskyite ways against Soviet Union.[29] Khrushchev told the Chinese that since Indians were killed in the border clashes (Longju and Kong-ka clashes), it meant China attacked India. For communists it was not important where the border ran.[30]

The Bucharest crisis was transmitted to the entire international communist movement. Sino-Soviet state-level relations had worsened with Soviet technicians and experts leaving China in July and publications devoted to Sino-Soviet friendship stopped. The CPI had chosen to overlook the new phase in the Sino-Soviet ideological dispute until its two delegates to Bucharest, leftist M. Basavapunniah and left-of-centre Bhupesh Gupta returned to tell the story. General Secretary Ghosh and a senior leader, S. A. Dange, had attended the Peking meeting of the World Federation of Trade Unions in June and knew about these developments but had chosen not to tell the party about them. After the Bucharest clash the CPI could no longer ignore the open Moscow-Peking conflict.

A world conference of communist parties was due in Moscow later in the year and the CPI had been invited to its preparatory meeting. So it had to declare its position on the ideological dispute. Its executive discussed the Bucharest crisis and the party found itself divided on ideological issues. The executive first endorsed the Bucharest communique without committing itself to the Khrushchevian thesis of peaceful co-existence or the Peking line opposing it. At a subsequent meeting, however, it adopted a more comprehensive resolution which took pro-Soviet positions on the issues. The left found itself in a minority and vacillating elements joined the majority. But the resolution made a significant observation : "The first breach in Indo-China friendship was created in the attitude and acts of the Indian government towards the counter-revolutionary uprising and aid given to the Dalai Lama to conduct an anti-China campaign in India." It also attacked the Chinese description of Kalimpong as the "commanding centre" of Tibetan rebels, their insistence that the Dalai Lama was making his statements under duress and their use of the term "expansionism" in relation to India. The Chinese were charged with making a "basically wrong assessment" of the Indian situation, and this without any effort to ascertain the views of the CPI. In contrast, the Soviet party was praised for its correct role treating the Sino-Indian border dispute as a conflict "between two countries of the peace camp and advocating restraint and settlement by negotiations". But for the Soviet role, the damage to the peace camp and Indian democracy would have been far greater. Hostility to China, the resolution said, would have grown into hostility towards the entire socialist camp had the Soviet Union backed the Chinese position.

The most important part of the resolution was its reference to the ideological roots of the Sino-Indian border dispute which was not just an issue between the two countries. The Chinese party's new assessment of the Indian national bourgeoisie's role had found its "sharpest and most devastating expression" on this issue. Indian communists were to know more about this new assessment later. Harekrishna Konar of West Bengal and K. Damodaran of Kerala attended the Vietnamese Lao Dang Party Congress in Hanoi in September and had gone from there to Peking. Konar returned to tell his colleagues about what the Chinese thought of the Indian situation: since capitalism was weak in Asian countries in relation to imperialism, the bourgeoisie and the governments of these countries would link up with imperialism. In India, the Nehru government was leaning more and more on imperialism.[31]

The Chinese, who were the first to recognise the potential anti-imperialist role of the national bourgeoisie of newly free countries like India in the Bandung phase, were changing their assessment. The Soviet drive for influence in the non-aligned countries began belatedly, after the Chinese had realised the importance of these countries. The Chinese now thought the national bourgeoisie of non-aligned countries were linking up with imperialism but the Soviets had innovated the peaceful coexistence theory with its two corollaries—peaceful transition to socialism and the state of national democracy through which such transition could come about.

The attitude to the national bourgeoisie in countries like India was an issue at the Moscow conference of world communist parties in November 1960, the Soviet and Chinese assessments colliding headlong. There was also a sharp Sino-Indian clash at the conference. The Soviets tried to enlist the support of other parties to isolate the Chinese. The Moscow conference itself was claimed by the CPI as the result of its initiative. The CPI, after its September resolution attacking the Chinese ideological positions, was of immense strategic use to the Soviet party in its effort. The CPI general secretary played an important role in the international commission which drafted the documents for the conference. The commission's work was based, among other things, on an eighty-four page letter from the CPSU to some of the fraternal parties, the hundred-page Chinese rejoinder to it, and the twelve-page CPI resolution of September.

The statement at the end of the conference contained a controversial formulation. It referred to the national democratic state, described as a form of transition to socialism in developing countries, especially in the non-aligned countries of the peace zone where the national bourgeoisie played an objectively progressive role and deserved the political and economic aid of the socialist camp. The national democratic state was one that had won complete economic independence from imperialism and was ruled by a broad anti-imperialist front including the national bourgeoisie, the peasantry and the proletariat. The working class was to evolve as its leader only gradually.

The concept of national democracy was an innovation of Soviet-Indian revisionism. It was at once a justification of Soviet aid to India and some other Asian countries whose bourgeoisie the Soviets considered objectively progressive, and an extention of the peaceful co-existence thesis. A CPI theoretician claimed that though "the state of national democracy" was a new concept in the international communist movement, his party had since 1956 put forward a programme and produced an analysis which was the same as the Moscow statement's. It was the culmination of a very precise formulation of the CPI.[32] The CPI had outlined the programme for a "national democratic" front as early as 1956 and anticipated the Soviet thesis. The Chinese attitude to socialist aid to countries outside the socialist camp precluded support to this concept. There was a veiled Chinese attack on the concept of national democracy on the eve of the 22nd Soviet party congress.[33]

The nature of the obligations of the developed communist world to the developing communist bloc countries had been one of the issues in the Sino-Soviet conflict. The Chinese thought that Soviet aid to China had been niggardly and the Soviet leadership had equated developing communist countries with developing non-communist countries like India in the matter of aid. The Soviet leadership pursued its national interest and sought a big power alliance with United States to gain world domination, the Chinese thought. They were to develop this theme in their polemics later, but certainly the concept of a national democratic state, to the extent it implied justification of Soviet aid to the bourgeoisie of a country like India was an irritant n Sino-Soviet relations.

A latter day Chinese assessment of Nehru suggested that they regarded India non-aligned during the Bandung phase (1954-58) and that India had compromised with imperialism thereafter. Nehru had "thrown away the banner of opposition to imperialism" and had "suited himself" to the needs of United States imperialism becoming its "busy spokesman". Bourgeois nationalism under different conditions had played different historical roles. Nehru "who once represented, to a certain degree, the interests of the Indian national bourgeoisie ... became a loyal representative of the big bourgeoisie and big landlords of India". When contradictions between imperialism and the Indian nation sharpened, the Nehru government, under the pressure of the masses, showed a certain degree of difference from imperialism. But the class nature of the big bourgeoisie and the landlords determined that Nehru depended on imperialism and served it more and more.

The assessment underlined the growing dominance of foreign capital in India's economy after independence and the growing dependence of the Indian government on foreign aid. At one stage, Nehru's role helped world peace (e.g. his refusal to joint military blocs, denial of bases to imperialists, his non-alignment, declaration of *Panch Shila,* and his positive role in sponsoring the Bandung conference). Nevertheless, he was subservient to imperialism, criticising it in a "small way" and "helping it in a big way". United States wanted to convert India into a market for its commodities and capital and therefore had shifted its attitude to Nehru's "non-alignment". From refusing to supply the Indian big bourgeoisie machinery and know-how, it was now keen on co-operation with it for joint exploitation of the Indian people. "In a word, U.S. imperialism pursues a policy of paying a high price to buy over the Indian bourgeoisie represented by Nehru."[34]

The Chinese were tracing India's hard line on the border to the class nature of its ruling alliance while the Soviet leadership was seeing immense national democratic virtues in the Indian bourgeoisie and gave it economic aid and diplomatic support. India had become the model of a country of the peace zone, in the process of peaceful transition to socialism. China did not consider India a non-aligned country of the peace zone any longer and did not subcribe to the peaceful transition thesis.

The attitude of India and its ruling class alliance became one of the issues in the Sino-Soviet ideological dispute which was to interact on the Sino-Indian border dispute pushing India and China towards a confrotation.

Notes

[1] *White Paper II*, New Delhi, Ministry of External Affairs, Government of India, pp. 27-33.
[2] Nehru admitted Indian withdrawal from a post in Tamaden near the western end of the McMahon Line because it was found to be north of the line. He also asked for similar Chinese withdrawal from Longju. Text of Nehru's reply in *White Paper II*, pp. 34-52.
[3] *The India-China Border Dispute and the Communist Party of India* (for party members only), New Delhi, Communist Party of India, 1963, pp. 44-50.
[4] *White Paper III*, pp. 45-46.
[5] *Ibid.*, pp. 50 ff.
[6] This was quoted by Sir Benegal's brother, B. Shiva Rao, "Nehru and the UN," *The Statesman*, 6-7 December 1965.
[7] R.K. Karanjia, "Good-bye Good Friend," *Blitz*, 18 September 1971.
[8] *Ibid.*
[9] *New Age* weekly, 8 November 1959.
[10] *New Age* weekly, 15 November 1959.
[11] *Link*, 15 November 1959.
[12] "On India-China Relations," Resolution of the CPI National Council, 11-15 November 1959.
[13] *The Hindu*, 22 October 1959.
[14] Address to Members of Indian Parliament on 10 December 1959.
[15] See "Letter to Fraternal Parties" dated 20 November 1962 signed by members of the CPI Secretariat. It was directed mainly to the ruling communist parties to secure their support to the Indian government's stand on the Sino-Indian border dispute.
[16] *U.S. Congressional Record*, 6 June 1958, 85th Congress, 2nd session, Vol. 104, p. 10396.
The resolution was passed in the Senate despite strong objections to the effect that India was getting precedence over the military allies of United States. It was later deleted at the joint House-Senate conference, the House agreeing in principle with the sentiments but opposing specific reference to India in a general aid act. See P.J. Eldridge, *The Politics of Foreign Aid in India*, New Delhi, Vikas, 1969, pp. 43-44.
[17] United States' private investment which totalled Rs 67.7 million in 1956 rose to Rs 1,930 million in 1965. United States aid became substantial

only after the 1957-58 foreign exchange crisis. This period also witnessed a major growth in trade with United States.

[18] Chou En-lai was to say later, in 1971, that Nehru knew about it first through a Chinese pictorial magazine. See interview with Neville Maxwell *Sunday Times*, 5 December 1971.

[19] "The Truth About How the Leaders of the CPSU Have Allied Themselves With India Against China," *People's Daily*, 7 November 1963. The Chinese were also to claim that Khrushchev had told their delegation at the Rumanian party congress in June 1960: "I know what war is. Since Indians were killed, this meant China attacked India....We are communists. For us it is not important where the frontier runs." *Ibid.*

[20] *Prime Minister on Sino-Indian Relations*, Vol. I, New Delhi, Ministry of External Affairs, 1961, p. 134.

[21] *Ibid.*, p. 148-49.

[22] Menon's biographer T.J.S. George has referred to this formula in *Krishan Menon—A Biography*, London, Jonathan Cape, 1964, pp. 254-55. Though the existence of such a formula was denied in the Indian Parliament (after the death of Pant and Nehru), Menon himself has been equivocal about it. He told Michael Brecher that he never provided his biographer with any material nor did he encourage him to write the book. "I would never discuss these questions outside Government. I am not prepared to say yes or no at this point. I am not prepared to continue talking about these issues." See Michael Brecher, *India and World Politics: Krishna Menon's View of the World* London, Oxford University Press, 1969, pp. 169-70.

[23] This is the account Nehru's intelligence brief, B.N. Mullik gives of the briefing in *The Chinese Betrayal*, New Delhi, Allied, 1971, pp. 263-64.

[24] Chou En-lai was perhaps referring to United States bases in Gilgit in Pakistani-occupied Kashmir.

[25] This account is from Pandit Sunderalal, veteran Congress leader who was connected with the India-China friendship movement and was President of All-India Peace Council. He was the only non-official to have met Chou during the Delhi talks. *Swadhinata*, 26 January 1966.

[26] The Chinese had stopped patrolling since the 1959 clashes.

[27] Pandit Sunderlal disclosed this in *Swadhinata*, 26 January 1966.

[28] Detailed earlier in this chapter.

[29] *Link*, 31 July 1960.

[30] "The Truth About How the Leaders of the CPSU Have Allied Themselves with India Against China," *People's Daily*, 2 November 1963.

[31] *Link*, 16 October 1960.

[32] *Maral*, January 1961.

[33] *People's Daily*, 10 October 1961.

[34] "More on Nehru's Philosophy in the Light of the Sino-Indian Boundary Question," *People's Daily*, 27 October 1962.

5 / The Road to 1962

The Chou En-lai-Nehru talks and the effort of the teams of officials following them up failed because each side approached the Sino-Indian border dispute on the basis of its own set of facts. Nevertheless, it was still a border dispute primarily and had not got enmeshed with the larger dispute of communist ideology. The Chinese objective was still limited to securing de jure possession of the Aksai-chin area.

Though the Tibet revolt had strained Sino-Indian relations and though India was becoming central to the Sino-Soviet ideological dispute, the Chinese did not appear anxious to settle any issue of ideology through the border dispute with India. However, shortly after the Chou-Nehru talks, the ideological dispute sharpened, drawing the Sino-Indian border dispute into its vortex, and complicating the situation. In its origin the border dispute was independent of the ideological dispute but the Sino-Indian military conflict in 1962 was unmistakably a function of the ideological dispute in the international communist movement.

When the Chou-Nehru meeting took place, it was a virtual stalemate truce on the border. Following the 1959 clashes at Longju in NEFA and at Kong-ka in the Ladakh area, China had suspended forward patrolling along the entire border. (The middle sector was free from clashes.) India had suspended patrolling on the eastern border after the Longju clash but theoretically had suspended it in the Ladakh sector.[1] The stalemate truce could have been stabilised into a formal disengagement pending solution of the border dispute. Chou was aiming at such disengagement when he proposed to Nehru the formal suspension of patrolling along the entire border. China was already in possession of the vital Aksai-chin area and a disengagement would have helped avoid clashes which culminated in the 1962 conflict but would have foreclosed India's right to advance into disputed area in the Ladakh sector. India was to assert this right through its "forward policy" initiated in November 1961 to outflank the Chinese posts and to displace the Chinese from Indian claimed territory.

Nehru's response to Chou's proposal for a formal suspension of patrolling was ambiguous. Accepting it would have exposed him to a fierce political onslaught at home and the critics would have seen in it a surrender of the right to regain Indian-claimed territory under occupation. So it was hardly surprising that the Chou-Nehru communique was vague on this issue. It merely said every effort would be made by either side to avoid friction and clashes in the border areas. Confronted with the question if it meant India cannot patrol its territory, Nehru told Parliament that they found it "very difficult and partly undesirable to be precise about it". He thought Indian patrols were free to move about these areas without coming into conflict.[2] Which meant India reserved the right to advance into the no-man's land between the lines of actual control and beyond to recover the Indian-claimed territory through an outflanking operation. In fact, India was to embark on such a "forward policy" in November 1961.

Between the Chou-Nehru talks and the initiation of the forward policy, the Sino-Soviet ideological dispute took a new turn, affecting the state-level relations further. The Sino-Soviet clash at the Rumanian party congress in Bucharest (June 1960) was to be followed by another at the 81 parties meet at Moscow towards the end of 1960 and again at the 22nd Soviet party congress in October 1961 where Khrushchev attacked Albania and denigrated Stalin. By the end of 1961, Premier N. S. Khrushchev had pulled off his summit meeting with President Kennedy in Vienna (in June) and had informed the Chinese (in October) of the Soviet decision to sign the partial nuclear test ban treaty. The cold war was thawing and both Soviet Union and United States had acquired a stake in the stability of the Indian subcontinent and were ready to back India against China.

At the beginning of 1961, Nehru's Congress party had declared the "resolve of the people and the Government of India" to defend the country's integrity, to repel aggression and to secure its vacation.[3] This clearly was a mandate to the government to recover Indian-claimed territory in Chinese occupation. On 21 February, Nehru declared that there was no border dispute as far as India was concerned and therefore no reason for negotiations. A settlement was possible only after China had acknowledged the Indian position and there would be no "horse trading".

Acting on intelligence reports of Chinese activity on the border (incursions, road building, etc.) the Indian government launched the forward policy by which armed forces were to be in effective control of the whole frontier and close all gaps by setting up posts or through patrolling. Both sides seemed to be trying to narrow down the unoccupied area between the respective lines of actual control. In the process India went about setting up posts to outflank the Chinese posts. In some places, Indian patrols even went behind the Chinese lines.[4]

Towards the end of 1961 India was preoccupied with the liberation of Goa to end the 451-year-old Portuguese colonial rule, and with the third adult franchise elections. Portugal was a NATO member and India was risking a wider conflict (NATO intervention) when it marched troops into the Portuguese pocket on 17-18 December 1961 after United States efforts to avert a military solution had failed. After the lightning operation in Goa, the Chinese Foreign Ministry expressed (on 19 December), its resolute support to India's action and assailed the United States role in the episode.

Nehru and His Critics

The country was moving towards the elections and Nehru and his party faced a serious challenge from the rightists and anti-communists who had made the border dispute an issue. Nehru and his colleagues were obliged to adopt a tough anti-China line to blunt the Opposition's campaign. On 28 December, Nehru said that unless there was a change in the Chinese attitude, the renewal of the 1954 India-China agreement on Tibet (due to expire on 3 June 1962) would not help. He ruled out its renewal until China vacated the Ladakh area.[5]

The right-wing Swatantra party, founded in 1959, was making its debut at the poll. Together with the Hindu nationalist Jana Sangh party and the social democratic Praja Socialist Party it was spearheading the campaign against V. K. Krishna Menon in his North Bombay parliament constituency. In 1957 Nehru had put up Menon from this constituency, one of the country's most cosmopolitan and literate, to seek a verdict on the government's foreign policy. Menon won against the candidate of the combined opposition. This time Nehru's party was divided on Menon's candidature from North Bombay. Menon got the nomination through Nehru's intervention. Anti-Menon elements who could not block the nomination joined hands with the combined anti-communist Opposition to back former Congress President Acharya J. B. Kripalani against Nehru's principal foreign policy aide. Failure to get the Chinese out of Indian-claimed areas was the campaign plank because Menon happened to be Nehru's Defence Minister.

Launching the campaign for Menon, Nehru thundered against his party men who professed loyalty to him (Nehru) but did not want Menon in his Cabinet. "I say go to hell," Nehru told the critics who did not like his team. On the same day, Menon appealed to the Chinese to withdraw from occupied territory in the interest of peace and socialism and in their own interest. Six days later, Nehru reiterated his resolve to get the Chinese aggression vacated by peaceful means. If necessary, "force will be used". This undercut the opposition. Menon won hands down but on the whole the right managed a breakthrough in the Parliament and replaced the communists as the principal Opposition. Nehru's critics who were assailing his foreign policy and wanted a hard line against China were gaining ascendency in the party.

Shortly after the elections, there was speculation in New Delhi that Nehru might go to Peking to meet Chou because the two Prime Ministers had envisaged another round of talks when the officials had drawn up their reports. But there were two incompatible reports by the officials, with no common ground. Warren Unna reported in *Washington Post* (25 February 1962) that Nehru, in an interview with him, did not discourage such speculation and that he had indicated Indian willingness to settle for a lease to China for the use of the Aksai-chin road in exchange for general sovereignty over Ladakh as well as all the territory up to the McMahon Line. Nehru contradicted the "lease" part of the report.[6] No such offer had been made to China and it was possible that his remarks were misunderstood, he told Parliament. He had merely said that the road could be continued to be used by the Chinese for civil purposes pending a discussion of the whole dispute.[7]

Meantime tension was mounting on the border. On 2 November 1961 China had demanded a "speedy change" of the "erroneous" Indian strategy. In the same month it warned it might cross the McMahon Line if India persisted in disturbing the status quo in the western sector. In the second week of January 1962, India reported a Chinese probing operation. On 30 April China protested against Indian "provocations" and demanded immediate dismantling of the posts and withdrawal of "intruding Indian troops" and warned of conflict. The warning was repeated on 11 May.

On 14 May India offered talks on the basis of Nehru's 16 November proposals, modified to let Chinese civilian traffic on the Aksai-chin road. Chou's reply on 2 June rebuffed the offer. "Is China a defeated country to accept such unilaterally imposed submissive terms?" he asked. "No force in the world can oblige us to do something of this kind." China could consider the proposal in the western sector only if India accepted the same principle in the eastern sector.[8]

But Nehru ruled out withdrawal in the eastern sector. Once more it was clear that Aksai-chin, through which the vital road ran, was the real Chinese stake in the dispute. The threat to cross the McMohan Line if India persisted in its "forward policy" in the western sector might have aimed at preventing an

Indian push into the Aksai-chin area.

Amidst these exchanges the 1954 agreement on Tibet lapsed quietly on 3 June though between December 1961 and May 1962 China had thrice proposed a new agreement. "Although the conclusion of such a new agreement would have nothing to do with the boundary question, it would undoubtedly have helped to improve Sino-Indian relations," Chou was to say later.[9] But India was linking an agreement on Tibet with the border dispute.

India's forward policy was making its impact on the situation in the Ladakh sector. On 10 July India alleged Chinese encirclement of its post in Galwan valley. On 21 July there was a clash in the Chip Chap valley, the first since the one at Kong-ka in October 1959. R. K. Nehru, Secretary-General of India's External Affairs Ministry, who happened to visit Peking on his way back from Outer Mongolia got the impression that the Chinese were willing to negotiate the border dispute. Chou was to disclose later that on 13 July, when China's ambassador in New Delhi, P'an Tzu-li made a farewell call on Nehru, he had been told that the two countries could discuss the dispute on the basis of the reports of officials. Chou also disclosed that on 23 July Foreign Minister Chen Yi who was in Geneva for the conference on Laos had suggested to Krishna Menon that they (he and Menon) issue a communique declaring that the two sides would hold negotiations on the prevention of a border conflict. Menon pleaded that there was not enough time to work on a communique because he had to go to New Delhi immediately and the two governments could do it after his return. But nothing came of it after Menon's return to New Delhi. Chou thought there was some "external" cause for this and it was not due to Menon himself.[10]

A few days after P'an Tzu-li's departure, Foreign Secretary M. J. Desai sent for the Chinese Charge d'Affaires in New Delhi to discuss the proposal for talks between leaders of the two countries. This information leaked out to the press and the leakage scuttled the proposed talks because a campaign against Nehru's "appeasement" policy began gaining momentum. Meantime, on 26 July, India had reminded China that it was ready for talks on the basis of the officials' reports as soon as tensions eased and a proper climate for talks was created. Read with the earlier correspondence, a "proper climate" meant withdrawal of the Chinese from Indian-claimed areas of Ladakh. But this particular communication did not reiterate this position in detail and Nehru's critics seized on this lapse. Perhaps Nehru wanted a meeting to discuss the officials' report and was not making Chinese withdrawal from Ladakh areas a precondition. In the wake of newspaper reports that Nehru had agreed to talks with preconditions, a campaign against him was gathering strength. The 26 July offer was assailed by newspapers. (One called it "the road to dishonour").[11] In Parliament there was a demand for breaking diplomatic relations with China. The talks offer issue was raised on the opening day of the monsoon session (13 August) and Nehru was obliged to clarify that total Chinese withdrawal from the occupied areas was the precondition for talks and there could only be minor modifications of the boundary. The talks could not relate great chunks of territory. The *People's Daily* snapped back:

> ... if the Chinese side could accept such conditions for negotiations, the Indian side would realise its territorial claims on China without any negotiations. In that case would not negotiations itself become unnecessary?[12]

To the Chinese, Nehru's proposals amounted to one for "one-sided withdrawal" and therefore unacceptable. Nevertheless, they were for negotiations in principle on the basis of the officials' report but without preconditions."

All the same Nehru was anxious not to give the impression that he was banging the door on talks leading to talks. Further discussions were envisaged by him and Chou but Nehru was maintaining that the talks could not take place because of tension on the borders and "further aggression" by China. But he was modifying his 26 July position when he drew a line between talks to end tensions and talks on the merits of the dispute. There could be no discussion on the merits of the dispute until the Chinese withdrew but he was ready to discuss measures to remove tensions and to create the climate for further discussions.[14] To Nehru, the issue was one of removing the tensions. After that the Chinese could withdraw so that the officials' report could be discussed.

This shift in Nehru's stand came after Chen Yi had told an Italian-Swiss radio-TV network in Geneva on 3 August that even if the incident of a local nature took place on the border, there would be no question of a widespread war between China and India. Chen blamed the border tension on India's refusal to negotiate and deep penetration of Indian troops into Chinese territory. Referring to Chou's 1960 New Delhi visit, he said, "from the point of view of courtesy alone, the Indian Prime Minister should have repaid the visit. But he did not do so, neither in 1960-61 nor 1962". About Indian proposals for Chinese withdrawal, Chen had said: "To wish that Chinese troops would withdraw from their own territory is impossible. That would be against the will of six hundred and fifty million Chinese. No force in the world could oblige us to do anything of that kind."

On 14 August Nehru sought and got a "free hand" from Parliament to secure a peaceful settlement of the dispute. His shift was more evident now. Asked if there would be no negotiations until the Chinese withdrew to the Indian-claimed line, Nehru said the situation was such they could not have serious negotiations but he did not specify what he thought could create the required situation beyond saying that if the stage was reached for talks on the basis of the official reports, both the reports would be discussed. He pilloried the Opposition for what he variously termed "childish," "infantile," "not very coherent," and "irrelevant" criticism. He blasted those who wanted India to "run to take shelter under the wing of some other country". This was "dishonourable". The basic reason they attacked his China policy was they were opposed to his non-alignment policy. They wanted the cold war to come to India. About talks and negotiations, he said talks were only exploratory and preliminary. Negotiations were formal. "I refuse to accept that we must not talk unless they vacate their aggression." But negotiations were different. They could be held only "when suitable circumstances existed".

Nehru was prepared to discuss steps to reduce tensions while pushing ahead with his forward policy in the western sector. The Chinese hold that the tensions were caused by India's refusal to negotiate and its forward policy. On 22 August, Nehru claimed in Parliament that the situation was turning in India's favour. About 2,500 square miles out of about 12,000 square miles in Chinese occupation had been "recovered" in the Ladakh sector—the immediate gain of the forward policy. But the Chinese would not have countenanced any threat to the Aksai-chin road and India seemed prepared for this eventuality and was going ahead with its outflanking moves with the objective of regaining "lost" territory.

Nehru's 13-14 August position was not to last long. Pressured by critics, he had to reverse the order of priorities in solving the dispute: he now insisted on Chinese withdrawal first, so that initial talks could relate only to withdrawal (and not *easing of tension*) as he had proposed earlier. The earlier position that talks could take place even before the Chinese "vacated aggression" was now gone. A note on 22 August made this change clear. Chen's remarks in his Geneva interview about Chinese refusal to withdraw were cited as "preconditions" that did not square with the professed Chinese desire for a peaceful solution through negotiations.[15]

Prelude to War

As these exchanges continued, tension was increasing in the western sector and just beginning in the eastern sector at Dhola, south of the Thagla ridge. There were two versions of the McMahon Line in this area and Dhola lay in the gap between the two. Of about a dozen new posts India had set up in the eastern sector under the forward policy, none was in this area. So when a post was set up in Dhola in July, the Chinese saw in it a violation of India's undertaking in 1959 after the Longju clash.[16] The Chinese invested the Dhola post on 8 September.

On 6 October India made the Chinese withdrawal from the south of the Thagla ridge an additional condition to its offer of talks (made on 19 September). Suprisingly the 19 September note had not mentioned the Dhola post issue though it later transpired that the day after the Chinese had invested it, a decision was taken in New Delhi to get the Chinese out of the area south of the ridge.

On 13 September, the Chinese had charged India with inventing excuses for not holding discussions and formally proposed a meeting between the representatives of the two governments from 15 October, first in Peking and then in New Delhi alternatively.[17] On 19 September, India agreed to the discussions but on its own terms—"to define measures to restore the status quo in the western sector which has been altered by force in the last few years and to remove the current tensions in that area".[18] The Chinese rejected this condition but reiterated their proposal for talks without preconditions: either side should be free to raise any issue it wanted.[19] The Chinese resumed patrolling along the entire border.

Whatever discussion India had offered or conditionally accepted so far related entirely to the western sector and the eastern sector was beyond discussion in the Indian view. Perhaps India wanted to freeze the situation in the eastern sector. But in July 1962, its forward policy was extended to the area between the two versions of the McMahon Line. The Chinese did not react to this until 8 September when they invested the post. They resumed general patrolling (suspended in 1959) on 20 September.

When India introduced on 6 October the new condition for talks, it had begun implementing its decision to throw the Chinese across its version of the McMahon Line. A special corps had been created under Lt.-Gen. B. M. Kaul. Indian personnel were already grouping on the banks of the Namkachu river. On 10 October there was a clash between Indian and Chinese personnel. On 12 October Nehru announced to newsmen in New

Delhi that the army had been asked to throw the Chinese out of NEFA "although I cannot fix the date for that" and it was entirely for the military to decide. Menon told partymen in Bangalore the next day that India was determined to throw the Chinese out and to "fight to the last man, to the last gun".

As an Indian commentator said, 8 September became "symbolic of the dividing line between the past and present". Menon had ordered troops at the India-Bhutan-Tibet trijunction to open fire "if necessary". Home Minister Lal Bahadur Shastri had declared that there was no alternative but to drive the Chinese out. Nehru, in London for the Commonwealth Prime Ministers conference, had said that Chinese incursion into NEFA was serious. The talk in New Delhi after 8 September was about "extreme steps" to get the Chinese out as well as of "restraint". The External Affairs Ministry at the same time was anxious that the press should not play up "alarmist" NEFA stories. The commentator, recounting all this, asked: "Is New Delhi firm or 'restrained' in relation to the crisis in NEFA? It is unlikely that anyone in Peking or in New Delhi knows the answer to this."[20]

After the 8 September clash at Dhola domestic opinion was dead set against negotiations and Nehru's 12 October statement had made the nation believe that India was militarily well-prepared to throw the Chinese out of NEFA even if it meant retaliation on the western sector. In fact one thought India was militarily in a better position in the eastern sector than in the western sector. There were further skirmishes in the eastern sector culminating in a full-scale conflict along the eastern and western borders on 20 October, each side charging the other with launching the attack.

The first four days of the conflict was a limited operation and the Chinese achievements included the capture of Towang in the eastern sector. On 24 October Chou proposed a cease-fire based on three points. (*i*) Both sides should declare that the dispute should be settled peacefully (Chen Yi had suggested this to Menon at Geneva in July) and agree to respect the line of actual control (clarified by Chou later to mean as of November 1959). (*ii*) Withdrawal of armed forces of each side by 20 kilometres. If India agreed to this, the Chinese would withdraw to the north of the McMahon Line; and *(iii)* the Prime Ministers of both countries should meet again to seek a friendly solution of the dispute.[21]

LIMITED CHINESE AIM

The Chinese seemed to have a limited objective at this point: to force negotiations. They had no military aim in the conflict. India did not reject the offer outright but proclaimed a "state of emergency" (which was to last until the end of 1967) on 26 October. On 27 October Nehru confronted the Chinese with the question, "What is this 'line of actual control'?" Was it the line of 7 November 1959 or the one created by the Chinese as a result of its military action? Chou explained on 4 November that the line of actual control basically meant the November 1959 line and that the Chinese would have to withdraw much more than 20 kilometres from their present position in the eastern sector but it appeared that they were anxious to retain the area gained in the western sector.

The fighting continued but on a low key. After India's Parliament had resolved "to drive the aggressor out", the Chinese stepped up their military campaign. On 14 November, Nehru wrote to Chou rejecting the 24 October cease-fire proposals and questioning the Chinese interpretation of the 7 November 1959 line to mean the line it had claimed as the boundary since 1960.[22] The 14 November letter seemed to have led the Chinese to believe that India did not want negotiations. They intensified their military drive, taking Walong in the eastern sector and making new thrusts at several points in the western and eastern sectors. The key eastern sector town of Bomdila was taken on 18 November when India sought United States and British military aid. On 21 November China repeated the 24 October proposals and announced a unilateral cease-fire to take effect from the next day to be followed by withdrawal of troops but not "civil police" by 20 kilometres behind the "line mean that Chinese forces would be far behind their 8 September 1962 positions, possibly to counter the Indian charge that China had its own version of the 7 November 1959 line.

It was a brief, desultory war on the Himalayas but it had the dimensions of a disaster for India, shattering many myths. Militarily it was a debacle, shocking the country into awareness of its vulnerability after having been fed on the illusion that military means could force the Chinese out of the Indian-claimed territory. After the Goa operation, Nehru had encouraged the belief that a military solution to the border dispute was possible and that it was merely a matter of choosing the appropriate time. Asked about use of force, as was done in Goa, Nehru had said it was "of course, open to us and should be used by us according to suitability and opportunity".[23] His top aide Lal Bahadur Shastri was more outspoken: "If the Chinese will not vacate the areas occupied by her, India will have to repeat what she did in Goa. She will certainly drive out the Chinese forces."[24]

When the Chinese unilaterally declared cease-fire on 21 November, they were militarily on top and the Indian army headquarters was thinking of pulling its forces out of Assam.[25] This betrayed a lack of appreciation of Chinese military aims in the conflict. The Home Ministry had already ordered the civil administration to evacuate Tezpur and this amounted to writing off Assam when the Chinese seemed to be knocking at the doors to the plains. It was generally presumed that the Chinese had territorial designs in the plains and were out to grab as much as they could before the war ended. Indian leaders had talked of a total war and the nature of the mobilisation and the character of the Government's emergency powers pointed to a conflict lasting years if not decades. A commentator, however, proved prophetic suggesting on 5 November that China might make a sudden and calculated withdrawal in NEFA to the positions they had held on 8 September.[26] (Nehru was already committed to negotiating with the Chinese if they pulled back to 8 September positions.)

The commentator's reasoning was that the Chinese could

enhance their tangible territorial gains in NEFA by persisting in their drive enlarging the area of both their threat and commitments. Such territorial advantage would be meaningful "only in the degree that they intended to proceed further into the sub-continent. But several factors would veto such a course—the cost and strain of a sustained campaign, the risk of alienating Soviet Union, the non-aligned allies, and India, and the resultant isolation. Conversely, if the Chinese objective in the war was specific and limited and a political one, they were likely to derive some political advantage by a sudden and calculated withdrawal.

The Indian government leadership knew about the Chinese cease-fire offer from the newspapers. Its intelligence chief says that he and others woke up Nehru on 21 November morning (after the newspapers had reported it) with the news and Nehru said, "I knew this. This had to happen. This was bound to happen. How could the Chinese come any further? They had already come too far. Our army was unnecessarily alarmed. The Chinese, now they are at the end of their supply routes, want to get a diplomatic victory over us. They may try to have their way but we will not give in to their demands."[27] In retrospect, judging by the nature of the cease-fire proposals, the Chinese had a very limited military objective. The had admitted advancing into the areas south of the McMahon Line to defeat Indians and "to shatter their plan for altering the border status quo by armed force, and to create conditions for a negotiated settlement".[28]

There are several theories explaining the abrupt end to the war: a stern Soviet warning coupled with troop movements in Sinkiang by way of diversionary action; stoppage of Soviet oil supplies; an implied United States warning by moving an aircraft carrier of the Seventh Fleet towards the Bay of Bengal in response to an Indian request, the failure of Chinese logistics, and the like. It is more plausible that China had the limited objective of using the border dispute to challenge some of the Soviet positions in the ideological dispute. In a sense that war itself was a function of the larger ideological conflict and the war in turn aggravated the ideological dispute. It would be well to remember that though independent in their origins, the Sino-Indian border war (20 October-20 November) and the Cuban missile crisis (22 October-28 October) got interwinged with each other and had a far-reaching impact on the ideological dispute leading to the international communist schism.

India Seeks Arms Aid

The border war put India's non-alignment to a crucial test by forcing it to seek arms aid from the Western camp, causing the Soviet leadership immense embarrassment because it had made India the model of non-alignment and peaceful transition to socialism via national democracy. The Chinese were out to prove that India was not really non-aligned and that its national bourgeoisie whom the Soviet leadership was pampering had long ceased to be progressive.

On 22 August 1961 Nehru had defended non-alignment rejecting the suggestion that India should seek military aid against China. "Taking military help meant practically getting aligned," he told Parliament when tension on the border was growing. "A few crores [ten millions] that we may save if we get these equipment [military equipment] as gift would be far outweighed by the tremendous loss in prestige and position and even in sympathy which we would have had from other countries."[29]

Nehru was to compromise his non-alignmnet barely 14 months later. On 29 October 1962, India formally decided to accept United States military aid, after Ambassador J. K. Galbraith had met Nehru. Galbraith had insisted with Foreign Secretary M. J. Desai that the press should be told clearly that request for military aid came from the Indian Prime Minister. President Kennedy promptly agreed to send arms to India without strings and the terms were to be settled later. Indian officials produced inflated lists of requirements and the baffled Americans were obliged to prune them drastically down to realistic limits.

Until about 1960, India had relied heavily on Britain and Europe for arms supplies. In 1951 it signed an agreement under the Mutual Defense Assistance Act with United States and got arms which could not be procured on good terms in Europe. These arms were used for self-defence and internal security. It was by no means a secret agreement and was published (though belatedly) in the United States treaty series.[30] United States had become the second largest source of arms for India until the United States-Pakistan defence pact in 1954. India rejected a similar offer of a pact by United States under the Mutual Security Act of 1954 because the provisions were unacceptable. The law provided for cash sales and gifts. Either was possible only when "the President shall have found that furnishing such assistance will strengthen the security of the United States and promote world peace". For cash sales, the recipient country had to undertake not to use the arms for aggression and to help promote world peace. For grants and deferred payment sales or prices below market value, the recipient had to agree to ten specific undertakings. India and other non-aligned countries were not given arms for these reasons. Further, the establishment of a United States military supplies and training mission in the recipient country was essential. Non-aligned countries, conscious of the political consequences of entertaining such missions preferred to go without United States arms.

But now, within days, emergency supplies of United States infantry weapons and light artillery weapons were ferried to India from depots in Europe and a United States Military Assistance Group began functioning in New Delhi. On 19 November India sought full defensive intervention by United States Air Force. The request was sent through the Indian Embassy in Washington but Galbraith had serious misgivings about the utility of such intervention. He claims to have restrained India from using the air force against China.[31]

After the cease-fire, President Kennedy responding to Nehru's appeal earlier despatched a high-powered team of State Department and Defence Advisers led by Averell Harriman. The team included Gen. Paul Adams, commander of the mobile strike force alerted for emergency ground action in the war. The British sent a similar mission, headed by Duncan Sandys to synchronise with the United States mission's stay in New Delhi. They together processed India's request for military aid for the next three years, formalised few weeks later at Nassau by President Kennedy and Prime Minister Harold Macmillan. The 120-million dollar aid package gave small arms, ordnance machinery and ammunition, the donors sharing the cost.

The flare-up on the Sino-Indian border on 20 October and the tension preceding it found the Soviet leadership in a fix. The beginning of the Cuban missile crisis synchronised with the beginning of the Sino-Indian border war. As early as 8 October (when India had decided to throw the Chinese out of NEFA), a Chinese leader told the Soviet ambassador in Peking that India was planning a massive attack along the border. China could defend itself against such an attack. He also pointed out that Soviet-made helicopters and transport aircraft were used by India on the border and this demoralised the Chinese troops. According to the Chinese, on 13 and 14 October, Khrushchev told the Chinese ambassador in Moscow that their information tallied with what the Chinese said. In a similar situation they (the Soviets) would have taken the same measures the Chinese had. If anyone attacked China, a neutral Soviet attitude was impossible and would amount to betrayal.[32]

SOVIET ATTITUDE

The Soviet response to the war appeared a makeshift one in the beginning though latter-day reconstructions indicate a pattern to it. On 20 October, Khrushchev wrote a "stiff" letter to Nehru on the border situation. On 22 October the Cuban missile crisis began deepening. On 24 October Chou offered India a three-point cease-fire proposal. On 25 October, *Pravda* in an editorial said the Sino-Indian border question was a "legacy" of the British colonial days when the map of Asia was cut and recut arbitrarily. The "notorious McMahon Line, which has never been recognised by China was imposed upon the Chinese and Indian peoples". The Soviet government and people had always advocated peaceful negotiations. *Pravda* also backed Chou's three point proposals for negotiations and observed that the conflict brought "grist to the mill not only of imperialism in general but also of certain reactionary circles inside India most intimately associated with foreign capital and imperialist forces inimical to the Indian people" and referred to "war hysteria" in India. *Pravda* also published that day a Chinese statement which held it "absolutely impossible to imagine the solution of the border question with the help of armed force". The Soviet people took the Chinese statement as an expression of serious concern for its relations with India and of its desire to end the conflict. The proposals were an "acceptable groundwork of negotiations".

The *Pravda* editorial no doubt irked New Delhi. The usual platitude about Nehru's role as "crusader of peace" was missing this time. Nehru had written to Khrushchev explaining the Indian position in great detail but *Pravda* was paraphrasing the Chinese stand on the McMahon Line and endorsing the proposal for negotiations. Worse, the editorial had charged the Indian "reactionary" circles with whipping up "war hysteria". However, New Delhi refrained from retorting on this issue because it badly needed Soviet support on the Kashmir issue.

The Soviet hands were full with the Cuban missile crisis and they could not have risked a split over it in the communist camp. The editorial was meant to convince the Chinese that if it came to taking sides in the Sino-Indian border war, Soviet Union would be with China.

The Chinese were forcing a more fundamental issue, of ideology, by challenging the Soviet assessment of India's ruling class alliance. Two days after the *Pravda* editorial came the Chinese assessment of Nehru and his government. Its title "More on Nehru's Philosophy in the Light of the Sino-Indian Boundary Question"[33] suggested an exercise at updating the previous analysis, of 1959 after the Tibet revolt. The latest analysis traced the Indian "invasion" of China now and the "interference" in Tibet earlier to the "class nature of the big bourgeoisie and big landlords of India" whose interests were closely connected with those of imperialists.

Nehru had gradually become a loyal representative of the

ruling class alliance and his government had substituted "reactionary nationalism" for the anti-imperialist and anti-feudal revolution. Nehru's anti-imperialist stance in the past was attributed to mass pressure whenever the contradiction between imperialism and Indian national interests sharpened. But the class nature of the ruling alliance determined that the Nehru government depended more and more on imperialism. The growing Indian dependence on foreign aid and failure to end the feudal system supported by the British for their own ends underlined this, the analysis said.

Like its domestic policy, the Nehru government's foreign policy reflected its "reactionary class nature". Its actions once helped world peace (refusal to join imperialist military blocs, denial of bases to imperialism, declaration of "non-alignment" and Panch Shila, positive role in sponsoring the Bandung conference). But Nehru had seldom voiced opposition to United States aggression and had come out against just struggles in various countries. On key issues Nehru had stood with imperialism (criticising it on "small issues" and helping it "in a big way"). With the changes in the domestic and international situation, "Nehru's foreign policy leaned more markedly on imperialism". There was intensified suppression and exploitation of the Indian people and greater reliance on imperialist aid to face the economic and political crisis at home.

The analysis linked the shift in Nehru's policy with the changed United States strategy towards India to counter the influence of China's revolution and reconstruction, to obstruct national liberation movements and to control the intermediate zone. As the general crisis of capitalism deepened daily, United States monopoly capital tried to penetrate India and turn it into a market for its commodities and capital. As a result, United States had given up opposition to India's non-alignment and its refusal to supply machinery and technical knowledge to the Indian big bourgeoisie. It was now co-operating with it in the joint exploitation of the Indian people. Over the past few years Nehru had given up opposition to imperialism and colonialism in international affairs, suited himself to the needs of United

States imperialism and had become its "busy spokesman" and even made "Indian troops serve as an international policeman" against the liberation movements.

In sum, the Indian national bourgeoisie which once played a progressive role had now gone over to imperialism. The attack obviously was on the continued Soviet prettification of the Indian bourgeoisie and Nehru as a progressive force that could be relied upon to complete the tasks of the democratic revolution with the diplomatic and economic support of the socialist camp. A paragraph in the analysis was unmistakably addressed to the Soviet leadership to underline the point:

Marxism-Leninism points out that bourgeois nationalism under different conditions plays different historical roles. Marxism-Leninism has always drawn a distinction between nationalism of the oppressed nations and the nationalism of the oppressor nations, between progressive nationalism and reactionary nationalism, and had taken different attitudes to nationalism in accordance with this distinction.[34]

The Soviet leadership was called upon to denounce the Indian bourgeoisie as the lackey of imperialism, which meant retreat from some of its ideological positions—on issues like peaceful transition to socialism and the national democratic state. The Soviet position in the border conflict was to change on 5 November, not in China's favour but India's. The Cuban missile crisis eased on 28 October after Khrushchev's climb down. He could now afford to get tough with the Chinese once again. His 31 October letter to Nehru was cautious and did not indicate any shift in the Soviet position. On 1 November, the Communist Party of India's resolution branded China aggressor, supported Nehru's terms for negotiations, and rejected the Chinese view that he was the leader of "reactionaries" and "expansionists" of the Indian government acting as a tool of United States to secure more aid. It did not expect a socialist country to settle the dispute with India by force of arms and "make astounding claims against a country which is engaged in peaceful consolidation of its newly-won independence, which belongs to the peace camp, which follows a foreign policy of non-alignment". The CPI supported the unity of all patriotic forces in the national emergency and was "not opposed to buying arms from any country on a commercial basis" but opposed induction of foreign personnel in the war. The resolution went beyond the Sino-Indian border dispute and attacked the Chinese on ideological issues:

> The behaviour of socialist China towards peace-loving India has most grossly violated the common understanding in the communist world, arrived at in the 81 Parties conference in 1960 in relation to peaceful co-existence and attitude to newly liberated countries and the question of war and peace. Socialist China has fallen victim to narrow nationalistic considerations at the cost of the interests of world peace and anti-imperialism, in its attitude towards India.[35]

The CPI resolution might have exerted some pressure on the Soviet leadership and contributed to the shift revealed in the *Pravda* editorial on 5 November calling for a cease-fire and negotiations without preconditions and was opposed to anything which would aggravate the situation. This amounted to criticism of the Chinese. There was no homily (unlike in the 25 October editorial) on the origin of the McMahon Line. Nevertheless the 5 November editorial fell short of the CPI's expectations because it did not brand China aggressor. The Soviet restraint here might have stemmed from the realisation that the entire socialist camp did not endorse its attitude to the Sino-Indian border dispute. The Soviet press not only ignored the CPI resolution but was critical of the Indian government's swoop on the CPI dissidents on 1 and 2 November.[36]

After passing the 1 November resolution, the CPI took upon itself the task of explaining the Indian government's stand on the border dispute to the ruling communist parties of Europe and to secure their support against China. To this end the party sent a long letter to "fraternal parties" and despatched Dange on a roving assignment. His long meeting with Khrushchev seems to have paid off for the Indian government.

Shortly after Dange's Moscow visit, an authoritative pronouncement marked a further pro-Indian shift. According to the Chinese Khrushchev went back on everything he had said two months ago. On 12 December he insinuated that the Chinese started the war.

> The areas disputed by China and India were sparsely populated and of little value to human life. The Soviet Union could not possibly entertain the thought that India wanted to start a war with China. The Soviet Union adhered to Lenin's views on boundary dispute. Its experience over forty-five years proved that there was no boundary dispute which could not be solved without resorting to arms. Of course, it was good that China had unilaterally ordered a cease-fire and withdrawn its troops, but would it not have been better if the Chinese had not advanced from their original positions ?[37]

Even before the CPI addressed its letter to fraternal parties and sent Dange on his mission, the changed Soviet stand revealed in the 5 November *Pravda* editorial was influencing several parties away from China. Early in November, at the Bulgarian party congress in Sofia, Chinese delegate Wu Shiu-chuan attacked the host party for "repeating the vicious [Soviet] practice" of criticising the Albanian party and for not supporting China against India. According to a pro-Moscow account, while there was no public reference to the CPI resolution condemning China, off-stage discussions made clear that the resolution had made a good impression. The 1962-63 congress of European parties were timed to discuss the Sino-Indian border dispute. It figured at the Italian and Hungarian party congresses in December. Frol Kozlov, Soviet leader, assailed the Chinese at the Italian congress. The East German party chief Walter Ulbricht was the first communist leader outside India to directly charge the Chinese with attacking India without informing his party.[38] (However, the Chinese maintain that India attacked China on 20

October and the Soviet leadership had been told about the developments preceding the attack.

Both the Chinese and Soviet parties were obliged to explain their respective positions on the Sino-Indian border dispute to the other ruling communist parties. A confidential memorandum from the Chinese party in late December 1962 devoted a whole section to argue that there was no aggression against India. China was forced to launch military action because its demands for return of "purely Chinese" territory were of no avail. Soviet Union, together with United States and United Kingdom was supporting India with guns and aeroplanes. This put Soviet Union on the side of imperialism. India was neither neutral nor pseudo-socialist and its government took orders from Washington and London. Soviet aid to India was equivalent to direct military aid to India against China. China would shortly suggest to India negotiations at the summit level and not objecting to the presence of neutral Asian nations. The next session of the memo charged the Soviets with cowardice over Cuba.[39]

The Soviet rejoinder to the Chinese memo said China had invaded India without informing them though they had offered to mediate. India was willing to negotiate and in all the past negotiations, Soviet Union had backed China which held talks only to gain time for aggressive designs. The unprovoked Chinese aggression on India put the Soviet Union in a difficult position. No doubt the McMahon Line was artificial but that did not warrant military operations which were bound to push India into the capitalist camp. India was following a neutralist and independent policy. Indian and Soviet policies had much in common. Their relations were friendly and had been built over years.

The Soviet letter disclosed that China had sought Soviet aid in the war knowing that Soviet Union was providing India defence equipment. (This was described as a victory over United States and Britain). The Soviets begged the Chinese to stop their military operations at once and offered mediation for which India was ready. They tried hard to prevent India from looking to United States and Britain. Thus, years of striving for

India's neutrality went waste and capitalists were supplying arms to India thanks to the Chinese aggression. Another disclosure was the Soviet concern over the ouster of Krishna Menon from the Indian government.[40] "The Chinese aggression also had the consequences that we lost one of our most faithful friends among the Indian leaders, and that because he relied on our help."

During the war the Soviet stopped deliveries of military equipment. Only after the Chinese stopped the war were the supplies resumed. The letter hoped China would leave aggression to capitalists and hold talks with India as an ally with an ally and a great power with a great power. India was genuinely neutral thanks to Soviet efforts before the war. India's neighbour [Pakistan] was a member of the aggressive SEATO pact but China was now negotiating a pact of friendship with "this appendage of the capitalists".[41]

Sino-Soviet exchanges of December 1962-March 1963 marked an unprecedented intensification of polemics forcing most Asian communist parties to give up their neutrality and take pro-Chinese positions. But the CPI, which had already supported the Soviet positions on ideology in 1960, pledged support to the Soviet general line and attacked the Chinese positions on 12 February 1963. The CPI was influenced by a subjective factor —the Sino-Indian border dispute—and made it the touchstone for Chinese positions on ideological issues.

The provocative CPI attack on the Chinese ideological positions and the accompanying charge of the violation of the 1957 Moscow declaration and the 1960 Moscow statement invited a sharp reply on 9 March in the form of "Mirror for Revisionists" the famous *People's Daily* attack on Dange. A day earlier, the Chinese party had replied to the Soviet party's letter of 21 February. The "Mirror" was a thundering denunciation of the "revisionist clique" headed by Dange which had embarked on the road to national chauvinism and class capitulationism with the intention of turning the party into "an appendage of India's big bourgeoisie and big landlords" and externally to serve the aims of United States imperialism "which is promoting neo-colonialism in India".

The specific attack was on the CPI's support to India's defence effort. The Dange leadership was trying to split the CPI with the Nehru government's help by getting party dissidents jailed and capturing the party machinery. The climax of the attack was the comparison of Dange to Tito. The Indian party like the Yugoslav party was the litmus test of Marxism-Leninism. The *People's Daily* wrote:

> The Tito cliques provides a mirror. It reveals how a group of renegades following a revisionist line corrupt a party and cause a socialist country to degenerate into a capitalist country.
>
> The Dange clique provides another mirror. It reveals how the leaders of the communist party in a capitalist country take the road of revisionism, slide down it and end up as the servants and the tail of the bourgeoisie.[42]

Before Dange could answer this, there was another Chinese broadside on the Nehru government and the Dange leadership. A *Red Flag* commentator said Nehru's socialist pattern was nothing but a capitalist society which, while assimilating the method of planning, preserved the basic characteristics of capitalism and developed bureaucratic comprador monopoly capitalism. But "some revisionists in India" had been asking people to rally around the socialist pattern without reservation.[43]

Defending himself against the Chinese attack, Dange charged them with attempting to split the party. He traced the Sino-Indian conflict to the changing approach to the basic problems of the present epoch and the manner of solving them. He stated:

> The Chinese Communist Party has gone into a head-on clash with the majority of the communist parties of the world and the common understanding that bound them all. The India-China issue became only an incident in the world controversy. From a local affair, it has been lifted into a question affecting the whole world communist movement and the Chinese way of thinking and action in world politics.[44]

Khrushchev's open support to India against China on 12 December 1962 ("we absolutely disallow the thought India wanted to start war with China") set the pace for skirmishes between the Chinese and others at the European party congresses in December 1962-January 1963. Meantime Soviet Union resumed arms supplies to India suspended during the war under Chinese protest. After December 1962 it was clear that Soviet relations with India would not be strained on account of the Chinese. Soviet identification with India was complete. The Sino-Soviet border dispute had become part of the major Sino-Soviet difference of principle related to it. The larger ideological dispute was being debated in the world communist movement.

Beginning with a polemic against the Italian leader Palmiro Togliatti on 3 December 1962 the Chinese had launched a new offensive against the Soviet leadership and by March 1963 had attacked the French leader Maurice Thorez, Togliatti a second time, Marshal Tito, and Dange. The Chinese attack was to extend to the microscopic Communist Party of United States of America and this was to make the Sino-Soviet border dispute public.

Save for the possibility of a few incidents in 1960 caused by nomadic herdsmen on the frontier, the Sino-Soviet border dispute was dormant until 1962 and had not become public. It was to be disclosed later that there was some trouble in 1962 when a large number of Kazhaks fled Sinkiang into Soviet territory. In July 1962, Soviet consulates in Sinkiang (at Urumchi and Kuldja) were closed down but all this was unpublicised then. The Chinese were to charge the Soviets later with subversion in Sinkiang.[45] A Soviet government statement on 21 September 1963 was to allege 5,000 Chinese violations of the Soviet border in 1962.[46]

The Chinese made the Sino-Soviet border dispute public on 7 March 1963 while replying to an attack by the Communist Party of United States of America. Showering praise on Khrushchev for his handling of the Cuban missile crisis the CPUSA attacked the "pseudo-left dogmatic and sectarian line of our Chinese comrades" which "dovetails with that of the most adventurist U.S. imperialists and gives the latter encouragement".[47] It was generally believed in the international communist movement that this was proxy for Khrushchev in reply to the Chinese charge of a Soviet sell-out of Cuba.[48] Part of Khrushchev's self-justification was his taunt at the Chinese over Taiwan, Hong Kong, Macao and other territory in foreign occupation. This invited a biting reply bringing the border dispute into the open. The Chinese said:

> With an ulterior purpose, the statement of the CPUSA referred to Taiwan, Hong Kong and Macao. It said the Chinese comrades were 'correctly not following the adventurist policy in Taiwan, Hong Kong and Macao that they advocate for others. Why this double approach?
> We know from what quarter they have learned this ridiculous charge. And we know too, the purpose of the person who manufactured it. ...
> We know very well, and that you know too that you are, to put it plainly, bringing up the question of Hong Kong and Macao merely as a fig-leaf to hide your disgraceful performance in the Caribbean crisis.[49]

The Chinese went on to list all the "unequal treaties" forced on China by imperialist and colonial powers before the victory of the revolution. This included treaties through which the Czars annexed territory that was now part of Soviet Union. The reply hinted that they would reopen all these treaties and would "recognise, abrogate, revise or renegotiate them according to their specific contents". But in this respect they would make a differentiation between socialist and imperialist countries. With regard to the outstanding issues, they should be settled peacefully through negotiations and pending settlement the status quo should continue.[50]

Turning the tablets neatly against Khrushchev, the Chinese warned that they intended to present at the appropriate moment, their claims to the territory now with Soviet Union.

You are not aware that such questions as those of Hong Kong and Macao relate to the category of unequal treaties left over by history, treaties which the imperialists imposed on China. It may be asked: in raising question of this kind, do you intend to raise all the questions of unequal treaties and have a general settlement? Has it ever entered your heads what the consequences would be? Can you seriously believe that this will do you any good?[51]

This warning appears to have hardened Soviet support to India in the border dispute with China. But long before this episode, the Chinese had made Soviet support and supply of arms to India an issue. The *People's Daily* hit out at French leader Maurice Thorez and others who had charged China with lacking in "minimum goodwill" for a settlement of the Sino-Indian border dispute. At the moment the situation on the border had begun to relax as a result of the Indian defeat and the cease-fire and the unilateral Chinese withdrawal "after having fought back successfully in self-defence". The three years and more of the dispute had proved conclusively that China had been "absolutely right" in its "necessary struggle against the reactionary policy" of Nehru. What surprised the Chinese was that when a fraternal socialist country was facing the Nehru government's provocation and attacks, certain "self-styled Marxists-Leninists" should abandon the principle of proletarian internationalism and assume a "neutral stand". In practice they had not only been giving political support to the "anti-China policy" of Nehru but had been supplying his government with war *material*. Instead of condemning these actions, Thorez and others had described them as a "sensible policy".[52]

Beginning with this the Chinese kept a steady attack on Soviet arms aid to India taking care to paint the Nehru government as reactionary and pro-United States. They tried to develop the theme that Soviet and United States interests were converging on India and Nehru was trying to use the border dispute with China to widen Sino-Soviet differences and use non-alignment as a lever to secure more arms from both the big powers. Typical of the Chinese attacks was the comment by an "Observer" who quoted Nehru as saying that Indo-Soviet friendship was worth twenty divisions and that "Soviet neutrality in the conflict was of greater help to India than all the military aid received from the West in those days". He said Nehru donned the non-alignment cloak to "bluff the world" and gain advantage from both United States and Soviet Union, using Soviet aid to cover up the fact India was a United States protege.[53]

The Chinese saw in Soviet military aid to India a "new chapter of collaboration" between Soviet Union and United States to ally with India against China. The famous 9 September 1959 *Tass* statement was still the irritant. When a capitalist country was making provocations against a socialist country, the Soviet government without distinction between right and wrong had expressed regret over the border incidents. In the three years that followed, whenever Nehru wanted support to enlarge the border dispute Soviet leaders went to India to "bolster them up". Soviet Union aided "Indian reactionaries" politically and stepped up assistance "economically and even militarily". During the 1962 war, India had used Soviet equipment against China together with United States equipment.[54]

The Soviet answer to the "collusion" charge came on 19 September in the form of a *Pravda* editorial urging an end to the Sino-Indian border conflict which had already caused "great damage to the unity of cohesion of the Afro-Asian countries in their joint struggle against imperialism and colonialism". The reactionary forces in India were using the conflict to "step up chauvinism, to attack the progressive forces of this country, to push India off the road to neutralism and to draw her into Western military political blocs". *Pravda* attacked China for not reaching a settlement with India and said "it is difficult to believe the sincerity of Chinese leaders who make assurances that they were trying to achieve a peaceful settlement with India".[55]

The rejoinder to *Pravda* constitutes the most comprehensive Chinese polemic on the Soviet attitude to India. It charged the Soviet leadership with bringing the Sino-Soviet differences on India into the open. It collected all available information dating back to 1959 to prove Soviet identification with India. By publishing the 19 September *Pravda* article, the Soviet leaders had discarded all camouflage and were openly siding with United States "in supporting the Indian reactionaries against socialist China".

The main point made was that the border dispute with India was a major one, involving 12,400 square kilometres and China was defending socialist territory from the imperialism of bourgeois reactionaries. But the Soviet leaders had failed to recognise that the responsibility for the armed clashes was entirely India's. India provoked China emboldened by the prospect of Soviet and Western support and adherence to the principles of peaceful co-existence by China in these circumstances would have amounted to capitulation. The crowning charge was that Soviet Union did not want a negotiated settlement of the dispute and this was evident from its statements blaming China, and its military aid to India. The Soviet leaders were also charged with exploiting the dispute to "sow dissension between China and other Asian-African countries, and to divert their peoples from the struggle against imperialism", and to "cover up the U.S. imperialist aggressive warlike activities". A report in the pro-Moscow Indian weekly *Blitz* was cited in support of the charge. *Blitz* had said Soviet Union had taken upon itself the task of explaining the Sino-Indian border issue to Afro-Asian countries who China claimed were critical of India's stand on the dispute. [56]

It was obvious that Soviet Union had launched a diplomatic offensive on India's behalf to isolate China on the border dispute. The reason was not far to seek. The Sino-Soviet border dispute had got enmeshed with the Sino-Indian border dispute. The issues were almost identical and India was the best stand in against China, from the Soviet point of view. Soviet support to India on the border dispute had crystallised even before the 1962 war but the war itself should have influenced Soviet Union to commit more military aid to India to confront China. It was in the Soviet interest to ensure a continued Asian confrontation between India and China.

Notes

[1] Following the Kong-ka clash, patrolling by armed police units of the Intelligence Bureau and the Assam Rifles was stopped. The task was entrusted to the army which could not undertake it immediately.

[2] Lok Sabha, 26 April 1960.

[3] The resolution was passed at the plenary session at Bhavanagar, 2-4 January 1961.

[4] According to B.N. Mullik, India's intelligence chief then, the army had accepted the forward policy in 1950 and Defence Minister V.K. Krishna Menon had been advocating it since the summer of 1960, that is, immediately after the Chou-Nehru talks. Cf. *The Chinese Betrayal*, New Delhi, Allied, 1971, pp. 304-06. Menon has disapproved the use of the term forward policy to describe this and has asserted that India setting up posts in its own territory or patrolling it cannot be called forward policy.

[5] Press conference in New Delhi.

[6] Lok Sabha, 13 March 1962.

[7] This offer had been made to the Chinese 18 months earlier and was renewed on 14 May 1962.

[8] On 19 May, China alleged a serious Indian violation at Longju. India had vacated this place after the 1959 clash. The Chinese who were in occupation of the place left after a while due to a plague epidemic there. But the 19 May allegation meant the beginning of tension in the eastern sector too.

[9] Letter to Heads of Afro-Asian States, 19 November 1962.

[10] Chou disclosed this in his interview to Neville Maxwell, *Sunday Times*, 19 December 1971.

[11] *The Hindustan Times*, 10 August 1962.

[12] 7 September 1962.

[13] *White Paper VII*, p. 18.

[14] Lok Sabha, 13 August 1962.

[15] *White Paper VII*, p 36.

[16] India had said it was ready to discuss "the exact alignment of the so-called McMahon Line at Kinzamane, the Longju area and the Tamaden area" and wanted status quo maintained at all these places. Chinese personnel should not alter the position by crossing the Thagla ridge and try to occupy any territory south of the ridge. Similarly, pending examination of the position at Tamaden force should not be used on the Indian posts there. As for Longju India was prepared not to send its personnel there provided the Chinese also withdrew their forces. *White Paper II*, pp. 9-10 (Note from India to China). Indians vacated Longju after the 1959 clash and the Chinese who occupied it pulled out a year later because of plague in the area.

[17] *White Paper VII*, p. 73.

[18] *Ibid.*, p. 76.

[19] *Ibid.*, pp. 96-8.

[20] N.J.N. [N.J. Nanporia], in *The Times of India*, 15 October 1962.

[21] *White Paper VIII*, pp. 2-4.
[22] *White Paper VIII*, pp. 10-17.
[23] Press conference, New Delhi, 28 December 1962.
[24] *The Hindu*, 6 February 1962.
[25] B.N. Mullik, *op. cit.*, pp. 429-33.
[26] N.J.N. [N.J. Nanporia], "A Trap in the Making," *The Times of India*, 5 November 1962.
[27] B.N. Mullik, *op. cit.*, pp. 438-9.
[28] *Peking Review*, 8 November 1963.
[29] Rajya Sabha, 22 August 1961.
[30] Ranjit Desai, "Arms Need and Non-alignment," *Mainstream*, 22 December 1962.
[31] J.K. Galbraith, *Ambassador's Journal*, excerpts in *Imprint*, April 1970, p. 115.
[32] "The Truth About How the Leaders of the CPSU Have Allied Themselves with India Against China," *People's Daily*, 2 November 1963.
[33] *People's Daily*, 27 October 1962.
[34] *Ibid*.
[35] *The India-China Border Dispute and the Communist Party of India* (for party members only), New Delhi, 1963, p. 67.
[36] Those believed to be in disagreement with the resolution were picked up in a countrywide swoop. The Chinese alleged that CPI Chairman S.A. Dange had provided the lists to the government. The arrests followed his meeting with Nehru to explain his party's resolution. It is widely believed that the draft resolution had the approval of Nehru before the national council passed it.
[37] "The Truth About How the Leaders of the CPSU Have Allied Themselves with India Against China," *People's Daily*, 2 November 1963.
[38] *New Age* weekly, 20 January 1963.
[39] Description of the Memorandum in David Floyd, *Mao Against Khrushchev*, London, Pall Mall, 1964, pp. 338-9.
[40] Menon resigned during the border war following an uproar in Nehru's Congress party against his handling of the defence portfolio which allegedly led to India's military debacle against China.
[41] Summary in David Floyd, *op. cit.*, pp. 362-7.
[42] *People's Daily*, 9 March 1963.
[43] "What Kind of Stuff is Nehru's Much Advertised Socialism?" *Red Flag*, 1 April 1963.
[44] S.A. Dange, "Neither Revisionism Nor Dogmatism Is Our Guide," *New Age* weekly, 21 April 1963.
[45] Chou En-lai told Neville Maxwell in 1971 that in 1962 the Soviet leadership indulged in provocation and subversion against China by getting many Chinese to leave Sinkiang. *The Sunday Times*, 19 December 1971. Cf. also "The Origin and Development of Differences Between the Soviet Union and Ourselves," *Red Flag* and *People's Daily*, 6 September 1963.
[46] *Izvestia*, 21 September 1963.

[47] *The Worker*, 13 January 1963.
[48] The Chinese called it "100 per cent appeasement, a 'Munich' pure and simple". "The Differences Between Comrade Togliatti and Us," *People's Daily*, 31 December 1962.
[49] "A Comment on the Statement of the Communist Party of the USA," *People's Daily*, 8 March 1963.
[50] *Ibid.*
[51] *Ibid.*
[52] "Whence the Differences? A Reply to Maurice Thorez and Others," *People's Daily*, 27 February 1963.
[53] "The Indian Reactionaries in the Anti-China Chorus," *People's Daily*, 16 July 1963.
[54] *Ibid.*
[55] "A Serious Hotbed of Tension in Asia," *Pravda*, 19 September 1963.
[56] "The Truth About How the Leaders of the CPSU Have Allied Themselves with India and Against China," *People's Daily*, 2 November 1963.

6/ The Price of 1962

To the Indian elite, conditioned to expect a war with China for years if not decades, nothing could have been more humiliating than the unilateral offer of cease-fire by the Chinese. The brief flare up had already taken its toll of India's non-alignment by forcing a compromise on arms aid. The cease-fire offer underlined the stunning military debacle, compounding the humiliation of defeat. It must have been a strange feeling of anticlimax and disorientation for Prime Minister Nehru because he had asked the army to clear NEFA of the Chinese in the belief that it could be done. As he was to admit later, he had ordered it because the army had advised the government that it could be done.[1]

As the Chinese began implementing their cease-fire plan, the mood in New Delhi was overwhelmingly against negotiations. A renewed conflict was taken for granted and even the formalisation of the cease-fire was opposed on the plea that it would undermine defence effort. United States and British arms aid missions had counselled against an immediate showdown and wanted an arms build up to prepare for the seemingly inevitable next round. India observed the cease-fire without formally accepting the Chinese proposals. Nehru's approach was three-pronged: to secure more arms from the West, to get diplomatic and arms support from the socialist bloc, and to secure non-aligned diplomatic intervention against China. This military-diplomatic approach was supposed to ensure continuity of non-alignment and not appear to conflict with it.

A dizzy procession of official and non-official missions went to Western capitals with shopping lists of military hardware. The Soviets and the pro-Moscow Indian communists had together taken upon themselves the task of persuading East European countries to back India against China. India directly launched a diplomatic offensive among Afro-Asian countries, sending out delegations to Indonesia, Cambodia, Burma, Ceylon, and United Arab Republic. Only UAR was on India's side. Others were closer to China, and concerned over the implications of Western arms aid to India and confused about the exact nature of the Chinese proposals for negotiations with India. India was insisting on the restoration of the 8 September 1962 positions while China wanted to return to the 7 November 1959 positions. At stake for India was the 43 military check-posts it had set up since 1959 and overrun by the Chinese during the war.

India's efforts with UAR[2] resulted in a move for a conference of six Afro-Asian powers (Burma, Cambodia, Ceylon, Ghana, Indonesia, and UAR) to discuss the cease-fire and the possible basis of negotiations. The conference met in Colombo on 10 December and only UAR backed India's demand for restoration of 8 September 1962 positions while Ghana and Indonesia were closer to India than to China. Ceylon was neutral and Burma and Cambodia were supporting the Chinese stand. The conference refrained from blaming either side for the conflict but did not endorse India's demand for return to the 8 September 1962 positions.

On 15 December the conference communicated its proposals to India. In the NEFA sector it wanted the line of actual control (that is, the McMahon Line) to be the cease-fire line, the specific areas in dispute as that below the Thagla ridge to be discussed later. In the Ladakh sector, the Chinese should withdraw 20 kilometres from the "line of actual control" but the Indian side could stay where it was (Chou En-lai had proposed this earlier); "pending final solution of the border dispute, the area vacated by Chinese military withdrawals will be a demilitarised zone to be administered by civilian posts of both sides to be agreed upon, without prejudice to the right of the previous presence of both India and China in that area".

In effect, the Colombo proposals sought a demilitarised zone in the Ladakh sector and New Delhi's response was mixed. It was to India's advantage in two respects: the Chinese were to withdraw from their positions and not India, and this released some of the 43 Indian posts. But this also had implications unacceptable to India: it did not ensure withdrawal to the 8 September 1962 line and bypassed India's point that the result of the Chinese push during the war had to be undone; only some of the 43 posts were released and the released posts were to be in the demilitarised zone.

A delegation of the Colombo conference led by Ceylon Prime Minister Sirimavo Bandaranaike visited Peking to discuss the proposals and reported a positive Chinese response. The Chinese, however, had two reservations: the proposals did not provide for Indian withdrawal; they proposed civilian posts for the demilitarised zone. But these reservations were not to be made the conditions for talks. Mrs Bandaranaike visited New Delhi from 10 to 14 January and India requested clarification of the Colombo proposals and they were given.[3]

The clarification in essence was: the demilitarised zone created by Chinese withdrawals in the Ladakh sector will be administered by civilian posts and this was a substantive part of the proposals. The agreement was to relate to the location, the number, and composition of the posts. Nehru accepted the proposals subject to this clarification because it came closest to India's demand and the ball was now in the Chinese court. Politically, India's attitude was one of "heads I win, tails you lose". If Peking accepted the proposals as clarified, it would be the loser. If it did not, it would be putting itself at odds with the Colombo powers and appear belligerent and unwilling to negotiate on reasonable terms. An Indian commentator summed up New Delhi's intentions as follows:

> ... all the evidence that is available suggests that New Delhi's manoeuvre of supposedly placing China in a position of having to accept something which it is reluctant to accept and therefore will not accept is liable to misfire. Peking's refusal so far to accept the Colombo proposals does not mean that there is anything in these proposals inconsistent with Peking's

interests. The supposition in New Delhi that there is nothing more than that is responsible for almost the complacent belief that Peking has been enwrapped in a dilemma.

According to this theory, India will benefit since a Chinese rejection of the Colombo proposals in the wrong and alternatively an acceptance *in toto* will be a triumph of Indian diplomacy. This is unconvincing in that it is quite unreal. Peking today can, any time it considers it advisable to do so, accept the Colombo proposals *in toto* without any damage to its interests and with the further advantage of being able to represent such acceptance as a major concession to peace. The initiative, as before, lies with the Chinese but not necessarily provided New Delhi prepares itself and the nation for the dangers of diplomatic negotiations.[4]

Domestic pressures had made it impossible for Nehru to negotiate the dispute with China since 1961 and there was little chance of he or his government preparing the country for such negotiations now.

The Chinese had at the outset signified "positive response" to the proposals and accepted them in principle. As clarified to India by the Colombo powers, they seemed to the Chinese loaded in India's favour because they denied them the fruits of victory. As Chou pointed out in his letter to Mrs Bandaranaike on 19 January 1963, the Colombo proposals required China to fulfil the cease-fire plan with no corresponding obligation on the Indian side. Chou suggested that the Indian forces should stay where they were, not only in the Ladakh sector but also in NEFA. Besides, Indian military or civilian personnel should not occupy the area in the Ladakh sector gained as a result of the forward policy. On their part the Chinese would withdraw all their military and civilian posts in the area.[5] To India, the 43 posts it had set up there between 1959 and 1962 was the crucial issue. The Chinese did not make these reservations a condition for talks.[6] Their contention was that the role of the Colombo powers ended with making the proposals as the basis for direct negotiations and the differences over the interpretation of the proposals could as well be part of the talks.

Colombo Proposals

On 28 January, *People's Daily* urged immediate talks. But India thought it had retrieved its diplomatic initiative by accepting the Colombo proposals (as clarified by Mrs Bandaranaike) *in toto* and made similar acceptance by China the precondition for talks. On 25 February, Nehru told the Lok Sabha that the proposals "fall to the ground" if China did not accept them *in toto*. Two days later he told the Lok Sabha that he would not rule out a negotiated settlement and reaffirmed that any conflict could be prolonged one. "I do not know what might happen in the next few weeks, in March-April." On 3 March he said in Amritsar if China did not accept the proposals, another conflict was likely before the monsoon.

As the Colombo proposals remained deadlocked, China released all prisoners of war and completed its withdrawals in keeping with its cease-fire offer. The alignment of the Colombo powers was shifting in its favour. Until January, Ghana was closer to India but moving away fast. On 23 January, Ghana's Justice Minister Ofori Atta, after he had discussed the Colombo proposals with the Chinese, said in Hong Kong that there was no need for the two countries to accept them *in toto* because they had different interpretations of the proposals which were based on two issues: cease-fire and a 20-kilometre withdrawal to create a demilitarised zone. He also said Chou had proposed to Mrs Bandaranaike some modifications of the proposals. About the same time, Ghana's President Nkrumah wrote to Nehru urging him not to insist on clarification of the Colombo proposals and to accept China's unreserved attitude as good enough and begin direct negotiations. Nehru replied that the very acceptance of the proposals was a major concession by India.

An Indian journalist visiting Djakarta got the impression Indonesia was not insisting on China accepting the proposals *in toto*.[7] Burma's Ne Win was just indifferent while Cambodia's Prince Sihanouk admitted differences among the Colombo powers. He said in an interview:

> We are favourable to the idea of giving Mrs. Bandaranaike a *carte blanche* in the matter. I am against a second meeting of Colombo conference nations because the more conferences we have the more divided the countries seem to get on this matter. I would like to serve the cause of India-China peace discreetly. If we make these individual efforts, my friend Sabry [United Arab Republic] says one thing and my other friend Subandrio [Indonesia] says another thing. This is all bad. Among ourselves there are different voices.[8]

India had laid down its conditions for formulating the cease-fire and holding talks early on 6 April: (*i*) China should accept the proposals without reservation as India has done; (*ii*) such acceptance can be followed by an official level meeting to settle various matters left by the Colombo powers for direct agreement and to decide details regarding implementation of the Colombo proposals on the ground; (*iii*) officials of both sides can then take action to implement these proposals on ground so that agreed cease-fire arrangements are established on ground; (*iv*) thereafter, India and China can take up the differences on the boundary question and try to reach a mutually acceptable settlement in one or more than one stage; (*v*) if the settlement is not reached in direct talks and discussions, both can consider the adoption of other methods, like referring the dispute to the International Court of Justice at The Hague and abiding by its decision. If China does not agree to this method of peaceful settlement, both can agree to international arbitration by a person or a group of persons nominated in an agreed manner by both the sides. The award should be binding on both.

On 8 September, India pressed China for a reply to its 6 April 1963 letter. China replied on 9 October, virtually rejecting India's suggestions. The Indian position was "hypocritical and an attempt to impose its own interpretation of the Colombo proposals on China". The task of the Colombo conference was to mediate and not to arbitrate. The proposals were only recommendations and not a verdict or an award which China must accept *in toto*. Although the Colombo nations hoped the proposals would be accepted on both sides, it did not mean that direct negotiations could start only when the proposals had been accepted *in toto*. Acceptance of the proposals without reservations actually meant acceptance of the proposals plus the clarifications produced in New Delhi which were in fact the Indian interpretation of the Colombo proposals.[9]

There might well have been two sets of clarifications by the Colombo powers on their proposals—one to China and one to India. It is possible the Ghanian and Indonesian representatives were responsible for the muddle. The crux of the Chinese contention was that its reservations related to details of the proposals and they would be brought up at the conference and not before. In India's perception, this did not amount to accepting the proposals *in toto*. Thus the proposals were dead, despite Chinese readiness to negotiate on the basis of the proposals which both sides had accepted in principle. But India, "owing to its internal and external political requirements" could not negotiate for the time being and China was willing to wait patiently.[10]

By June India had lost initiative. Nehru's party was trounced in a series of by-elections and the entire non-communist Opposition, aided by a strong lobby in his own party, was clamouring to get the Chinese occupation of Indian-claimed territory vacated. Mrs Bandaranaike proposed lower level direct Sino-Indian talks, in Colombo if necessary. But in the Indian view, even these talks amounted to negotiations which *per se* were not compatible with the defence effort. However, Afro-Asian countries were unimpressed by India's rigid posture and its feverish quest for military hardware. None of the Colombo powers was prepared to force China to accept the proposals *in toto*. They gradually lost interest in the dispute because it was virtual disengagement of the worder now, about a year after the war, despite mutual charges of incursions into the demilitarised zone and into each other's area.

Early in April 1964, Nehru told the Lok Sabha that talks

could be held if China dismantled its posts in Ladakh but the question of negotiations had gone beyond the point of return because it had been drawn into the Sino-Soviet ideological dispute and the international communist movement was on the verge of an open split.

The last Chinese attempt to solve the problem was in October 1964 amidst the second Cairo conference of the non-aligned nations despite the Indian Prime Minister Lal Bahadur Shastri's anti-China stance there. The Chinese government declared its readiness to negotiate any time at any place "with the Colombo proposals as the basis" (which meant either side was to be free to raise any issue). The non-aligned powers were welcome to promote direct negotiations without involving themselves in the dispute but there was no question of mediation by anyone. Nor could the Colombo proposals become an "arbitral award".[11] On the whole, the Chinese tone was mild and the border situation itself had eased and Soviet and Western arms aid to India should not have worried China much.

A little later, Chou reiterated at the first session of the Third National People's Congress in Peking his desire to settle the dispute peacefully "but if India is determined not to have negotiations, no matter we can wait", he said.[12] The Chinese have waited since and have made no serious attempt to alter the status quo.

Kashmir Issue

When the war broke out United States was worried that the Pakistani press was echoing Chinese propaganda on their war with India. India feared that Pakistan might exploit the situation for a military adventure to settle the Kashmir issue. President Kennedy, and later Premier Khrushchev tried desparately but without success to secure from Pakistani President Ayub Kahn an open declaration freezing the Kashmir issue for the duration of the war. Moreover, the Shah of Iran had even suggested committing Pakistani troops to fight China under Indian command as a gesture of goodwill. (Iran and Pakistan are CENTO allies.)

The Price of 1962

Pakistan asked United States to propose to India a reasonable stand on Kashmir in return for a Pakistani assurance not to complicate matters. As the war wore on, Pakistan began a dialogue with China and there was even talk of a non-aggression pact. Though Ayub Khan assured United States in private that he would not attack India he was sore about supply of arms to India. Galbraith, United States Ambassador in India, lobbied in Nehru's Congress party for reconciliation with Pakistan. He got Nehru to write a friendly letter to Ayub Khan while the United States Ambassador in Pakistan was busy convincing Ayub Khan that the Chinese were now a threat to the whole subcontinent.

Though United States and Britain responded promptly to Nehru's appeal for emergency arms aid, neither of them was prepared to make a long-term commitment on defence aid without extracting a political price. The Averell Harriman mission and the Duncan Sandys mission together processed India's request for military aid for the next three years. By mid-December 1962, President Kennedy and Prime Minister Macmillan decided on a 50-50 United States Commonwealth sharing of the 120-million-dollar outlay for small arms, ordnance machinery and ammunition for India. But this was after they had forced an Indo-Pakistan dialogue on the Kashmir issue in an effort to unite the two neighbours against China. India's defence effort vis-a-vis China was linked with a solution to the Kashmir problem.

The ten-day gap between the Chinese cease-fire announcement (21 November) and its implementation (1 December) was the twilight of India's non-alignment policy. The Harriman and Sandys missions were in New Delhi and later in Rawalpindi and it was feverish diplomatic activity in the two capitals. United States revived the joint Indo-Pakistani defence idea (mooted by President Ayub Khan of Pakistan two years earlier) while Sandys wanted India to join a military alliance with the West and come under the protection of a NATO nuclear deterrent.

Both the missions were keen India should settle the Kashmir issue with Pakistan. Harriman and Sandys managed to secure

Ayub's consent to a draft Indo-Pakistan declaration agreeing to talks on Kashmir, first at the ministerial level and later between Ayub and Nehru. On 29 November, Sandys got Nehru's consent to the substance of the draft. Ayub had wanted talks on Kashmir but Nehru wanted this to be enlarged into "Kashmir and other matters". As a compromise, the statement referred to talks on "Kashmir and related matters".

Though neither of the Western powers had a specific formula on Kashmir, India agreed to talks, first at the ministerial level and later at the summit level, as a concession to the aid donors. The talks were held alternatively (six rounds) in Indian and Pakistani cities in 1962-63 and did not yield any tangible results. The plan for a plebiscite in Kashmir was revived by the mediators but India's firm rejection inhibited them from pressing it. The more important fact here was that India could discuss Kashmir as an issue with Pakistan though it did not recognise any Pakistani claim to it and there was little political opposition to these talks. Only a Chief Minister from the South (Kamaraj of Madras) is believed to have told the party leadership that if it meant parting with territory there was little to choose between Pakistan and China. Pakistan was in illegal occupation of Kashmir areas and it was not a border dispute. Yet China was regarded a greater enemy than Pakistan. United States Secretary of State Dean Rusk told Nehru later that his country firmly believed that China's aggressive and expansionist policies posed a threat to the entire subcontinent and therefore wanted India and Pakistan to settle the Kashmir dispute.

The Eisenhower Administration outgrew the Dullesian pactomania and non-alignment ceased to be a dirty word in Washington as the Sino-Indian border dispute grew in importance. India qualified for massive United States economic aid and was even offered military assistance against China in 1959. As the cold war thawed the Kennedy Administration reviewed its Asian policy. When Nehru visited Washington late in 1961, non-alignment had become respectable there but with some reservations. On the eve of the Sino-Indian border war, these reservations were not many but vital.

First, a friendly, non-aligned country like India was expected to look to the West rather than to the communist countries for its security. Indian action in Goa in defiance of United States advice, and the MiG aircraft deal with Soviet Union when United States had refused to sell similar supersonics, were irritants.

Secondly, non-aligned countries getting large-scale military aid were expected to show concern for United States interests. The resolution on the United States base at Guantanmano passed at the Belgrade non-aligned conference in September 1961 angered Washington. India had supported the resolution rather haltingly and Washington appreciated this fact.

Thirdly, though non-alignment was no longer unacceptable, United States did not approve of Indian attempts to win other countries over to its creed.

UNITED STATES MANOEUVRES

With the 1962 war, United States achieved in no time all its objective vis-a-vis India at minimal cost in terms of military aid. When India turned to United States for emergency arms supplies, Kennedy did not insist on a formal military alliance because all his reservations had disappeared overnight.

Not only did India ask for emergency military aid from the West but wanted United States air force to defend Indian cities. India feared a renewed flare up in the near future. Within four weeks of the cease-fire Kennedy and Macmillan decided at Nassau on aid to equip six mountain divisions India had proposed. India had overcome its inhibitions about long term military aid. United States contrived to station a military mission in New Delhi with least embarrassment to India. The Military Assistance Advisory Group was called by a different name and was attached to the United States embassy. On 27 January Secretary of State Dean Rusk said that aid beyond the Nassau commitment would depend on "future developments" which could only mean the fate of the Colombo proposals. A few weeks later he was to hold talks with Nehru in New Delhi

United States was more interested in pushing the plan for

an "air umbrella" which would have been less expensive from its point of view. On 27 January Dean Rusk announced that a United States-Commonwealth air defence team was going to India. The timing was significant. Nehru had just got Parliament's support for the Colombo proposals. On 21 February Kennedy said that United States would be "responsive" to any Indian request for air cover in the event of sudden Chinese attacks on Indian cities and the response would be decided in the light of the air mission's report. On the same day, Nehru, justifying the air mission's visit, ruled out stationing foreign air forces in Indian bases.[13] When the Chinese stormed Sela and advanced towards Assam in November 1962 United States and Britain were ready to defend Indian cities if the fighting were to spread to the plains. A United States aircraft carrier with 80 jets was ordered into the Indian Ocean and supersonic jets in Western Europe were alerted.

After the cease-fire, India began drawing up shopping lists of military hardware, giving supersonic aircraft high priority. United States and Britain were not ready to commit long term military aid without political strings and a dialogue with Pakistan towards a settlement on Kashmir was forced on India while the supersonics issue was kept in abeyance. The joint air defence team (of United States, Britain and Canada) was to look into India's request for supersonic fighters. The team visited India in January-February 1963 and concluded that India did not really need supersonics at this stage; some radar and communication equipment for an "early warning system" would suffice and that the Indian Air Force could be strengthened with a few Hunter aircraft and air-to-air missiles.

A team of Indian officials headed by S. Bhoothalingam visited Washington and London in April, followed by Minister T. T. Krishnamachari. Neither of the missions could convince the West of India's case for a supersonic force. Instead India was asked to stage a joint air exercise without prejudice to its plan for a supersonic force.

The joint air defence team's visit to New Delhi was directly linked to the United States plan for an "air umbrella". A powerful lobby in New Delhi including a section of Nehru's party was trying to canvass this plan on the following arguments: it would be inexpensive and obviate the need for a huge army; it would save India the worry about its immediate future, pending build-up of its own air force because even the Soviet-aided MiG project would take four years to build; and a Western air umbrella with its swift and shattering strike power might prove decisive against China's might.

Britain was not too enthusiastic about the umbrella plan because that would affect the traditional outlet for its military aircraft. United States favoured it because it would reduce the military aid burden and would be the best way of carrying Pakistan (which was protesting against direct United States arms flow to India) with it. The air umbrella plan, as publicised in the Indian newspapers, involved the following: (i) the operational control of certain types of military equipment and specialised weapons given to India should remain not in Indian hands but in foreign hands; (ii) an air umbrella should be provided over India by foreign air forces, employing foreign pilots and technicians but based in Indian airfields and installations; and (iii) India should permit such foreign air forces or aircraft carriers to be based on the Andaman and Nicobar islands.

The basic objection to the plan was that the air umbrella would not be in Indian control and would be subject to Pentagon's overall global strategic needs. Even if the umbrella was based in the Arabian Sea, Bay of Bengal, or Pakistan its radar centres would have to be in Indian soil and manned by foreign personnel. This would violate India's sovereignty. Besides, the air umbrella project would affect India's relations with Soviet Union and its allies and might even jeopardise the MiG project. Worse, acceptance of Western air cover would lower India's standing in the non-aligned world.

Even the Communist Party of India which had identified itself closely with the government was worried about the implications of the plan and sent a deputation of its Members of Parliament to seek a clarification from Nehru. In Nehru's own party there was a storm over the plan compelling him to deny that there was any such plan. He said he had not asked for an air umbrella, but only an appraisal of India's air defence needs by a high-powered Western team. However, New Delhi seemed to have an open mind on the plan and preferred to await the report of the joint team.

Soviet Attitude

Meantime, Soviet Union had agreed to give India ground-to-ground and ground-to- air missiles and fulfilled its MiG delivery commitments, setting at rest all doubts about its support to India against a socialist country.[14] There were also offers from Eastern Europe to assist India's defence build up.

Assured of Soviet MiG 21s, India had no difficulty accepting the joint air defence team's report and entering an agreement on joint air exercises plan which provided for a consultation clause in the event of a threat, which amounted to underwriting India's air defence in the short run. This plan was more acceptable than the air umbrella project because it would provide radar and other installations while in the long-run India would develop its own supersonic force.

While accepting the joint exercises offer, India made clear that its defence including air defence was solely its responsibility. The exercises named Operation Siksha took place in November, with the participation of a United States Air Force F 100 subsonic squadron and Royal Air Force Javelins. Indian Air Force men could handle the radar equipment "more or less independently". Operation Shiksha was meant to prove that India did not need supersonics to defend its skies and subsonics could do the job.

United States and Soviet interests were converging on India on a new plane. The fresh Soviet commitment on arms which came amidst the air umbrella debate amounted to renewal of support to India against China. A few weeks later, Kennedy's message on "Free World Defence and Assistance Programmes" to the Congress [15] mentioned India but only to stress that any "additional efforts on our part" to bolster India's defence would be on the crucial condition that "these efforts can be matched in an appropriate way by the efforts of India and Pakistan".[16] It was now clear that a settlement on Kashmir was expected as a precondition to military aid. The Indo-Pakistan talks on Kashmir begun under pressure were still going on, and in May Lord Mountbatten visited India to persuade Nehru to agree to partition as a solution to the Kashmir dispute. Military aid was linked with Kashmir.

United States refused to believe that the Chinese would launch an attack in NEFA and was not convinced of India's claims in the Ladakh sector. So when India embarked on an ambitious plan to strengthen its military capability, United States was noncommittal about further military aid to India. Defence Minister Y. B. Chavan said that the army strength would be doubled in the next few years, six new ordnance factories set up, and the air force modernised.[17] In April, a team of officials led by S. Bhoothalingam went to Washington to plead for aid. In May, Minister for Economic Co-ordination, T. T. Krishnamachari, followed on a similar mission to convince the State Department that a renewed conflict with China was imminent in the near future and India was the real bulwark against China. United States defence experts began analysing the six billion dollar plan (a fourth of it in foreign exchange) to modernise and strengthen India's defences over a three-year period but no commitment on aid was forthcoming.

By mid-1963, United States' attitude to India's needs seemed to have changed. An indication of this came in President Radhakrishnan's communique with President Kennedy on 4 June in Washington. Kennedy rejected the Pakistani thesis that China was no threat to India and shared India's "mutual defensive concern to thwart the designs of Chinese aggression against the subcontinent". He promised "effective assistance" in India's development and defence.[18]

Indian Communist Split

The Sino-Soviet ideological dispute was heading towards an

open showdown by September. Soviet leaders were planning a world conference to excommunicate the Chinese and retain their hegemony of the movement. The Soviet-Yugoslav rapprochement, the decision to sign the partial test ban treaty ignoring the Chinese opposition, and the failure of the Moscow talks in July between the Soviet and Chinese parties, together worsened relations between the two at all levels. Soviet attitude to the Sino-Indian border dispute had transcended the state of neutrality and was one of open support to India's case.

From now on Soviet effort aimed at securing the CPI's support to Nehru and to prevent it from taking a pro-Chinese stand in the ideological dispute. Soviet backing to India in the border dispute eased pressure on the CPI which now cited the Soviet attitude to rationalise its own support to Nehru in the name of national defence. The CPI was useful to the Soviet leadership because it could keep pressure on Nehru to confront China. In these circumstances the ascendency of the hard-lining left group in the CPI would have weakened the Soviet position in the ideological conflict. The Soviet party and government had special reasons to force the pace of the CPI right group's drive to isolate the left and liquidate it through an organisational crisis. The CPI's dominant right group found an alibi for its offensive against the left in the Soviet party's "Open Letter" to its ranks on 14 July which climaxed the polemical offensive against the Chinese.[19] The specific charges against the Chinese included "organising and supporting various anti-party groups of renegades who are coming out against the Communist Parties in the United States, Brazil, Italy, Belgium, Australia and India". Significantly the letter ignored the New Zealand party which had been openly pro-Chinese since 1960 but levelled the vague charge of subversive activities by the Chinese in the communist parties of Asia, Africa, and Latin America. Ceylon was singled out for special reference and for the first time the Chinese were accused of having links with a Trotskyite faction of the Fourth International.

But certain aspects of the charges were intriguing. The letter grouped India with countries where the Chinese were charged with "organising and supporting various anti-party groups of renegades". But the version of the letter published by the CPI replaced the term "renegades" with a milder term: "dissenters".[20] Secondly, before the CPI had said anything about its dissenters, the CPSU had branded them as "anti-party group organised by the Chinese. Thirdly, while the letter detailed alleged splitting activities of the Chinese in other countries it gave no details of such activities in India. The differences in the CPI at this point related to an old issue—the attitude to Nehru and the Congress party—and no member of prominence had been expelled from the party or had formed a rival group. Even the CPI right group's leadership could not have believed what the letter had said about India. Nevertheless, it welcomed the letter, supported the Soviet general line but refrained from referring to "splitters" and "Trotskyites" if any in its own ranks.[21]

There was no threat of a Chinese-engineered split in the CPI but the right group was forcing the party to the brink by leading a stampede in support of the Nehru government and its complete identification with what the left group called bourgeois nationalism. The November 1962 resolution on the Sino-Indian border and defence effort provided the alibi for the stampede. Many of the right group leaders called the Chinese cease-fire proposals "treacherous" and "diabolical" through the Chinese had unilaterally announced the ceasefire and begun implementing the proposals. Again the party had no independent stand on the Colombo proposals and would not support them until after Nehru had decided to accept them. Thereafter, the CPI began echoing the Government's demand that China also accept them *in toto*.

The CPI's uncritical support to Nehru's stand on the border dispute inevitably led to what the leftists called class collaboration. Through its distorted interpretation of the Vijayawada line to facilitate a united front with the Congress, the majority right faction tried to force the politico-ideological crisis and convert it into an organisational crisis. Most of the leftist leaders were absent from the scene (40 of the 110 National Council Members were in prison). There was a "spontaneous" demand for "stern measures" against the "pro-China" and "anti-patriotic" elements (that is, those who disagreed with the rightist leadership) and General Secretary E. M. S. Namboodiripad who represented the minority view, resigned signalling an organisational deadlock. The right group pressed its offensive further and committed the party to Soviet ideological positions. It was acting in the belief that the Soviet leadership was determined to excommunicate the Chinese from the world communist movement and therefore a split in India to liquidate the left group was quite in order. The Soviets, in a bitter attack on the Chinese, had indirectly denounced as "splitters" all the parties and groups which did not back the Soviet general line. The Soviets said that 65 parties were on its side, claiming the CPI among them.[22]

The communist parties in India, Ceylon and Outer Mongollia were the ones in Asia to fall in line with the Soviet party in the polarisation that had begun. Soviet bitterness at this failure in Asia found expression in an article which presumed the imminence of an open, world-wide split and alleged that there was an attempt in Peking to "knock together an international bloc out of groups and groupings" comprising largely of people who have been expelled from the communist parties and "all possible unprincipled and corrupt elements". The Soviet leadership was perhaps unnerved at the growing left challenge to the CPI leadership and thought an immediate split was the only way of carrying the CPI majority on its side. Significantly, the Soviet attitude to the Indonesian party (which had taken a pro-Chinese stance in the Sino-Indian border, the Cuban missile crisis, and the test ban treaty issues) was different. There was no attempt to split it. The CPI split vertically in 1964. The breakaway wing later came to be known as the Communist Party of India Marxist.

In September 1964, Soviet Union entered a major military agreement with India to provide MiG fighters, transport aircraft, light tanks, and naval equipment, on deferred payment basis. The deal for a MiG manufacture complex for India was also clinched. As for United States. Kennedy had begun a reappraisal of his Asian policy. When the Sino-Indian rift widened with

India becoming one of the issues in dispute, it was not in United States' interest to narrow the Sino-Soviet differences on India. Nehru was not averse to exploiting these differences. There was a tacit United States-Soviet understanding on military aid to India to confront China, neither of them seriously objecting to India getting aid from the other.

By mid-1964 United States had decided on a hard line towards China and wanted India to play a key role in its "containment" strategy. Secretary of State Dean Rusk reaffirmed on 18 June the importance of his country remaining "steadfast in its support" to India's economic development and defence efforts during the coming year. He mentioned some "key problem areas where United States aid is a factor". They included Vietnam, India, Brazil, Africa, and Cyprus.[23]

In September, Senator Hubert Humphrey, a Vice-Presidential candidate, was harping on the theme of "a coalition of Asian powers with India as the main force" to counter-balance China's power.[24] Soviet interests were similar and United States realised this. David Bell, head of USAID, told the Senate Foreign Relations Committee on 5 May 1965, that the economic effect of Soviet aid to India may be beneficial to India and, in a sense, to long term United States interests in India.[2']

SINO-PAKISTAN RELATIONS

United States and Soviet Union developed parallel policies towards India because of their attitude to China. United States found India a better ally than Pakistan against China. Despite its membership of CENTO and SEATO, Pakistan had been moving closer to China since the early 1960s.

Just as it was the first to realise the anti-imperialist potential of the newly-free Afro-Asian countries in the Bandung phase and thereby set the pace for the Soviet friendship drive with them, China was also the first to realise the tenuousness of Pakistan's alliance with United States. Sino-Pakistan relations began warming up at Bandung where Prime Minister Mohomed Ali of Bogra denounced Soviet Union as imperialist and colonialist but referred to China as a friendly and peace-loving neighbour. He convinced Chou that Pakistan's membership of the SEATO did not mean hostility towards China and if United States were to embark on aggressive action under the treaty or launch a global war Pakistan would not involve itself in it.[26] Mohomed Ali even offered to mediate between United States and China to solve outstanding issues (especially the Taiwan issue) but Washington cold-shouldered him. Chou was convinced that Pakistan, despite its participation in the SEATO, had no objective reason to be hostile to China. So much so, Sino-Pakistani relations began improving and Pakistan's entry into the Middle East Defence Organisation (MEDO) in July 1955 did not deter the process.

An Indian scholar surmises that Pakistan might have known about the Sino-Indian differences over the border because it had repeatedly proclaimed that there was no conflict of interests between itself and China and that the two countries met "peacefully at an undisputed border in the south-west".[27] About this time Soviet Union had launched a diplomatic offensive in South and South-east Asia to counter the Chinese triumph at Bandung. Prime Minister Bulganin and party secretary Khrushchev visited India at the end of 1955 and Khrushchev declared that Kashmir's accession to India was final and complete.[28] Pakistan reacted sharply to this "unfriendly act" detrimental to its "sovereignty". The unequivocal Soviet support to India contrasted with United States equivocation on Kashmir.

China withheld support to India on Kashmir and kept its options, underlining its independence of Soviet Union on foreign policy issues. Pakistan came under military rule in October 1958. The new regime entered a bilateral defence agreement on 5 March 1959 enabling United States to have military bases in Pakistan. This and the military regimes crackdown on communists earlier proved a setback to Sino-Pakistani relations though China did not protest formally against the defence agreement. The Lama revolt in Tibet (1959) found Pakistan condemning China. President Ayub Khan's foreign policy showed a strong pro-Western inclination. When Sino-Indian relations turned critical in the wake of the Tibet revolt and the border dispute sharpened, President Ayub Khan proposed a joint defence plan for the subcontinent.[29] Nehru rebuffed this, asking rhetorically: "Against whom" Sino-Indian border incidents disturbed Ayub and he was turning belligerent towards China.

Soviet Union was trying to befriend Pakistan with the offer of economic co-operation. A barter agreement had been concluded in 1959 and negotiations were on for Soviet technical assistance in oil and mineral exploration when the United States U-2 spy plane was shot down over Soviet territory on the eve of May Day 1960 and it was found to have taken off from the Peshawar base in Pakistan. Yet the negotiations continued and ended successfully in December.

Pakistan was obliged to reformulate its China policy when United States changed its attitude to India's non-alignment. The Kennedy Administration decided on large scale economic aid which directly helped India's military capability. Pakistan feared that the military balance in the subcontinent might change. Though a military ally, United States was taking Pakistan for granted while India, which had been non-aligned, was now qualifying for additional aid to supplement Soviet supplies because it had a border dispute with China. In a mood of disenchantment, Pakistan tilted towards China. Surprising its allies, in 1961 Pakistan supported a Soviet draft resolution in the General Assembly for China's admission to United Nations. Pakistan was developing close relations with China without prejudice to its relations with United States.

Early in 1961 Pakistan had sounded China about a border agreement but did not get any response until February 1962 when the Sino-Indian border dispute was heating up after a two-year lull. On 3 May, China announced negotiations with Pakistan on China's border with "the contiguous areas, defence of which is under the control of Pakistan", and that "after the settlement of the dispute over Kashmir between Pakistan and India, the sovereign authorities concerned shall reopen negotiations with the Chinese government regarding the boundary of Kashmir, so as to sign a formal boundary treaty to replace the provisional agreement".[30]

India protested against the negotiations. India's claim was to the whole of Kashmir and there could be no Sino-Pakistani border or a border dispute as such unless it was conceded that the areas bordering China in Pakistan's occupation belonged to Pakistan. China rejected the protest pointing out that the negotiations were needed "to settle the question of the actually existing common boundary so as to maintain tranquillity on the border and amity between the two countries". China responded to Pakistan's overture almost a year later and only when its border with India and Soviet Union had become tense. Sino-Pakistan negotiations began on 12 October 1962 when the Indian army had just been asked to clear NEFA of the Chinese. On 26 December, an agreement on principle was reached "on the location and alignment of the boundary actually existing between the two countries". The agreement was signed on 2 March 1963 after detailed negotiations when India and Pakistan were going through a series of ministerial level talks on "Kashmir and related matters". The agreement was no doubt provisional, pending final solution of the Kashmir dispute. India protested against the agreement and refused to recognise it. Nehru said that in its anti-India hysteria, Pakistan had parted with 13,000 square miles of Kashmir territory to China[31] but Pakistan, refuting this said that not only did it not lose territory but gained about 750 square miles in the demarcation.

But according to an Indian estimate China gained 2,500 square miles of Kashmir area in addition to 1,600 square miles of area Pakistan was not effectively controlling.[32] The Chinese maintain that the Karakoram range is the boundary between Sinkiang and Kashmir. Their claim to Aksai-chin is based on this argument. By securing Pakistani recognition to their claim line, the Chinese were seeking justification of their claim on Aksai-chin which they already possessed. In any case, China had become a third party to the Kashmir dispute because the accord took place when Pakistan and India were discussing the dispute.

The convergence of United States and Soviet interests on India demonstrated effectively during and after the Sino-Indian border war pushed Pakistan and China closer. The border agreement was followed by a trade agreement, an air transport agreement, a barter deal, and a sixty-million-dollar interest-free loan for Pakistan's development.

Chou visited Pakistan in February 1965 (his first visit was in December 1956) and Pakistan pulled off a diplomatic coup. The Chou-Ayub communique hoped "the Kashmir dispute could be resolved in accordance with the wishes of the people of Kashmir as pledged to them by India and Pakistan".[33] China was exercising its option on Kashmir in Pakistan's favour and challenging the Soviet position on Kashmir.

United States was disturbed over the growing Sino-Pakistan amity and tried to use the aid lever against Pakistan. It stopped further economic aid early in 1965 and prevailed upon the Aid Pakistan Club to postpone its meeting to decide the quantum of aid. United States-Pakistan relations worsened on the eve of the Indo-Pakistan war in 1965. An armed clash in the disputed Kutch border in April-May preceded the September-October war. During the clash, China came out in open support of Pakistan, charging India with carrying out the "U.S. scheme of making the Asians fight Asians, thereby disrupting Afro-Asian unity".[34]

Khrushchev's ouster in October 1964 had softened Chinese attitude to Soviet Union and India in the hope that the Brezhnev-Kosygin leadership was less revisionist and less friendly to India. When they realised that the new leadership was no different from the old, the hard line against both Soviet Union and India was resumed. When President Johnson escalated the Vietnam bombings early in 1965, Prime Minister Lal Bahadur Shastri initiated a couple of peace moves which invited sharp Chinese attacks. When Shastri visited Moscow in May, the Chinese were convinced that India continued to follow the Nehru line. "India's 'non-alignment' policy has long become so much a sham as the emperor's clothes in Hans Christian Anderson's fairy tales," wrote the *People's Daily* commentator. United States imperialism was highly appreciative of Shastri's role on Vietnam because he was a "rare anti-China cavaliar" as well as Washington's pet. Alignment with the Indian reactionaries against China was "an integral part of Khrushchevian revisionism". The formation of an anti-China alliance made twin-brothers of Khrushchev and Nehru. "Now one of them is fallen and other is dead' but Khrushchev's successors were pursuing his line to "form an anti-China alliance with Nehru's successors", he said.[35]

Shastri's communique with Tito in Belgrade was assailed for its support to Johnson's "peace swindle" and the "Tito group" and the "Indian reactionaries" were denounced as "American agents".[36] This was followed by a withering attack on non-alignment. "By receiving 'military aid' from the Soviet Union the Indian government hopes to conceal its alliance with Washington claiming that between the two it is 'non-aligned' and 'neutral'." Military aid from both the sources were of the "same nature"—both served India's purpose of opposing China and arms expansion and war preparations, "all of which endanger the security of India's neighbours and peace. ... Thus India's acceptance of Soviet military 'aid' does not mean that Indian reaction has changed its allegiance to Washington, but on the contrary, it has strengthened such an allegiance".[37]

Indo-Pakistan War and China

Meantime, when there was an armed clash on the disputed Indo-Pakistan border in Kutch sector in April-May, Chinese came out in open support of Pakistan, charging India with carrying out the "U.S. scheme of making the Asians fight Asians, thereby disrupting Afro-Asian unity".[38]

In August India reported large-scale infiltration into Kashmir by Pakistani irregulars, but before the trouble there took a serious turn India and China had been charging each other with border violations and incursions. Soviet and Chinese attitudes to the Kashmir developments collided at the very outset. On 24 August *Pravda* blamed the imperialists who "more than once" had tried to set India and Pakistan against each other, and called the Kashmir problem a "grim colonial legacy". But China's Foreign Minister Chen Yi, on a visit to Karachi, backed Pakistan's "just action in Kashmir to repel Indian armed provocation". An ominous Peking statement on 7 September warned that "Indian aggression against any of its neighbours concerns all its neighbours" and of a "chain of consequences" if New Delhi did not mend its ways.[39] Chou, on 9 September, condemned "Indian aggression against Pakistan" as a threat to Asian peace and saw United States support and Soviet encouragement behind the "serious military adventure".[40] On the same day Vice Premier Hieh Fu-Chich told a Lhasa rally of "wanton incursions" on China's border and "naked aggression on Pakistan" by "Indian reactionaries" and asked the people and armed forces of Tibet to be vigilant. Following this, a Chinese note alleged intrusions across te Sikkim-Tibet border and demanded Indian troop withdrawal from the contested posts on the Sikkim border.

In this situation the Soviet Union was quick to support India against China. Brezhnev, on 11 September, warned India and Pakistan against "third forces" which tried to gain from an aggravation of the conflict and urged a cease-fire.[41] Three days later the Soviet leadership repeated its warning against those who made "incendiary statements" and again called for a peaceful end to the conflict.[42]

The Chinese attitude did not change. On 11 September *People's Daily* backed "Pakistan's just struggle against aggression and the Kashmiri people's struggle for national self-determination". Another comment three days later attacked the United Nations as the "sanctuary for Indian aggressors". On 18 September *People's Daily* returned to its old theme of United States-Soviet backing for India. "Who are the backers?" it asked rhetorically and answered the question: United States hoped to cut Pakistan down to size through Indian "military aggression" because it cannot bear Pakistan's independent policies. Soviet leaders pretended to be impartial but actually favoured "Indian reactionaries" and were "not one whit inferior to U.S. imperialists" in this respect. They had tried to cover up "Indian aggression" to defend India's non-alignment describing it as a policy of "peace and peaceful co-existence", and had slandered countries supporting Pakistan, namely, China. The attack was on Soviet responsibility for the conflict and failure to distinguish between a "just and unjust war".[43]

As the war moved to its climax, China virtually threatened to open a second front in Pakistan's support when it issued a 72-hour ultimatum on 16 September demanding demolition of the alleged Indian military structures on the Tibet-Sikkim border and the return of 800 sheep and 59 yak alleged to have been taken away by Indian soldiers from Tibetan herdsmen. Prime Minister Shastri warned China that if India were attacked it would "fight with grim determination"[44] but his government agreed to the Chinese demand for joint inspection of the alleged installations while rejecting the charges of incursion. India reported large-scale Chinese troop movements all along the border, and firing on 20 September along the Ladakh border and in the Sikkim region. On 19 September India alleged Chinese incursions while the next day China extended the ultimatum by 72 hours. Meantime, India had alerted five of the six Colombo powers (Cambodia was the one left out) and pointed out that any military action by the Chinese on the Sikkim border or elsewhere would be a breach of the undertaking China had given these powers. The suggestion of this *demarche* was that the Colombo powers should try and restrain the Chinese, particularly after India had agreed to neutral or joint inspection of the complaint.

On 22 September, China announced that the military installations had been demolished while Indian officials maintained that the so-called fortifications were a myth and the Chinese announcement a "climb-down" to prepare for Pakistan's acceptance of the Security Council resolution of 20 September calling a cease-fire. A more plausible reason for the Chinese stance could be the fact India had accepted the cease-fire call. Chinese choice of the Sikkim-Tibet border as the subject of the ultimatum is significant in the context of a latter-day disclosure. China had warned India through United States not to extend the conflict to East Pakistan (which was separated from West Pakistan by 1,200 miles of Indian territory).[45] To this extent the Chinese ultimatum achieved its objective because the war did not extend to East Pakistan and India and Pakistan responded to the

Security Council's cease-fire call.

The check-mate war did not solve the Kashmir problem but gave Soviet Union a long-awaited opening to establish its Asian presence. It proposed an Indo-Pakistani meeting with Soviet participation to solve the immediate problems thrown up by the war and to evolve a procedure to settle the outstanding bilateral issues. India accepted the proposal but Ayub Khan could not accept it until after he had discussed it with the State Department in Washington.[46]

The tripartite meeting at Tashkent (3 to 10 January 1966) formalised the cease-fire in the undeclared war and secured withdrawal of troops to 5 August 1965 positions. Trade, travel and cultural relations were resumed but only formally. The Kashmir issue remained. The declaration at Tashkent provided for joint meetings and joint bodies to look into common problems. However, the much eulogised Tashkent "spirit" had turned sour before the declaration was a year old. Shastri died of a heart attack within hours of the declaration and Ayub Khan back home faced severe criticism on the Tashkent accord.

The Chinese saw unmistakable evidence of United States-Soviet collusion over the Indo-Pakistan war. A *People's Daily* editorial on 27 December 1965 said the United Nations had become the "market place" of such collusion and charged the two powers with behind-the-scene bargaining over Vietnam, endrosing United States intervention in the Dominican Republic, taking a biased stand favouring "India's aggression" against Pakistan; authorising Britain to "quell" the situation in Rhodesia, working actively to set up a permanent United Nations force, preventing nuclear proliferation and consolidating nuclear monopoly, and raising an anti-China chorus.

Another "model" of United States-Soviet collaboration was produced on the question of the India-Pakistan war, the editorial said, and attacked all Security Council resolutions on it.

First of all, they did not condemn the Indian reactionaries as the aggressor. Secondly, they disapproved of Pakistan's counter-attack in self-defence. Thirdly, they did not allow other countries to support Pakistan. On the Kashmir question, the Security Council ignored the right of self-determination of the Kashmiri people and simply shelved its own previous resolution on holding a plebiscite in the area. It is widely known and evident to all how the United Nations had done everything it can to side with India. Unashamed in this indecency, the Soviet leaders came out openly to act as the protectors of the Indian reactionaries. They have behaved more blatantly than even the U.S. imperialists. It is nothing to be wondered at when Lal Bahadur Shastri and the Indian press declare with moving gratitude that the Soviet Union 'has stood firmly by India'. ... in the Security Council, Russia simply refused to agree to any resolution or motion which was not acceptable to India. [47]

The Tashkent declaration was denounced with equal vehemence. The talks initiated by Soviet leaders was also a product of "joint" United States-Soviet plotting. The Johnson Administration lost no time in acclaiming the declaration. The accord was imposed on Pakistan by the super powers motivated by selfish ends. *People's Daily* wrote:

During the Indo-Pakistan conflict both U.S. and the Soviet Union instigated and encouraged the Indian aggressors, and brought crude pressure to bear on Pakistan which was acting in self-defence by safeguarding its own sovereignty. Why afterwards did they work hard in close co-ordination to bring the Indian and Pakistan leadership together to 'make peace'? The truth is the Soviet leadership went to all that trouble to conjure up a so-called 'Tashkent spirit' for the simple reason they want to continue backing up the Indian reactionaries and use the spirit to publicise their general line of 'peaceful co-existence' in order to take the edge off the united struggle against imperialism in Asia and Africa. As far as U.S. imperialism was concerned, its purpose was to make common cause against China and push ahead with its global strategy utilising the Soviet leaders' intervention in Asian affairs.[48]

United States Pressures

Even before the 1965 war the Indian economy was in a crisis, its growth rate slowing down in mid-1964. The crisis was partly due to diversion of resources for the defence effort after the 1962 war with China. Partly it was due to poor crop weather and bottlenecks in transport and power generation. United States lost no time telling India that aid would be forthcoming only if it behaved properly and directed the aid to agriculture, public health and education and not for industrial development. United States and the World Bank were moving in concert on this. In August 1964 a World Bank team led by David Bell had visited India and made its report (still a secret document). Its main points were made known. It asked for general liberalisation of controls on the private sector, particularly with regard to licensing procedures and policies; devaluation of the rupee, and if this was unacceptable, the control of balance of payments through import duties rather than physical controls, and greater emphasis on agriculture and "infrastructure" projects rather than heavy industrial projects.

The 1965 Indo-Pakistan war gave United States the opportunity to arm-twist India. Economic aid was suspended when the war began. Besides the war, another disaster hit the Indian economy. The summer rains failed causing a severe famine in a country already dependent on PL-480 foodgrain imports. The Food for Peace programme under which these supplies were being made expired in June 1965 and a new agreement was not forthcoming. Shipments were put on a month-to-month basis to hold India on the short leash despite the danger of mass starvation in the country. Then when the war broke out, President Johnson suspended all aid. The United States-controlled World Bank tightened the squeeze by slowing down loans India needed to repay its old "time plan" loans.

Food was the Achilles heel of the Indian economy. A growing grain deficit had to be made up by imports that had already reached the six-million-tonne level even in 1964-65, a year of bumper harvests. The Indian government had launched a crash programme to build new fertiliser plants that would help raise agricultural production. But India could never borrow enough on its terms from the Western lenders to finance these projects. Western oil and chemical combines wanted to build and run these plants themselves, on their own terms. By December 1965 the Indian government was obliged to liberalise its policy for foreign investors in the fertiliser industry. They were allowed to fix their own prices and handle their own distribution. This might have been adequate a year earlier but not now. United States investors held back and Johnson added to the pressures by withholding aid to India. More liberal terms for the investors was made the condition for food and economic aid resumption.

This was the picture when Mrs Indira Gandhi, who had succeeded the late Lal Bahadur Shastri as Prime Minister, decided to go to Washington in March 1966, mainly to secure United States aid resumption. Johnson had set his price: India should make use of more private capital and relax the myriad controls to encourage production. Besides, India should use more fertiliser to grow more food.

At the end of her five day sojourn in Washington, Johnson announced on 30 March a 3.5-million-tonne foodgrain aid to India. He also announced help to India's agricultural development and appealed to other countries to help with foodgrains. He reiterated United States' decision to provide India through the consortium headed by World Bank economic assistance "on a scale that is related to the needs of our sister democracy". But the price of all this was indeed heavy in terms of India's economic and foreign policies. Though Mrs Gandhi had earlier denied that her United States visit was to solicit aid, her joint communique with Johnson gave priority to economic assistance and India's foodgrain needs.[49] Then followed Johnson's proposal for an India-United States Educational Foundation to India to utilise the staggering accumulation of PL-480 counterpart rupee funds.[50] Then came references to foreign policy items such as the Tashkent declaration, Vietnam, and China.

On Vietnam the communique recorded known positions of both India and United States. India had been silent on United

States' role there but according to reports, when Mrs Gandhi discussed it with Vice-President Humphrey in February, there was no serious difference between them on any aspect of the Vietnam conflict. Mrs Gandhi agreed with Humphrey that North Vietnam was completely under the influence of China and Hanoi was in position to make an independent move to seek a peaceful solution. India's Foreign Minister Swaran Singh had stated that when United States ordered a one-month bombing pause after the January escalation, North Vietnam did not respond or indicate a desire for a peaceful settlement. Therefore, India did not see any need to condemn United States resumption of bombing.[51]

On China, the communique agreed that aggressive Chinese policies threatened world peace, "especially in Asia". Earlier, Mrs Gandhi had told the Washington Press Club that by offering a viable "Asian" alternative of democratic socialism to China, India had incurred its wrath, which presumably explained the Chinese invasion of October 1962 as well as Chinese attempts to subvert Indian unity. She had also said the best bulwark against China would be strong nationalism and socio-economic development in conditions of freedom in countries around China.[52] In connection with this a well connected New Delhi columnist wrote:

> A noteworthy feature of Smt. Gandhi's diplomacy in America has been to underline the danger from China, and to link it up with Kashmir for enlisting American support for India's stand. She has gone to the extent of referring to India's dispute with China having its roots in ideological divergence—a line of approach which Nehru always combated even in the crisis days of 1962. Nehru's point was that the Chinese aggression on India had nothing to do with communism as such but was inspired by China's aggressive militarism seeking world domination. Smt. Gandhi has throughout touched on India and the U.S. having a "common way of life"—a point which smacks too much of the "Free World" jargon, a rather awkward angle for a Prime Minister who chose to return home from Washington via Moscow in a Soviet plane.[53]

India had in the past used its non-aligned foreign policy as a lever to get economic aid from both the camps. With the erosion of its non-alignment, United States could now use aid as a lever to influence India's foreign policy. There was now tacit understanding that India should refrain from criticising United States foreign policy, especially its Vietnam policy. This was only a part of the price of United States aid. Within weeks of Mrs Gandhi's return from Washington, there was a dramatic shift in India's economic policies. United States investors who had demanded liberal terms in the fertiliser industry had their way. The government entered a controversial deal in May with an American firm for setting up a fertiliser plant in Madras. The American company had only 49 per cent equity share and the Indian government 51 per cent. But the management control was with the foreign investor. This amounted to dilution of India's basic industrial policy. As the *New York Times* said:

> Many of the new trends now evident had their origin in the last months of Prime Minister Lal Bahadur Shastri's life.
>
> Much of what is happening now is the result of steady pressure from the United States and the International Bank of Reconstruction and Development, which for the last year, have been urging a substantial freeing of the Indian economy and a greater scope for private enterprise.
>
> The United States pressure, in particular, has been highly effective here because United States provides by far the largest part of the foreign exchange needed to finance India's development and keep the wheels of industry turning.
>
> Call them 'strings', call them 'conditions,' or whatever one likes, India has little choice now but to agree to many of the terms that the United States, through the World Bank is putting on its aid. For India simply has nowhere to turn.[54]

The climax was yet to be. On 6 July, India agreed to devalue the rupee by 57 per cent as required by the World Bank. New Delhi knuckled under United States pressures on its foreign and domestic policies and let Washington's strategy work out its own logic on the Indian economy. The devaluation decision marked the new policy slide back. United States political and economic intervention was triumphing in India, and distorted its declared policies.

India's equivocation on Vietnam marked this new phase. Foreign policy came to be subordinated to the dictates of aid realities. To those who knew the pressures operating even before Humphrey's New Delhi visit in February, India's Vietnam policy was losing whatever independence it had. Over a year earlier, the late Lal Bahadur Shastri had denounced United States bombing in Vietnam but later talked India into silence as the price of aid. In the process of finding a new equation, the domestic and foreign policies had been whittled down to absurd proportions.

After devaluing the rupee, Mrs Gandhi chose to go to Moscow via Cairo and Belgrade. On the eve of her departure, she ventured some proposals on Vietnam: the two co-chairmen of the Geneva conference should reconvene the Geneva conference to "guarantee the integrity and independence of neutral Vietnam and indeed the neighbouring states of Laos and Cambodia as envisaged in the Geneva Agreement"; immediate ending of bombing in Vietnam; cessation of hostilities, and withdrawal of foreign forces from Vietnam.[55]

United States welcomed the proposals the very next day while President Nasser of United Arab Republic supported on 9 July the call for a Geneva conference. On 10 July, China rejected the proposals. Chou said they were designed only to "sap the fighting will of the Vietnam people and help United States". Unless United States troops were withdrawn unconditionally, immediately, completely, and thoroughly, the total reconvening of the Geneva conference was out of question.[56]

In Moscow, Soviet leaders rejected Mrs Gandhi's proposals and wanted United States to get out of Vietnam first. They said even the initiative for peace must come from the Vietnamese.[57] This rebuff from the Soviet leadership came after Mrs Gandhi had indirectly accused China of seeking to undo the Great Power detente by aggravating tensions in Asia and had repeated her proposal for stoppage of bombing of North Vietnam, cessation of hostilities, and return to the conference table.[58] It was not merely a question of the tardiness on Mrs Gandhi's part in condemning the bombing: she was equating United States and China. The following record illustrates the equivocation: on 7 July Mrs Gandhi wanted the two co-chairmen to convene a meeting of the Geneva conference; on 16 July her joint communique with Alexei Kosygin in Moscow said "the resolution of the problem of Vietnam can be found only within the framework of the Geneva Agreements of 1954 on Indo-China; and on 25 July Mrs Gandhi told Parliament: "A peaceful solution can be reached only at the conference table, and hence the necessity for a co-chairmen to convene a Geneva-type conference to which we attach great importance."

"Geneva conference", "framework of the Geneva Agreement", and "Geneva-type conference" were used by Mrs Gandhi without regard to their connotations. On the whole, her proposals which were a non-started pleased neither United States nor even Soviet Union.

India had lost contact with Peking and its voice was no longer heard with more than politeness in Hanoi. Economic failures at home had made it hopelessly dependent on United States aid. Besides, India thought it should not let Vietnam go under Chinese influence. Mrs Gandhi's foreign policy aides believed United States presence and role in Vietnam really helped India's national interests vis-a-vis China. They knew that United States escalation of the Vietnam war did not disrupt the larger United States Soviet quest for a detente and this did not affect India's non-alignment which in practice lapsed into double alignment after the 1962 India-China war.

India's foreign policy now relied on the postulate that the Sino-Soviet rift would widen and India's pro-United States policies would not inhibit Soviet Union from going the farthest to help India. India got the best of both worlds to confront China: continued military and economic aid from Soviet Union and resumed economic aid from United States at the cost of proclaimed basic policies.

Notes

[1] "Otherwise I would not have said it," Nehru told Parliament. Lok Sabha, 27 February 1963.
[2] Asoke Sen, India's Law Minister who led the delegation to Cairo claimed that the UAR move was in fact India-inspired. Cf. Kuldip Nayar, *Between the Lines*, New Delhi, Allied, 1970, p. 185.
[3] *White Paper IX*, p. 186.
[4] N.J.N. [N.J. Nanporia], *The Times of India*, 11 March 1963.
[5] *People's Daily*, 28 January 1963.
[6] Chou En-lai's letter to Nehru, 3 March 1963, Text in *White Paper IX*, pp.3-5.
[7] K. Krishna Murthy, "The Fatal Clarification," *Far Eastern Economic Review*, 14 November 1963.
[8] *Ibid.*
[9] Neville Maxwell says the clarifications were drafted by the Indian government and released by Mrs Sirimao Bandaranaike on 7 March 1963. Cf. *India's China War*, Bombay, Jaico, p. 430.
[10] *White Paper X*, pp. 3-6.
[11] *Peking Review*, 16 October 1964.
[12] *Peking Review*, 1 January 1965.
[13] Lok Sabha, 21 February 1963.
[14] *Link*, 10 February 1963. The Soviet commitment followed the visit to Moscow of R.K. Nehru, Secretary-General of the External Affairs Ministry.
[15] 2 April 1963.
[16] "American Aid Politics," *Link*, 21 April 1963 for an account of the arm-twisting over economic and defence aid to India.
[17] Lok Sabha, 8 April 1963.
[18] Text of communique in *Asian Recorder*, Vol. IV, no 33. p. 5332.
[19] "Open Letter from the CPSU Central Committee to the Party Organizations and all Communists of the Soviet Union," *Pravda*, 14 July 1963. This was in obvious response to the Chinese party's letter of 14 June expounding its alternative general line and assailing Soviet domination of other parties.
[20] *New Age* weekly, 21 July 1963.
[21] "Statement of the Central Secretariat of the CPI," *New Age* weekly, 28 July 1963.
[22] "Marxism-Leninism is the Basis of the Unity of the Communist Movement," *Kommunist*, 18 October 1963.
[23] Quoted by Z.A. Bhutto, *The Myth of Independence*, London, Oxford 1969, p. 71.
[24] *New York Times*, 13 September 1964.
[25] U.S. Senate Committee on Foreign Relations, Foreign Assistance Act of 1965, Washington DC, 1965.
[26] *New York Times*, 25 April 1955.
[27] B.N. Goswami, *Pakistan and China*, New Delhi, Allied, 1971, pp. 43-44.

[28] N.A. Bulganin and N.S. Khrushchev, *Speeches During Sojourn in India, Burma and Afghanistan*, New Delhi, Representative of *Tass* in India, 1956, pp. 83-6.
[29] *Dawn*, 27 October 1959.
[30] *NCNA*, 3 May 1962.
[31] Lok Sabha, 5 March 1963.
[32] *Link*, 10 March 1963.
[33] *China, India and Pakistan*, Karachi: Pakistan Institute of International Affairs, 1966, p. 425.
[34] *Peking Review*, 14 May 1965.
[35] "What Shastri's Soviet Trip Reveals," *People's Daily*, 27 May 1965.
[36] "Poor Salesman for an American Plot," *People's Daily*, 9 August 1965.
[37] Shish Yen, "Non-aligned India's Double Alignment," *Peking Review*, 13 August 1965.
[38] *Peking Review*, 14 May 1965.
[39] *China, India and Pakistan*, op. cit., pp. 428-31.
[40] *Peking Review*, 17 September 1965.
[41] *Pravda*, 11 September 1965.
[42] *Ibid.*, 14 September 1965.
[43] "Who Backs India's Aggressors," *People's Daily*, 18 September 1965.
[44] Lok Sabha, 17 September 1965.
[45] According to Z.A. Bhutto, the Chinese threat was conveyed to India through the United States representative at Warsaw. Pakistan National Assembly 15 March 1966. Azizur Rehman said in the Pakistan National Assembly on 14 March 1966 that China directly warned India through its Charge d'affaires in Peking that it would intervene if East Pakistan was attacked.
[46] M.J. Desai, then India's Foreign Secretary corraborates this. Cf. T.F. Tsou (ed.), *China in Crisis*, Vol. 2, Chicago, University of Chicago Press, 1968, p. 439.
[47] "The United Nations is an American-Soviet Market Place," editorial in *People's Daily*, 27 December 1965.
[48] "Who is the Soviet Leadership Talking of United Action With?" *People's Daily*, 2 February 1966.
[49] Text of communique in *The Hindu*, 31 March 1966.
[50] Though Mrs Gandhi initially welcomed the plan, following strong domestic protests, the plan was abandoned.
[51] See K. Rangaswamy in *The Hindu*, 24 March 1966.
[52] Reported in *The Statesman*, 30 March 1966.
[53] N.C., "Balance Sheet from Washington," *Mainstream*, 9 April 1966.
[54] *The New York Times*, 28 April 1966.
[55] Broadcast to the nation, 7 July 1966.
[56] *The Hindu*, 11 July 1966.
[57] *Ibid*, 15 July 1966.
[58] *Ibid*.

7/ Continuing Deadlock

The Cultural Revolution phase (1966-69) found China's foreign policy at a low ebb though a major foreign policy debate had been up in Peking since mid-1965. It could not give shape to a new-look policy until after the ninth party congress in April 1969 which marked the end of the cultural revolution. During this interregnum, Lin Piao's strategy of linking all people's wars in the Third World into a global front against United States found acceptance as a result of the debate. Lin's strategy, first spelt out in 1965[1] commended to the Third World the Maoist theory of people's war based on guerilla tactics. It took the Chinese leadership two years to call for the implementation of this strategy. In June-July 1967, China stepped up support to national liberation movements already on and called for the armed overthrow of the regimes in Burma, India, and Indonesia.

In Lin's analysis, United States imperialism was divisible and could be destroyed bit by bit through people's war in the Third World. When United States was dreading people's war most, the "Khrushchev revisionists" came to its rescue by debunking it and "scheming to undermine" it. The revisionists had no faith in the masses, had succumbed to United States nuclear blackmail and were afraid people's wars against United States aggression would involve them in a conflict smashing the dreams of Soviet-United States co-operation to dominate the world. Lin also challenged the Soviet theory that a nation without nuclear weapons cannot defeat an enemy with nuclear weapons and ridiculed the belief that a single spark anywhere could touch off a world nuclear confrontation. People's war was the answer to all the issues in a changed world environment.

Lin's thesis was thus a frontal attack on Soviet ideological positions and the general line of the three peacefuls—peaceful co-existence, peaceful competition, and peaceful transition. The strategy aimed at a combined onslaught on United States imperialism and Soviet revisionism in the Third World through an escalation of the national liberation movement. Asia, Africa, and Latin America had become the focal point of the fundamental contradictions in the world and were the weakest sectors of the imperialist colonial empire. The contradiction between the oppressed nations and imperialism was the major and the most acute one. The contradictions centring on Viet Nam were being successfully resolved through armed struggle. The war itself proved that United States, however powerful, could be defeated.

While the debate continued in Peking, the changing Indian situation (the economic recession resulting from the wars of 1962 and 1965, and two successive drought years) did not go unnoticed by the Chinese leadership. A few months before the fourth elections (February 1967) there was a general deterioration in law and order amidst the serious economic crisis. The Chinese saw in this a "sharpening of class contradictions" and "the inevitable outcome of the reactionary policies" of the government at home and its kow-towing to United States and Soviet Union abroad.[2] On the eve of the elections there was gushing optimism in the Chinese reading of the "revolutionary situation" in India which had been swept by a series of a "stormy struggles" during 1966 when the people had demanded the exit of the Congress government propped by United States and Soviet Union.[3]

The Congress party which had a monopoly of power suffered a shattering defeat, losing nearly half of the 17 states and managing to return to office at the federal level with a shrunken majority. The Communist Party of India (Marxist), which had come into being in 1964 as a result of the split in the pro-Moscow Communist Party of India[4] emerged the dominant partner in the non-ideological coalition ministries in Kerala and West Bengal states. Except in Madras (now Tamil Nadu) where the separatist DMK could form a one-party government, there were non-ideological coalitions in the states which the Congress lost. It took the Chinese leadership a month to react to the election results. The new Congress government at the federal level was "more reactionary than ever and still more subservient to Soviet revisionism". The Congress party, a tool of the ruling classes for 20 years, "has now become ineffective in the face of the people's resistance", the *Peking Review* commentary said. "The general elections in India show that when the internal class struggle becomes acute, the reactionary rulers often throw to winds the sham 'democracy' which they use to deceive the people", it said referring to Rajasthan where the Congress had lost, but the federal government proclaimed its direct rule to prevent a non-Congress ministry from taking office. The "reactionary rule was running into a serious crisis and "it is certain that revolutionary flames will rage throughout the vast territory of India". The review mentioned the two CPI-M dominated Kerala and West Bengal ministries without much enthusiasm.[5]

The CPI-M's assessment of the election results, however, was at variance with the Chinese leadership's. It did not, for instance, share the latter's optimism about the "revolutionary flames" raging throughout the country. The only basic point of agreement was on the maturing political crisis. The CPI-M saw in the defeat of the Congress a "qualitative change" in the situation "which should be characterised as beginning of a political crisis". In objective terms it was a verdict against the policies of the government of the bourgeois landlord classes bringing a new confidence to the people, facilitating the acceleration and advance of the democratic forces in the country.

The CPI-M thought its own key role in forming and running the non-Congress governments in Kerala and West Bengal was of "special importance and significance" because the party could set the tone for other non-Congress ministries and force a new alignment and regrouping of forces on a higher plane. It was conscious of the limitation of the "class" state and the concentration of power in the federal government and understood the two united front governments as "instruments of struggle". In class terms, participation in such governments was one specific form of struggle to win support for the proletariat and its allies in the struggle for people's democracy, and at a later stage, for socialism.[6]

As it turned out, the Chinese party did not regard the united front ministries in Kerala and West Bengal even "instruments of struggle" and assailed the CPI-M's participation in them as a revisionist tendency, hitherto regarded the sin of the CPI. A Peking commentary branded the new six-week-old Indira Gandhi government in New Delhi as a United States-Soviet pawn against China.[7] "India's key position in the strategy of the United States imperialists and Soviet revisionists prompts them to spend freely and make all efforts to try and control India and enslave its people." The two big powers were trying to make India their military base against China. The one-party rule in New Delhi was "increasingly shaky", with people forced more and more into violence to meet its tyranny, "angry masses" rising to seize food and arms in some states. For the first time, Peking also supported the Naga and Mizo ethnic groups "persevering in their anti-government armed struggle'.[8]

Initially, Peking did not attack the CPI-M directly; it chose to make the CPI the surrogate target. Chairman S. A. Dange provided the opportunity. *People's Daily* attacked his 24 April statement to the effect that peaceful transition to socialism was possible in India and that the elections had changed the power structure, raising hopes of such transition. Dange had also said his party would seek talks with the CPI-M and others for an "alternative government" in New Delhi toppling the existing one by peaceful means. The fear that the CPI-M might succumb to the temptation of the revisionist short cut suggested by Dange prompted a bitter denunciation of the peaceful transition line. Dange's views were "hackneyed phrases" of old revisionists Bernstein and Kautsky and modern revisionist Khrushchev, and nothing but the Indian version of the theories of "growing into socialism peacefully and winning a stable majority in Parliament, thus enabling it to realise the socialist transformation of society".

The new Indian government was still "a reactionary regime of the dictatorship of the big landlords and big bourgeoisie". The non-Congress governments which had emerged in some of the states had not changed the "reactionary nature of the political game". In the place of the Congress party of the reactionary ruling class, the local comprador forces held sway from top to bottom in the non-Congress state governments. As for the CPI-M dominated governments, they were

> component parts of the state apparatus of India's big landlords and big bourgeoisie. Under the direct control of the Central government, they are completely unable to either introduce any reforms in substance to shake the foundations of the capitalist and feudal relations of production. Furthermore, whenever the Central government deems it necessary, it can use the gimmick of "President's rule" to take over all State government functions.[9]

Maoist Line for India

Short of calling for people's war, the Chinese party suggested the alternative course for the CPI-M:

> The facts prove that without a people's revolution, without the seizure of political power by force and without smashing of the old state apparatus there can be no change in the social system and in the nature of the political regime, and there can be no real social reform. There is no precedent in history, nor will there be any in the future.[10]

The Chinese party's fight against revisionism was acquiring a new edge as its Third World strategy was about to get off the ground:

> The Dange clique is the running dog fostered by imperialists and the Soviet revisionist ruling clique to sabotage the revo-

lution in India.... To fight for their liberation, the Indian people must resolutely smash this renegade clique and the revisionists of all forms and wage revolutionary struggles.[11]

"Revisionists of all forms outside the Dange clique" obviously meant the section of the CPI-M leadership which was sold on the peaceful transition idea and wanted to settle for bourgeois parliamentarism.

A miniscule peasant-tribal revolt in Naxalbari, a 270-square-mile enclave of 80,000 people in Darjeeling district of West Bengal provided the Chinese party the occasion to implement its strategy of transferring its struggle against United States and Soviet Union to the Third World by activating and intensifying the national liberation movement. It also provided it the occasion for a fundamental evaluation of the Indian revolution and to spell out the Maoist line for India.

An authoritative Chinese party pronouncement, lyrically titled "Spring Thunder Over India" saw in Naxalbari the emergence of a "red area of revolutionary armed struggle". It went on to provide guidance, both in theory and practice, to the revolutionary groups of the CPI-M which were leading the struggle and revolting against their party's parliamentarism. The Chinese laid down the broad strategy for India's people's war against the four "big mountains"—imperialism, Soviet revisionism, feudalism, and bureaucrat-capitalism.

India was only "nominally independent, in fact nothing more than a semi-colonial, semi-feudal country". Its revolution must rely on the peasants, establish base areas in the countryside and use the countryside to encircle the cities through people's war. The specific feature of the Indian revolution, like that of the Chinese revolution, was armed revolution fighting armed counter-revolution. Armed struggle was the only road for India, the article declared. More specifically, it meant arousing the peasant masses and using the "whole set of flexible strategy and tactics of people's war personally worked out by Chairman Mao, and to persist in protracted armed struggle and seize victory of the revolution step by step".[12]

Continuing Deadlock 183

The Chinese party was queering the pitch for the CPI-M by attacking the West Bengal government which had to handle the Naxalbari trouble. The united front ministry, in which CPI-M's Jyoti Basu was the police minister, either obliged the federal government by crushing the revolt or faced dismissal for its failure to fulfil its law and order obligations as a state government. The CPI-M could not ignore the implications of open Chinese support to the "adventurists" of Darjeeling district who had led the Naxalbari uprising. The CPI-M's stance not only amounted to disowning the Naxalbari revolt but abdicating its own political role in support of the peasant demands. By acquiescing on police excesses through which the revolt was suppressed, it was placing the survival of the ministry above everything.

Peking's support to the Naxalbari uprising aimed at pressuring the CPI-M out of the united front ministry and the parliamentary system. When there was no response, the Chinese party moved a step further, extending the attack to "some revisionist leaders" of the West Bengal CPI-M who were "opposing the revolutionary line of armed struggle" and persisted in the "revisionist line of peaceful transition". The Chinese seemed to have calculated that the majority of the CPI-M following could be persuaded to revolt against its leadership and disown it. It turned fire on the "handful of revisionists" who were "oppressing, deceiving and betraying the revolutionaries in the party and in sabotaging the revolution and oppressing the peasant movement".

The question of armed struggle was once again posed as the touchstone of the CPI-M's revolutionary bona fides. After setting up the area of armed struggle in Darjeeling, "the real revolutionaries and real Marxist-Leninists in India will resolutely stand for armed struggle, lead and support it and thus gain the support of the broad masses of revolutionary people".[18] The CPI-M's weakness for the parliamentary system and its repudiation of armed struggle irked the Chinese leadership, inviting sharper attacks. In August came the call for a Maoist party, splitting the CPI-M if need be. The call was for demarcation with the revisionists "politically, ideologically and organisationally" to wage a resolute struggle against modern revisionism. "The revolutionaries in the Indian Communist Party will surely close their ranks in the struggle and build a *genuinely revolutionary* party of Marxism-Leninism, Mao Tse-tung Thought.[14]

The Chinese leadership was convinced that the objective conditions for people's war existed in India and the subjective need was a Maoist party. The victory claimed for the first round of the Naxalbari uprising was expected to take peasant armed struggle to the next stage of guerilla warfare and lead to the creation of revolutionary bases all over the country. But the Naxalbari movement was crushed in no time.

In the Chinese view, the Naxalbari uprising took place in a new strategic environment. By mid-1967, China thought the revolutionary situation lad turned "excellent" amidst sharpened international class struggle, with more revolutionary wars and counter-revolutionary wars than eight years ago. "The world is full of the smell of gun-powder," wrote the *People's Daily* and the commentary "To Hell With the Theory of 'Dying out' of wars!" reflected Chinese optimism and confidence. Soviet Premier Alexei Kosygin's call for "an end to the war" at this juncture, the commentary said, aimed at greater United States-Soviet collusion against the revolutionary struggles.[15]

This was the new strategic environment in which the Chinese leadership called for armed revolutions in India, Burma, and Indonesia in June-July 1967. A *People's Daily* article credited to a "Red Guard" on 10 June called for "relentless armed struggle" to overthrow the Indian government and "forcibly seize power". The Chinese saw in Naxalbari the first spark of revolutionary armed struggle that could start a prairie fire in India. Naxalbari represented the general orientation of the Indian revolution.[16]

In Burma, open support to armed struggle and a call for overthrow of Gen. Ne win's military regime followed deterioration in state-level relations. The shift came on 30 June after China, following anti-Chinese riots in Rangoon, decided that its ambassador would not return.

About the same time, China also called for the overthrow of the regime in Indonesia. The authoritative *Red Flag* said that the Indonesian communist party faced a difficult task (after the 1965 coup and the massacre of communists that followed) because it had to switch from cities to the countryside, from peaceful struggle to armed struggle, from legal to illegal and from open to secret activity. But the objective realities of the revolutionary struggle would compel people to make the change, and master armed struggle because there was no alternative to it.[17]

New Low in Relations with India

Implementation of the new line strategy for the Third World synchronised with an aberration in China's state-level relations with several countries. The Cultural Revolution had begun affecting the functioning of the Foreign Office which recalled almost all its ambassadors (the one in Cairo being a notable exception). China was to return these ambassadors only after the Cultural Revolution.

China's call for the overthrow of the regimes in India, Burma, and Indonesia, the new Third World strategy and China's state-level relations began interacting on each other. Sino-Indian relations were never too good after the 1959 Tibet revolt and there was an outstanding border dispute to be settled. The overseas Chinese populations in Burma and Indonesia were the immediate cause of the diplomatic rupture with them.

Two events highlighted this phase of Sino-Indian relations. In June, China expelled two Indian diplomats on charges of spying and this invited Indian retaliation. Indira Gandhi's government came under heavy political pressure to break off with China. In September there was a skirmish at Nathu La on the Sikkim-Tibet border followed by another at Cho La nearby. But India viewed them as more border incidents and treated them as such.

Early in 1967, India's attitude to China was hardening further. On 10 February, an Indian note (reply to China's 4 May 1966 note charging violations and provocations on the border) objected to the reference to the Sikkim-Tibet border[18] because this was one sector of the Tibet border China had not disputed earlier. India significantly dropped a diplomatic courtesy in practice for 15 years: the phrases the Indian government "presents its best compliments" and "has the honour to say" were missing.

India continued to believe that China was an aggressive power. External Affairs Minister M. C. Chagla said on 14 March that India's position had not changed.

> We are prepared to respond to any gesture that might be made by that country but judging from the present indications China continues to maintain the same bellicose and threatening posture which she has done for some time past.

Four days later, President Radhakrishnan told Parliament:

> With China we too would like to live in peace. But the aggressive acts and postures of the People's Republic of China coupled with their rejection of the concept of peaceful coexistence continue to be the major obstacle to an improvement of relations with China.

Meantime, following a demonstration of Tibetan refugees in front of the Chinese embassy in New Delhi, a *People's Daily* commentator charged "Indian reactionaries" with "interference in China's internal affairs using the Tibetan bandit traitors from China to carry on anti-China activities," and said this was part of the anti-China campaign engineered by United States imperialists and the Soviet revisionist leading clique.[19]

"Down With Indian Reactionaries" posters had appeared outside the Indian embassy in Peking on 22 March following the 21 March Chinese note to India about the demonstration. On 23 March, NCNA charged India with preparing a large-scale military attack against China. President Radhakrishnan's 18

March statement had "viciously" slandered China to "curry favour with US imperialists and Soviet revisionists".

Chagla, on 27 March, promised Parliament "another look" at the government's Tibet policy in view of the "gruesome conditions" there and pledged continued support to Tibetan rights.

Following Peking's support to the Naxalbari uprising and call for an armed overthrow of the Indian government, there was a Red Guard seige of the Indian embassy in Peking and expulsion of two Indian diplomats on spying charges, bringing the state-level relations to near breaking point. On 12 June there was a Red Guard demonstration in front of the embassy and on 13 June, Peking Radio said that K. Raghunath, second secretary, and P. Vijai, third secretary, had been ordered to leave China at a "people's public trial" on 13 June. The two officials had been charged with spying. They left for India on 14 June and India alleged they were manhandled and subjected to humiliating treatment all along the way out of China. India hit back on 13 June, depriving first secretary Chen Lu-chih of his diplomatic status for his "military intelligence" and other "grossly subversive activities". Third secretary Hsieh Chenghoa was declared persona non grata.

In Parliament, members including those of the ruling party wanted India to snap diplomatic relations with China. The demand was repeated amidst much excitement the next day, when members wanted a "new" China policy. Chagla turned down the demand for severence of relations.

On 16 September there was a demonstration in front of the Chinese embassy in New Delhi and some demonstrators violated the Chinese premises. The Indian embassy in Peking came under a Red Guard seige the very next day. On 18 June, India warned of "counter measures" against the seige. The next day, armed guards were posted around the Chinese embassy in New Delhi to enforce restrictions on persons entering the premises and coming out. (These restrictions were to continue until after mid-1971.) A Chinese note on 19 June demanded an open apology for the 16 June incidents and action against the culprits. The seige on the embassy in Peking ended on

20 June.

The hawks in the Congress party, backed by the rightist Swatantra Party and the Hindu nationalist Jana Sangh party exploited the Raghunath-Vijai episode to whip up anti-China hysteria in the country and tried to force the government to break off diplomatic relations with China. They were trying to achieve what they could not do over five years ago when Jawaharlal Nehru was Prime Minister. They were taking advantage of Indira Gandhi's weakness as the leader of a party with a slender Parliament majority.

A well informed Indian commentators noted that the Prime Minister was pleading for a rapprochement with China when the episode occurred. There was talk of rapprochement even in the Foreign Office and C. S. Jha's posting as ambassador to France was meant to help such a dialogue through his counterpart in Paris. The tension had only heightened the urgency of such talks when even United States had been obliged to hold talks with China at the ambassador level in Warsaw.[20] The Prime Minister refused to oblige her critics because she was sure what had happened in Peking was only a temporary affair.[21]

The clash at the 14,500-feet Nathu La Pass on 11 September was the most serious border incident since the war in 1962. On 11 August, NCNA alleged that India had created a tense situation along the border and there was a "fresh military incursion". On 1 September it was reported in New Delhi that the Chinese army on the other side of the Nathu La had attempted to stretch its lines of communication into the Indian side of the watershed which marked the boundary between Sikkim and Tibet. Indian soldiers laid a barbed wire fence for a long stretch indicating the location of the border.

A scuffle there on 7 September (coinciding with the visit to India of the ruler of Sikkim and his wife) was followed by an exchange of fire on 11 September, with heavy casualties on both sides.[22] On the same day Indian proposed an immediate cease-fire and a meeting of sector commanders at Nathu La. A protest note charged China with seeking to build tension at a point on the border which had never been disputed. The Sikkim-Tibet boundary was a "well defined international border, and has been recognised as such". India once again proposed an unconditional cease-fire (on 12 September) and though there was no formal Chinese response, a twelve-hour lull was reported until shelling was resumed on 13 September. Gangtok, Sikkim's capital, ordered a black out and the civil defence machinery was mobilised fearing a Chinese air attack.

There was a lull on 14 September, but for a half-hour of Chinese shelling which Indians did not return, and on 15 September. The next day, arrangements had been made between the Indian and Chinese sides for the exchange of the dead and wounded as from that day.

Later, on 1 October, there was another clash, at Cho La, about 3.5 miles northwest of Nathu La. Each side blamed the other for the clash in which there were casualties on both sides.[23]

Late in August, a statement by Chagla seemed to presage a flexible China policy. He was reported as having said that despite tense relations between them, India was ready to enter a dialogue with China as soon as it showed the slightest intention of it. He hoped China would see reason and soon join India at the conference table and settle all disputes and normalise relations. It was precisely for this reason India had not broken off diplomatic relations with China despite all the unpleasant things in the past. This was the reason India did not want to take an extreme position against China.[24]

On 2 September, a spokesman of Chagla's ministry clarified in New Delhi that the minister had merely "restated" India's general position "in regard to its willingness to keep the door open for a peaceful settlement of its problems with China through appropriate negotiations". He would not clarify it further. On 3 September, Chagla explained his statement to the Cabinet but two days later he resigned from government on the issue of India's official language.

The Chinese were quick to assail Chagla's statement. Peking Radio on 10 September saw "counter-revolutionary dual tactics" in the peaceful settlement line, "assuming a gesture of relaxation so as to deceive Indian people and world opinion". Differences over the attitude to China were surfacing in Indira Gandhi's Cabinet. While Chagla was talking of negotiations with China, his colleague, Finance Minister Morarji Desai, was talking about "two Chinas" being a reality.

At this stage there was an in-depth discussion on foreign policy in the Indian Cabinet and new ideas on China were reported to have emerged. The younger officials had pointed out that the rigid posture (no talks until the Colombo proposals were accepted *in toto* would not help break the deadlock. But it was felt that the internal situation in China did not warrant a fresh approach and it would be well to wait for the "power struggle" in China to be over. The officials thought United States and China were working for identical aims in South and South-east Asia.[25]

Indira Gandhi visited Ceylon in September and discussed a regional co-operation plan which officials in New Delhi maintained was "not an anti-China alliance". Officials thought regional economic co-operation was possible because the two power blocs were loosening and even Japan was becoming assertive. But Morarji Desai's statement in Tokyo that regional co-operation among South and South-east Asian countries would provide a "democratic alternative to China" gave rise to suspicion that India was probably acting as a cover for a United States-sponsored alliance.

Soviet Arms for Pakistan

Sino-Indian relations were uneventful after the two clashes on the Sikkim border but Soviet overtures to Pakistan seemed to cause anxiety in New Delhi. These overtures began after the Tashkent Agreement in 1966 when Soviet Union tried to establish its "Asian presence". This development can be traced directly to the new Soviet policy of befriending South Asian countries—Iran, Pakistan, and Afghanistan, amidst a sharp deterioration in its relations with China and a growing detente with the West. Growing Soviet concern over Sino-Pakistani amity made Pakistan the focus of Soviet diplomacy after the 1965 Indo-Pakistan war.

Indira Gandhi had gone to Moscow four times as Prime Minister and New Delhi was keen that Premier Alexei Kosygin should visit India at least once before he went to Pakistan. Kosygin visited India in January and went to Pakistan in April, a few days after President Ayub Khan had served notice on United States that Pakistan would not renew the lease of the intelligence base at Badabar near Peshawar.[26] He hopped to New Delhi on his way back home for a short meeting with Indira Gandhi though the visit was officially described a "refuelling stop-over".

Kosygin had to do a great deal of explaining in New Delhi. India was apprehending Soviet arms supplies to its belligerent neighbour while Pakistan had all along thought Soviet Union had been violating the Tashkent agreement. Soviet Union had veered to a neutral position between India and Pakistan when it staged the Tashkent summit. India's fears about Soviet policy began in May 1967 when Pakistan's Foreign Minister Sharfuddin Pirzada visited Moscow and Ambassador Kewal Singh asked Soviet leadership about its arms policy towards Pakistan. The Soviet leadership equivocated. India's fears grew when Soviet Union decided to give arms to Iran which was a CENTO ally of Pakistan. India was assured that Iran would not divert Soviet arms supplies to Pakistan.

Kosygin merely told Indira Gandhi about the arms Pakistan had asked for and this was hint enough that some day Soviet Union would be giving Pakistan arms. There had been an outcry in the Pakistani press on the eve of the Soviet Premier's visit about the rumoured sale of 100 to 150 Sukhoi-7 fighter bombers, several hundred surface-to-air missiles, five naval aircraft and six submarines.[27] This was the major subject of discussion between Kosygin and Ayub Khan who saw little chance of Soviet Union stopping arms supplies to India and therefore found it more useful to demand Soviet arms.

India's relations with Soviet Union had a big setback in mid-1968 when it became known that Pakistan had succeeded in wresting a promise of Soviet arms. This was a major breakthrough for Pakistan to the extent it represented a significant shift in Soviet attitude to it. Soviet Union was keen on befriending Pakistan, which had become an ally of China, and ostensibly without prejudice to its relations with India. Kosygin had declared in Pakistan:

> The Soviet Union has good normal relations with all these West Asian and South Asian countries including the close neighbours of Pakistan. ... We are strangers to designs for using the relations with the country to the detriment of its relations with others...to sow seeds of discord between the states and peoples which have freed themselves, to seek to confront each other is the favourite policy of colonisers. They seek to pursue it now after they have been thrown away.[28]

A few weeks later, Gen. Yahya Khan, Pakistan's army chief, led a mission to Soviet Union (28 June-7 July) to seek military equipment. It became clear on 8 July that he had secured a promise of arms.

There was deep concentration in New Delhi. Prime Minister Indira Gandhi wrote to Kosygin on 10 July about the report of arms sale. Kosygin assured her the next day that his government continued to attach "utmost importance to Indo-Soviet friendship" and Soviet Union would do nothing to undermine its very close and cordial relations with India. He did not refer directly to the reported Soviet decision on arms for Pakistan but repeated that even if Moscow decided to give some military hardware to Pakistan, it would be done only in the larger interest of peace in the region. President Zakir Husain had gone to Soviet Union on 7 July on a 10-day official visit and it suited the Indian government to build a press campaign against the impending Soviet arms deal. Perhaps it aimed at forcing Soviet Union to retract. The Indian government gave the impression that it knew of the coming shift in Soviet policy (including the equivocation on Kashmir which was discernible now) but did little to counter it. The press campaign was becoming counter-productive because alongside the anti-Soviet sentiment a move against Indira Gandhi was gaining strength in her party. It was solemnly suggested by the government that there should be no recrimination against Soviet Union which implied that there should be no postmortem of these developments. From the reports New Delhi had, it appeared that the supplies to Pakistan would be very small and limited and the situation would not be so serious as to warrant an open condemnation. There was no question of the Indian government revising its attitude to the Soviet Union. The effort at this stage was to blunt the edge of domestic criticism and the impending Opposition attack on the government at the monsoon session of Parliament. An agency reporter covering Zakir Husain's tour claimed, on the basis of Indian briefing in Moscow, that Soviet Union had secured an assurance from Pakistan that the arms to be supplied would not be used against India. In fact, no such assurance had been sought or given.

Parliament debated the issue on 22 and 23 July. Indira Gandhi wrote another letter to Kosygin on 22 July conveying India's unhappiness over the reported decision. In the Parliament debate she hinted at a more flexible attitude to Pakistan and China. She admitted that there had been a certain amount of rigidity in India's policy towards her neighbours because of their aggression on India's borders. India, however, would like to keep the door open and keeping the national interest in view "we would like to create an atmosphere whereby the rigidity could be loosened and we would have more flexible relations". She reiterated this later when she addressed the Foreign Correspondents Association on 5 October.

Significantly, the first hint of a flexible attitude to Pakistan and China came in the context of Soviet arms to Pakistan, after the Opposition had assailed her foreign policy. She was to follow this up on 1 January 1969 at a formal press conference in New Delhi. She now visualised the possibility of resolving the frozen border dispute with China. However difficult the situation would seem, it was always possible in a changing world situation to find a way out. She qualified this saying whatever steps were taken obviously had to be in keeping with India's national interests and honour. She was not committing herself to a dialogue with China and what she said perhaps aimed at sounding public opinion on a dialogue, or putting pressure on Soviet Union for more arms, or to prevent further arms deliveries to Pakistan. She also said one cannot take any relationship for granted in world affairs and was obviously referring to United States attempts at a rapprochement with China. This carried the hint that if Soviet Union did no freeze arms supplies to Pakistan or step up supplies to India, a shift in India's China policy could not be ruled out.

Finding no change in the Soviet position, Ambassador D. P. Dhar took up the matter in Moscow in February and the Soviet leadership mooted a treaty with India as the answer. More disquieting was the apparent slow down in Soviet arms deliveries to India though everything had been straightened out at the bilateral consultative talks in New Delhi in September 1968. Within weeks Soviet Defence Minister Marshal Grechkov was in New Delhi (2-9 March 1969), to check the deterioration in India's relations with Soviet Union. There was trouble along the Sino-Soviet border and the famous Ussuri clash took place the day Marshal Grechkov reached New Delhi.

The trouble on the border preceding the Ussuri clash might have brought home to the Soviet leadership the need to enlist India's support against China by raising the bogey of Chinese aggression across India's borders. Marshal Grechkov is believed to have offered to step up military aid to enable India to meet any new threat from China; and to eliminate all bottlenecks in the way of supplies already committed to strengthen India's military capability. In return he expected India's support to Soviet Union in its border confrontation with China. A treaty of peace, friendship, and co-operation was proposed.

Soviet Union, for the first time, directly charged China with engineering a conflict with India on 19 March, after its own border confrontation with China had taken a serious turn. In the past, Soviet references were to "China-India border conflict" and the "expansion of conflict with India" but a Soviet commentary entitled "Geography, Peking Style—Maoist Bandit Attacks on Ussuri River are no Chance Occurrences," accused China of having attacked India.[29]

The treaty proposed by Marshal Grechkov did not make much headway because Indira Gandhi's Congress party faced a serious crisis in July-August over the election of a new President following the death of Zakir Hussain on 27 May. The party split vertically depriving Indira Gandhi of her majority in Parliament. She had to survive one vote after another with the support of Opposition parties, groups, and individuals, particularly the pro-Moscow Communist Party of India. Had she signed the treaty, she might have been toppled on the issue because the Opposition was already assailing growing Indian dependence on Soviet economic and military aid. Kosygin, on his way to Hanoi for Dr Ho Chi-minh's funeral in September had discussed the treaty with Indira Gandhi but there it stood.

Brezhnev's Collective Security Plan

The Soviet concept of a regional security system for India, Pakistan and Afghanistan as part of a plan to "contain" China had crystallised in May 1969 when Kosygin visited Afghanistan and Pakistan. He had mooted something approximating this plan through his statements in Kabul and Islamabad. *Pravda* followed this tour up with an anti-China tirade. In an assessment of Kosygin's tour, *Pravda* noted on 1 June that "the peaceful Soviet-Afghani border became an important factor in the stability in this area of Asia". This could have been dismissed as an innocuous platitude but there was something more to the reference to "some forces in Asia" which "obsessed by great power chauvinism, renounced the principles of peaceful co-existence of states with different social orders and are even resorting to force in futile attempts to achieve 'world leadership'. In reality their actions play the game of imperialism in its striving to arrest the rapid progress of liberation of the people of the East, consolidation of their national independence, of their economic and cultural development".[30]

The answer suggested by *Pravda* was a motley assortment of

countries forming a bloc depending on Soviet arms. The very next day, *Pravda* charged China (euphemistically described as "the new hegemonistic forces") to set Afghanistan against Pakistan and Pakistan against India. Perhaps, *Pravda* did not know that the Afghan rulers were hostile to Pakistan at the instance of India in 1947 when the Chinese were still fighting the Chiang Kai-shek regime. *Pravda* dropped its inhibition about mentioning China directly when it said:

> The perfidy of the Maoist instigators consists in the fact that with the aid of loud "left" phrases they may, sometimes, deceive people who have not passed through the school of political struggle and make them unwitting participants in adventurist actions that have no prospects. But events have frequently shown that adventurism has never led to anything good.[31]

This unmistakably was an attack on the Chinese general line for the international communist movement. In the *Pravda*-eye view there were two tendencies influencing the situation in West Asia and South Asia:

> On the one hand, the need is arising and objective prerequisites are being created for the co-operation of India, Pakistan, Afghanistan, Iran and other States both in the economic field and in the struggle for the preservation of universal peace.
>
> On the other hand certain forces are trying to whip up chauvinist hysteria, resort to threats, aggravate tensions and create a deadlock atmosphere which, sooner or later, may give rise to an armed conflict dangerous to peoples, to peace in the given area and universal peace.[32]

Soviet ideologies had taken it for granted that the real threat to the independence of Asian nations was from China and not United States. An authoritative Soviet article on the eve of the Moscow world communist conference in June asserted that "Mao and his henchmen entertain quite definite designs on a number of countries in this part of the world. The author, V. Matveyev, also said that "the main thing is that the Maoists are intensively exploiting the numerous Chinese communist in several Asian countries for the purposes that have nothing at all in common with the sovereignty of these countries". This was clear indication that the collective security plan would not be limited to West Asia and South Asia but would extend to South-east Asia. Matveyev noted that "there is a dismantling of foreign military bases" in Asia and added that a collective security system backed by Soviet Union would contribute to the security of the region and prevent any aggressive power from filling the "vacuum".[33]

Soviet party chief Leonid Brezhnev told the world communist conference a few days later that "the burning problems of the present international situation do not push into the background more long-range tasks, especially the creation of a system of collective security in those parts of the world where the threat of unleashing of a new world war and the unleashing of armed conflicts centred". He referred to Asia where he thought "the course of events also places on the agenda the task of creating a system of collective security in Asia".

Reporting to the Supreme Soviet about a month later, Foreign Minister Gromyko reiterated the proposal and emphasised that Soviet Union was both a European and Asian power and wanted all the people of Asia to live in peace as they had "common interests". He pleaded that the proposal should be studied by the interested states in all seriousness.

President Nixon announced his new doctrine for Asia at the Guam base island on 25 July, a few days before his visit to India. The Guam doctrine envisaged a new United States relationship with its Asian allies to obviate its direct involvement in any future Vietnam-type conflict. However, it did not mean the end of United States involvement in Asia: it only meant an intent to avoid further entanglements of ground forces on mainland Asia.

When Nixon came to India early in August, his administration had three widely discussed options before it. United States could continue its military role in Asia and draw some more countries into an anti-China alliance and keep up hostile pressure on China. It could attempt a detente with China and build a triangular equation with Soviet Union and China and bring about a new balance and gradually disengage itself militarily from Asia. But this would not be welcome to Soviet Union because it would mean recognising China as the principal Asian power. Or, United States could come to an arrangement with Soviet Union whereby both could be present in the region.

This was the time the State Department in Washington was divided into a China lobby and a Taiwan lobby amidst a serious debate on the options. On the eve of his long tour, Nixon had lifted certain trade and travel embargoes relating to China. Soviet displeasure at the signs of a coming United States-China rapprochement was clear. There were open Soviet warnings and pressure against Rumania coinciding with Nixon's visit to Bucharest (the first visit by any United States president to a communist country).

In New Delhi, Indian spokesmen paraphrased and annotated the Brezhnev plan to Nixon's aides, presenting it as something innocuous and without military overtones. The only tangible gain from the visit was India could persuade Nixon to continue the embargo on arms to Pakistan (imposed during the 1965 war but lifted in October 1970 after Pakistan had promised elections to end the military rule). The Indian side raised the implications of a major nuclear power like China attacking a non-nuclear power like India and United States showed interest in helping in such an eventuality. The discussions revealed a certain confusion on the Indian side because India had not decided to sign the treaty proposed by Soviet Union, and an equal lack of clarity on the United States side because its new Asian policy was still under formulation.

Predictably, China saw sinister designs behind the Brezhnev plan. The plan had been mooted after the Ussuri clashes, following which Soviet Union had raised its troop deployment in the Far East from 15 divisions in 1968. (This rose to 30 divisions in 1970, 33 in 1971 and 41 in 1972 totalling over a million troops). The Chinese saw in the plan a design to unify "all the puppets and lackeys" of United States in the region into "a general anti-China system" which would serve as a "tool for US imperialism and Soviet revisionism" to jointly oppose China and suppress the revolutionary struggle of the Asian people".[34]

Indira Gandhi's reaction to the plan must have added to Chinese apprehensions about it. While External Affairs Minister Dinesh Singh said on 23 June that he had no idea of the plan ("We have to discuss the matter before I can make any comments"), Indira Gandhi said just two days later in Tokyo that the plan was practically meant to restrain United States and China from making inroads into Asia. Kosygin had told her that Soviet Union was not thinking of any military security set up for Asia. But she seemed to subscribe to the dangerous United States theory of filling the vacuum, of Dullesian vintage: she referred to the proposed British pull-out from the East of Suez (since reversed) and possible United States pull-out of the Vietnam conflict, which she expected sooner or later. China showed a desire to spread its influence in Asia and to prevent this from happening it was necessary for all regions in Asia to have political and economic stability. Whatever the Soviet motivation behind the plan, Indira Gandhi, convinced of the need to contain China, saw immense possibilities to that end in the plan.

The Chinese saw in the Brezhnev proposals a plan to control Asian countries for pushing Soviet policy of "aggression and expansion" in Asia further and for opposing China. It was an "unbridled step in collusion with US imperialism in recent years to rig up an anti-China ring". United States had been asking Japan to "rig up a crescent" to encircle China and now Soviet Union was asking India to do the same.[35] The Chinese charged Indira Gandhi with peddling the plan on her visit to Indonesia (28 June-2 July) but Asian countries had cold-shouldered it. Only Indonesia's Suharto was interested in it. Her communique with him suggested an Asian council of ministers "as a prelude to the establishment of an anti-China military alliance manipulated by US imperialism and Soviet revisionism".[36]

About two weeks later, Chou En-lai compared the Brezhnev plan with the SEATO which was an "ignominous failure".[37] A major Peking commentary a few weeks later said the plan threatened Asian independence and sovereignty because it sought to expand Soviet colonial influence in Asian countries and contended with United States imperialism for hegemony in the Asian region. Mongolia was already a Soviet "military base" and Soviet arms were flowing to India, Indonesia, and Burma to crush the revolutionary movements there which China supported. "For the masses of the people in Asia such 'security' meant misery, disaster and the biggest insecurity." The plan was compared to the Warsaw pact and the COMECON which in the Chinese view violated the sovereignty and national independence of the member state.[38]

Indian equivocation on the plan seemed to follow the poor response it got from the rest of Asia because neither Japan nor Indonesia (the countries Indira Gandhi visited after the plan had been announced) was enthused about such a collective security system. Dinesh Singh's statement late in July was significant: "We are not aware of any proposal made by the Soviet Union on an Asian collective security system".[39] He was to discuss the plan with Soviet leaders later but Soviet Union had already proposed a bilateral treaty with India.

China's New Foreign Policy

China's foreign policy, a low-profile one during the Cultural Revolution phase, got a new orientation on the basis of the Lin Piao report to the ninth party congress in April 1969. The report indicated a major departure in the Maoist class analysis and assessment of the contemporary world since the last analysis (of 14 June 1963) which had identified the following fundamental contradictions: between the socialist camp and the imperialist camp; between the proletariat and the bourgeoisie in capitalist countries; between the oppressed nations and imperialism; and between the imperialist countries and among monopolist groups.

The Lin Piao report, discussing the possibilities of war and revolution revealed a new analysis and a new order of priorities when it listed four major contradictions in the world; between oppressed nations and imperialism and social imperialism; between the proletariat and the bourgeoisie in the capitalist and revisionist countries; between imperialist and social imperialist countries and among imperialist countries; and between socialist countries and imperialism.

The new analysis, bracketing imperialist and social imperialist countries, reduced the contradiction between them into an inter-imperialist one. The foremost contradiction was no longer between the socialist camp and the imperialist camp but between oppressed nations and imperialism and social imperialism. The socialist-imperialist contradiction was but the last of the four. The new analysis also innovated the term "revisionist countries" and avoided any mention of the *socialist camp* but referred to *socialist countries*. It reflected the escalated Sino-Soviet confrontation climaxed by the Ussuri clashes. Soviet intervention in Czechoslovakia in late 1968 gave China the occasion to brand Soviet Union a social imperialist country. The growing Soviet detente with United States and its plans to quarantine China were behind Peking's rising fears of Moscow.

China was now poised for a peace offensive to launch a new-look foreign policy which Lin Piao spelt out as follows:

To develop relations of friendship, mutual assistance and cooperation with socialist countries on the principle of proletarain internationalism; to support and assist revolutionary struggles of all the oppressed people and nations; to work for peaceful co-existence with countries of different social systems on the basis of the Five Principles of mutual respect for territorial integrity and sovereignty, mutual non-aggression, non-interference in each other's internal affairs, equality and mutual benefit, and peaceful co-existence, and to oppose the imperialist policies of aggression and war. Our proletarian foreign policy is not based on expediency; it is a policy in which we have long persisted. This is what we did in the past and we will persist in doing the same in the future.

The restated policy, which reiterated the five principles while pledging support and assistance to revolutionary struggles of all the oppressed peoples and nations, ruled out Chinese interference in the affairs of other countries. The Lin Piao report also spelt out China's approach to outstanding boundary disputes, now limited to two neighbours—Soviet Union and India. The dispute with Soviet Union had immediate relevance in the wake of Ussuri clashes. Lin Piao said that like boundary questions between China and some of her other neighbouring countries, the Sino-Soviet dispute was also "one left over by history". The Chinese party and government had so consistently stood for negotiations to settle them. Pending a settlement, "the staus quo of the boundary should be maintained in order to avoid conflicts'". China had settled the question with all her neighbours—Burma, Nepal, Pakistan, Mongolia, and Afghanistan. Lin Piao blamed India for the deadlocked dispute with China but the reference was on a low key:

> The Chinese government held repeated negotiations with the Indian government on the Sino-Indian boundary question. As the reactionary Indian government had taken over the British policy of aggression, it insisted that we recognise the illegal 'McMahon Line' which even the reactionary governments of different periods in old China had not recognised, and moreover, it vainly attempted to further occupy the Akasi-chin area, which has always been under Chinese jurisdiction, thereby disrupting the Sino-Indian boundary negotiations.

Late in 1969, Chinese diplomats in important world capitals began attending receptions held by Indian missions and Indian diplomats reciprocated this gesture. Chairman Mao reserved a big smile for the Indian Charge d'Affaires at the 1970 May Day reception in Peking and had asked him to convey his good wishes to Indira Gandhi. Mao also expressed his desire for friendly relations between India and China. New Delhi pegged a trial balloon for a dialogue with China on the much publicised Mao smile. To observers it seemed a response to an impending United States aid cut or the proposed delivery of some new range of arms to Pakistan. At the Congress party's session (AICC) in June, there was a well-articulated demand for a dialogue with China to solve the border dispute. The only jarring note came from Nalinaksha Sanyal of West Bengal. Indira Gandhi attacked his demand for "containment" of China and pointed out that even United States had not alleged Chinese troop presence in Cambodia, something Sanyal was trying to establish.

A section in the Foreign Office and some in the Congress party thought India could not allow the border dispute to continue indefinitely, if only because India had to regain some leverage vis-a-vis United States which was attempting a rapprochement with China, and Soviet Union which was making Pakistan the focal point of its diplomacy in South Asia despite Pakistan's close ties with China. Assessments that a Chinese diplomatic offensive was in the offing and that their foreign policy, at least their attitude to neighbours, was becoming more flexible added to arguments of those who favoured a dialogue with China. At the political level, thinking in favour of an early settlement with China was growing even inside the breakaway faction of Indira Gandhi's party (branded by her supporters a "reactionary" rump). There was growing apprehension over the increased Indian dependence on Soviet military and economic aid.

When the Indian Charge in Peking, Brajesh Mishra, rushed home for consultations after the Mao smile, a far-fetched interpretation of New Delhi's stance was that Indira Gandhi was activating the "settle with China" group in her party to mount pressure against Soviet arms to Pakistan. Assuming this theory had no basis and she was keen on a diplomatic initiative to settle with China, the odds were against her, heading as she did a minority government. In the past, it had suited the government leadership to condone United States-inspired lobby campaigns in New Delhi for a total break with China and to recognise Taiwan. Those actively campaigning for severance of relations with Peking and for the two-China theory were to be found not only in the rightist and social democratic parties, but right inside her own party even after the split.

When United States was not keen on activating the Taiwan lobby, the anti-China campaigners seemed to derive their inspiration from Soviet tirades against China. A Soviet article was timed to warn India and other countries against any detente with China. It referred to alleged Chinese interference in the affairs of Bhutan and Sikkim, things that even India had not said.[40]

The Soviet reading was roughly this: China was out to force an anti-Soviet united front in South and South-east Asia, and a front on a global scale though China's final confrontation would be with United States. Granting this premise, it should be in China's interest to respond to any initiative by India and try to isolate Soviet Union on the border issue. India would have to eliminate the influence of at least one super power to be able to enter a serious dialogue with China. Diplomatically it should help China to isolate Soviet Union and point out to the world that a non-socialist country like India could settle its border dispute with China but Soviet Union was not prepared for such a settlement.

Mishra returned to Peking with the understanding that India aimed at restoring ambassador-level relations first, and if possible a dialogue towards settling the border dispute. G. Parthasarathy returned in 1961 and India did not fill the post. Several months later, for reasons of protocol, the Chinese were obliged to recall their ambassador in New Delhi. Relations have remained at the Charge level since.

Amidst the euphoria in the Indian press about chances of a dialogue with China, the government's own attitude did not appear clear. Diplomatic and political assessments had for a long time ruled out any military threat of a joint Sino-Pakistani push into India which the press had been predicting for every summer with monotonous regularity. In August the lack of clarity in India's assessment became evident. Defence Minister Jagjivan Ram returned to the worn theme of a twin-threat to India when he said he could not rule out a Pakistani attack with Chinese help.[41] This tallied with the usual military asesssment but not the diplomatic and political assessments.

But the tone of Peking broadcasts had changed. A commentary described Japanese Foreign Minister Aichi's visit to India as a "counter-revolutionary mission" aimed at rigging up an anti-China military alliance under the cloak of an Asian collective security system paving the way for Japanese militarism's growing power. But contrary to practice, the commentary did not attack India or accuse it of complicity in the anti-China plot.

A subtle shift in India's border stand was revealed by External Affairs Minister Swaran Singh's statement in Parliament on 26 August. He said India was prepared to negotiate with China on the basis of respect for India's integrity and renunciation of force. There was no mention of the Colombo proposals, which meant India no longer insisted on the acceptance *in toto* of these proposals as the precondition for a dialogue. He admitted a slight change in China's propaganda against its neighbours "but no substantive change in its attitude to India". India would not be lacking in response to any Chinese step towards normalcy.

Observers in New Delhi read signs of a thaw in Sino-Indian relations when a senior secretary of the External Affairs Ministry, S. K. Banerji, along with two officials represented the government at the National Day reception in the Chinese embassy on 1 October. Since 1962, Indian representation at this reception was limited to the Deputy Chief of Protocol. Besides, the Indian government did not insist this time that the embassy should route all invitations through it. (This curb had followed similar Chinese restrictions on the Indian mission in Peking in 1967). Around 20 October, reports from London claimed that China had quietly invited India to discuss restoration of full diplomatic relations. Contacts between Indian and Chinese envoys in several capitals were also reported. But an official spokesman in New Delhi denied on 22 October any formal move of this kind. On 27 October, Indira Gandhi, returning from New

York said she did not know "how soon" India and China would exchange ambassadors, and such an exchange by itself would not be enough.

Bangladesh Crisis

The political instability caused by the split in Indira Gandhi's party left her government little room for manoeuvre on major issues and despite signs of thaw at the diplomatic level, there was no initiative from the Indian side. The instability ended with Indira Gandhi winning a landslide victory at the March 1971 elections to Parliament but her new ministry had hardly settled down to work when there was turmoil in East Pakistan which eventually led to the emergence of Bangladesh.

Pakistan had its first adult franchise elections in December 1970 and they were meant to bring to an end the military rule. In the Bengali-speaking eastern wing (separated from the polyglot western wing by 1,200 miles of Indian territory), the National Awami League of Sheikh Mujibur Rehman made a clean sweep of the polls on a six-point plank for autonomy for the Bengali-speaking region which accounted for over half of Pakistan's 130 million people. The Sheikh's party also won a clear majority in the Pakistan National Assembly. The military president, Gen. Yahya Khan, showed no desire to accept the results of the election or to respect the verdict in favour of autonomy for the eastern wing. After successful political manoeuvres to retain its dominant position, the military junta ordered a crackdown in the eastern wing on 25 March 1971 and imprisoned the Sheikh. The autonomy demand turned overnight into one for secession.

The Sheikh, who had sworn by Gandhian non-violence in the past, called for resistance to the army crackdown and the result was a massacre of the civilians which continued for months as the guerillas offered feeble resistance. The Sheikh's following formally proclaimed an independent Bangla Desh. Millions fled the military terror, crossing into India. India and Pakistan were drifting towards a war over Bangla Desh.

India had tried to internationalise the refugee problem by warning of unilateral action to reverse its flow if the world community failed to act in time. External Affairs Minister Swaran Singh returned in June from a round of the major Western capitals (including Moscow and Washington) with the claim that United States had assured India that no arms had been licensed after 25 March for Pakistan, and in no circumstances would they be licensed in the future. But he was confronted with reports of fresh United States arms shipment to Pakistan.

United States equivocation on arms to Pakistan (outright denial first, an unconvincing explanation blaming it on some "bureaucratic muddle" later, and finally a declaration that it would meet all commitments made in the past) had strained Indo-United States relations when Henry Kissinger, President Nixon's foreign policy aide, arrived at New Delhi on 7 July. His mission to India and Pakistan were ostensibly to get first hand reports for President Nixon on the Bangladesh crisis. Obviously, he could not be expected to give India any assurance on arms to Pakistan because he was not the decision maker.

New Delhi's appreciation was that there was no unified United States policy on arms supplies to Pakistan after 25 March and the Administration was divided between "hawks" and "doves". The hawks of the Pentagon wanted to underwrite the military regime in Pakistan while the doves, who in New Delhi's view included Kissinger, were not for giving arms to Pakistan. New Delhi thought that if shrewdly tackled, Kissinger would advise Nixon to stop arms to Pakistan. The totality of the pulls would determine the United States policy on Bangladesh.

There was dismay among Indira Gandhi's aides when it was disclosed on 15 July that Kissinger was on a secret mission to Peking after his smokescreen visits to India and Pakistan. President Nixon announced his visit to Peking to take place before May 1972.

On the eve of the 25 March military crackdown in East Pakistan, Indian opinion hailed Sheikh Mujibur Rehman as an apostle of Gandhian non-violence and thought Pakistan would disintegrate in days. Exaggerated reports of the exploits of the Mukti

Fauz (liberation army) of the Bangladesh fighters flooded the newspaper columns. The Pakistani army began its counter-offensive a little before the Bangladesh government was proclaimed from Mujibnagar, a makeshift town on the border. When the refugee influx swelled into a formidable tide and the Mukti Fauz found itself fighting a well-equipped Pakistani army, India found itself face to face with an unforeseen problem. The threat of unilateral action if the world community failed to reverse the influx had no effect on any of the major powers, including Soviet Union. New Delhi did not seem to believe seriously that the guerillas could force a solution and make it possible for the refugees to go back. A large section of the National Awami League leadership in exile in India did not believe it either. This section was keen on military intervention so that they could return to Dacca as early as possible. The longer the struggle, the lesser were the chances of the Awami League retaining its leadership and preventing it from slipping into the hands of extremists.

India had not recognised the Mujibnagar government, but was extending all help to the guerilla struggle. Domestic opinion was pushing Indira Gandhi towards recognising Bangladesh and extending open military aid to help liberate East Pakistan so that the refugees could go back. This was the situation when Kissinger visited New Delhi and Nixon announced plans for his visit to Peking a few days later. Nixon's announcement was followed by Gen. Yahya Khan's threat three days later of a "total war" if India tried to liberate any part of East Pakistan. In the event of such a war, Pakistan would not be alone. Referring to this threat, Swaran Singh told Parliament on 21 July that India would not be alone either if Pakistan were to attack India.

India's Treaty with Soviet Union

It would seem that India decided to sign a treaty with Soviet Union sometime between 15 July (when Nixon announced his visit) and 21 July (when Swaran Singh said India would not be alone in the event of a war). Any reservation Indira Gandhi might have had about signing the treaty immediately disappeared when it was known that Pakistan might attack on 12 August (that was the appreciation in New Delhi) and Kissinger's hint to India's ambassador in Washington, L. K. Jha, that United States would not intervene in a war but he was not too sure about China's neutrality. Up to this point of time, New Delhi had gone about it on the assumption that China would not intervene in a war.

Shortly after India had decided to sign the treaty, former ambassador in Moscow, D. P. Dhar, was contacted in Kashmir where he was holidaying. He left for Moscow unannounced, with a copy of the latest draft of the treaty so that it could be signed before the expected Pakistani attack on 12 August. Dhar's brief is believed to have covered three points besides the finalisation of the treaty. He was to ascertain from the Soviet leadership (a) whether India could expect more arms; (b) whether India could expect Soviet Union to exercise its veto at the Security Council in India's favour if the Bangladesh issue was raised by one of the members; and (c) whether Soviet Union would go with India if the latter recognised Bangladesh in the near future. The Soviet response was positive on the first point and ambiguous on the second and the third.

When Dhar was despatched to Moscow, New Delhi thought Kosygin would come down to sign the treaty. But shortly after Dhar had completed his mission, it was announced that Soviet Foreign Minister Andrei Gromyko would be visiting New Delhi, in response to an old invitation from his counterpart Swaran Singh. Swaran Singh had already announced his visit to Djakarta, also on an old invitation. His Djakarta programme clashed with Gromyko's sojourn in New Delhi beginning 8 August. Swaran Singh was obliged to put off his departure so that he could sign the treaty with Gromyko on 9 August.

Indira Gandhi had called a mammoth public meeting in New Delhi on 9 August, anniversary of the 1942 Quit India movement, mainly to blunt the Hindu nationalist Jana Sangh party's campaign for immediate recognition of Bangladesh. The organisers of the rally had no inkling of the treaty to come. The treaty was signed in the morning; the rally had been scheduled for the afternoon. The rally was supposed to endorse the government's handling of the situation as a rebuff to Indira Gandhi's critics who wanted premature recognition of Bangladesh.

From Indira Gandhi's point of view, the treaty could not have been timed better. The government and the mass media had created among the people the impression that Soviet Union was India's only friend on the Bangladesh issue and United States and China were backing Pakistan and therefore hostile to India. India, therefore, faced the threat of a war from Pakistan in which China might intervene against India.

The new level of Sino-United States relations opened for India options it could not have dreamt of in years. Here was an opportunity to regain the lost leverage vis-a-vis the super powers by making a gesture towards de-freezing relations with China. Instead, New Delhi rushed into a long term treaty with Soviet Union. After the treaty had been signed, Indira Gandhi called in the opposition leaders in Parliament to tell them that China might support Pakistan in the event of a war with India.

The treaty was Soviet Union's check-mate on the new Sino-United States relations. The Bangladesh crisis and India's fears of a new war with Pakistan and possible Chinese intervention used in justification of the treaty, Swaran Singh announcing the signing of the treaty, told Parliament that it was not a defence pact and was not aimed against anyone. But he was sanguine that it would deter any country that might be thinking of committing aggression on India. He hoped it would stabilise peace in the region.

The treaty met with minimal resistance from the confounded Opposition in Parliament when it debated it the next day. It was a 20-year treaty and the nation was repeatedly assured by the government leadership that it had nothing to do with Bangladesh. The treaty had been under discussion for over two years. All the same it suited the leadership to make the nation believe that but for the treaty, Pakistan would have attacked India. About eight weeks after the treaty, D. Sanjivayya, president of the Congress party told partymen in Simla on 7 October that Pakistan was about to attack India but the treaty with Soviet Union deterred it from such misadventure.

But the treaty did not prevent a war between India and Pakistan. It was to break out four months later, over Bangladesh.

Notes

[1] "Long Live the Victory of People's War," *People's Daily*, 2 September 1965.
[2] "Indian People Will Rise Up in Resistance," *Peking Review*, 16 November 1966.
[3] "India: Anti-tyranny Struggles Rock Reactionary Rule," *Peking Review*, 24 February 1967.
[4] The CPI split did not represent a straight Moscow-Peking polarisation though it synchronised with the international communist schism. The CPI-M was at best anti-revisionist without being Maoist. For a detailed study of this development, cf. Mohan Ram, *Indian Communism: Split Within a Split*, New Delhi, Vikas, 1969.
[5] "After the Indian Elections: A Still More Reactionary Government," *Peking Review*, 24 March 1967.
[6] Central Committee, CPI-M, *New Situation and Party's Tasks*, Calcutta, 1967, p. 39.
[7] "After the Indian Elections: A Still More Reactionary Government," *Peking Review*, 24 March 1967.
[8] *Ibid*.
[9] "Dange's Plot to Sabotage Indian People's Revolution Will Surely Fail," *People's Daily*, 4 June 1967.
[10] *Ibid*.
[11] Radio Peking, 10 June 1967.
[12] "Spring Thunder Over India," *People's Daily*, 5 July 1967.
[13] "Indian Revolutionaries Say 'It's Fine', The Revisionists Say 'It's Terrible'," Radio Peking, 1 August 1967.
[14] Observer, "Historical Lessons of Telengana Uprising," *People's Daily* 3 August 1967.
[15] Radio Peking, 1 July 1967.
[16] NCNA, 27 June 1967.
[17] *Ibid.*, 27 June 1967.
[18] *Ibid.*, 8 July 1967.
[19] When India became independent in 1947, it assumed responsibility of Sikkim's external affairs, defence and communications under a standstill agreement. A treaty on 5 December 1950 regularised this. Sikkim is a protectorate of India.

[20] "Indian Reactionaries Ugly Anti-China Farce," *Peking Review*, 24 March 1967.

[21] N.C., "New Delhi Skyline," *Mainstream*, 24 June 1967.

[22] *Link*, 25 June 1967.

[23] India: 65 dead 145 wounded; China: 88 dead, about 200 wounded.

[24] India: 21 dead, 21 wounded; China: 40 dead, number of wounded not known.

[25] United News of India, 29 August 1967.

[26] *Link*, 10 September 1967.

[27] The United States spy plane (a U-2) shot over Soviet Union in May 1960 took off from the Peshawar base. The incident tarpedoed the Khrushchev-Eisenhower summit in Paris a few weeks later.

[28] Initially, India admitted buying the submarines but not the other items. Admission of buying the Sukhois was to come two years later, and indirectly. The list of aircraft for the Republic Day fly-past on 26 January 1970 included the Sukhois. But the fly-past was cancelled due to bad weather.

[29] *Dawn*, 18 April 1968.

[30] *Komsomalskaya Pravda*, 19 March 1969.

[31] *Pravda*, 1 June 1969.

[32] *Ibid.*, 2 June 1969.

[33] *Ibid.*

[34] *Izvestia*, 28 May 1969.

[35] NCNA, 19 June 1969.

[36] *Ibid.*, 26 June 1969.

[37] *Ibid.*, 3 July 1969.

[38] *The Statesman*, 15 July 1969.

[39] NCNA, 4 September 1969.

[40] Rajya Sabha, 24 July 1969.

[41] *New Times*, 9 June 1970.

8 / Elusive Detente

Its treaty with Soviet Union in August notwithstanding, India's relations with China were moving towards a breakthrough until mid-November. Indira Gandhi mentioned at a press conference in New Delhi on 19 October the possibilities of exchanging ambassadors with China without discussing substantive issues like the border question. She repeated this in Paris on 9 November. Asked if India would resume normal relations on the basis of a status quo on the border and in regard to the Aksai-chin area, she said the question could be discussed. On 25 November External Affairs Minister Swaran Singh told Parliament that the likelihood of India unilaterally sending an ambassador to China was not "excluded". Indian envoys in various world capitals had conveyed to their Chinese counterparts India's desire for normal relations with China.

India's China policy seemed to be overcoming its rigidity. The border dispute was the least important factor now. The absence of criticism of Indira Gandhi's statements was proof that public opinion was no longer belligerent and did not oppose a dialogue with China on the basis of a status quo. One no longer heard the familiar demand that India should get the Chinese-occupied areas of Aksai-chin vacated before any negotiation. India was now prepared for a step-by-step normalisation of relations with China and Indira Gandhi's supreme position as the government leader and a mellowed public opinion gave her the options no Indian Prime Minister had since the late 1950s and a new China policy looked possible.

Back in 1961, India's rigid stand on the border dispute and belligerent public opinion brought the dialogue with China to an end. As R. K. Nehru, a former ambassador to China, was to recall later:

Our insistence on Chinese withdrawal from Aksai-chin, except for the use of their road for 'civilian traffic', which had no existence in fact, brought the dialogue to a premature end. Parliament was, in any case, opposed to a dialogue. ....[1]

R. K. Nehru visited Peking in 1961 as Secretary-General of the External Affairs Ministry, and Prime Minister Nehru described the visit as "infructuous". The Chinese proposal for renewal of the Tibet agreement was rejected and no new ambassador was appointed to Peking in the place of G. Parthasarathy who had returned in 1961. "What followed step by step was a military confrontation," according to R. K. Nehru. In Peking he got the impression that the Chinese leaders made some alternative proposals as the basis for further negotiations and were "apparently prepared either to negotiate on the basis of the experts' reports, or 'to agree to disagree' for the time being on the border problem while trying to improve relations in other directions or to settle the problem on the basis of the acceptance of our (Indian) sovereignty over Aksai-chin, subject in all cases to a standstill agreement, pend'ng a final settlement". The Chinese had also indicated readiness to recognise India's sovereignty over Jammu and Kashmir as part of an overall settlement. They were also anxious that the Indian ambassador's post in Peking should not be vacant.[2]

It was a full circle now. India wanted in 1971 what China had proposed in 1961 but found the dialogue ended abruptly. Soon after Henry Kissinger's visit to Peking (July 1971), Indira Gandhi had written to Chou En-lai offering to discuss Bangladesh and other subjects of mutual interest at any level China might choose. The letter had indicated that while Bangladesh was the main subject for discussion, India was willing to initiate a dialogue towards normalisation of relations on terms honourable to both the sides.

The letter was not meant to be a response to the Sino-United States move for a detente because similar approaches had been made to China in May, when ambassador D. P. Dhar had a couple of meetings with his Chinese counterpart in Moscow. Among the points raised were the terms of starting negotiations between the two countries and the return of ambassadors who had been withdrawn before the 1962 conflict. The Chinese side had promised to consider the suggestions and inform New Delhi in due course.

Ironically, India and Soviet Union signed the treaty within four weeks of Kissinger's mission to Peking and this development could hardly have enthused China to respond immediately to India's overtures. The treaty had far-reaching implications for the Bangladesh issue and China seemed keen on keeping its options open until the issue had worked itself to a decisive stage and the fuller implications of the treaty became known. The initial Chinese silence over the treaty and the significant reduction in China's anti-Indian propaganda (there was hardly any adverse comment on India's internal situation) led New Delhi to believe that China had taken the treaty into account both strategically and tactically and therefore would be compelled to respond to its overtures.

By mid-November, the Bangladesh issue was pushing India and Pakistan into an armed conflict and China could no longer keep its options open when India evoked a vital clause in the treaty. The Chinese saw far-reaching Soviet designs in their support to India on the Bangladesh issue.

Indira Gandhi was to attribute the setback in Sino-Indian relations to China's unreserved support to Gen. Yahya Khan's campaign against Bangladesh and India.[3] To what extent India's treaty with Soviet Union could have caused this setback is not a matter of mere conjecture. It was between a Third World country and a big Western power which had no common frontier with India and had deployed over a million troops along China's borders, and had proposed a collective security system for Asia which in the Chinese view was directed against them. It could well have been that China's attitude to the Bangladesh issue was determined by its perception of Soviet aims in the subcontinent and India's role in the Bangladesh crisis. China's attitude to India and Bangladesh, predictably, was a function of the larger Sino-Soviet ideological dispute.

CHINA AND PAKISTAN

China was silent on the developments in East Pakistan following the 25 March 1971 military crackdown there. It broke the silence only after Soviet President Nikolai Podgorny's 2 April letter to Yahya Khan asking him to stop repression and seek a peaceful settlement of the problems for that would "accord with the interests of the entire people of Pakistan". On 5 April, Peking Radio, which did not comment on the East Pakistan events as such, attacked "Indian interference" and India's "expansionist" aims. The following day, a Chinese note to India protested against the demonstrations in front of their embassy in New Delhi. On 11 April, an authoritative commentary in *People's Daily* attacked the resolutions passed in India's Parliament (31 March) and by the working committee of the Congress party, and charged India with "interfering in Pakistan's internal affairs" and "Indian expansionists" with seriously prejudicing Pakistan's security by "massing troops on East Pakistan's border". The commentary, citing the Podgorny letter and a U.S. spokesman, said "the two super powers, working in close co-ordination with the Indian reactionaries, crudely interfere in the internal affairs of Pakistan" and pledged China's support to "the Pakistani government in their just struggle for safeguarding national independence and state sovereignty". At this stage China was looking at the Bangladesh crisis as an internal affair of Pakistan, as India and Soviet Union indeed maintained in public. On 12 April Chou En-lai was reported to have sent a letter to Yahya Khan suggesting that he should continue negotiations with leaders of all sections. The letter also said the Chinese believed the developments were "purely an internal affair of Pakistan which can be settled only by the Pakistani people themselves and which brooks no foreign interference whatsoever". It also said the Indian government had been exploiting Pakistan's internal problems and Soviet Union and United States were doing alike. It was more important, the letter said, to differentiate between the broad masses of the people and a "handful of persons who want to sabotage the unification of Pakistan". Should India "dare to launch aggression against

Pakistan the Chinese government will, as always, firmly support the Pakistani government and people in their struggle to safeguard their state sovereignty and national independence".

China, Soviet Union, and India seemed to agree on the need for a negotiated settlement in East Pakistan, and at least theoretically, all of them maintained that it was an internal matter of Pakistan. Even India had not advocated secession of the eastern wing from the rest of the country. The difference, however, lay here: China had attacked all external interference and pledged support to Pakistan against any threat.

In the weeks that followed, Indo-Pakistan relations worsened as millions of refugees swarmed into India adding to its economic and social strains, and India stepped up aid to Bangladesh guerillas. Chinese pronouncements did not indicate any perceptible shift in attitude to India or the Bangladesh crisis.

The annual report of India's Defence Ministry in July indicated a softening of India's attitude to China which had returned over 50 of its ambassadors to various capitals since October 1970 as part of its diplomatic offensive. The report, amidst tough references to Pakistan, for the first time in years skipped specific reference to China which was now referred to as only an "unfriendly" neighbour. In contrast, it cited Pakistan's "colonial designs" in the eastern wing and the "imperialist" role of its army. To Indian analysts, the report suggested an India less concerned about China's threat than in previous years. China's utterances on the Bangladesh crisis showed Peking less hostile to New Delhi than before and during the 1965 Indo-Pakistan war. In 1965, China had declared that Indian aggression against any of its neighbours was of concern to all its neighbours but this conviction was scarcely evident in Peking's statement on Bangladesh. Instead China had chosen to project the possibility of outside interference in Pakistan's internal affairs as a matter concerning all "justice loving countries of the world". In 1965 China had attacked a whole range of India's foreign and domestic policies but criticism was now limited to Indo-Pakistan issues. Lately, India had been spared the charge of forging an "anti-China clique" until recently a favourite Peking theme. However, China had kept up its charge that India was in league with the super powers, but this in turn, according to Indian analysts, pointed to a marked change in Peking's thinking: such charges appeared directed more at Moscow and Washington, particularly Moscow, than at New Delhi.

Yet the implicit condemnation of the Bangladesh freedom movement was half-hearted. At a banquet on 21 May in Peking to celebrate the 20th anniversary of Sino-Pakistani diplomatic relations, Vice Foreign Minister Han Nein Lung avoided reference to Bangladesh or to India. At the same dinner, the Pakistani ambassador had said that "today our very existence as a nation has been threatened by hostile outside interference.... China has come out with unflinching support for our national solidarity".[4]

Through the Bangladesh crisis there was no sign of new Chinese hostility towards India before the signing of the treaty with Soviet Union or in the weeks following it. When President Nixon announced his visit to Peking "to seek normalisation of relations between the two countries", India's reaction was none too friendly to China. External Affairs Minister Swaran Singh would not discount the possibility of a Sino-United States detente at the expense of other countries including India. Nevertheless he reiterated India's desire for normal relations with China. He said:

> I entirely agree. We should not only defuse but also try to normalise relations with China. However, normalisation does not depend on one party alone. There has to be a mutual normalisation. If and when the Government of the People's Republic of China will be willing and ready to take concrete steps towards normalisation we should be equally willing and ready to do so. It must, however, be clearly understood that normalisation can take place only on the basis of mutual respect of each other's integrity and sovereignty and on the principle of non-interference in the internal affairs. We welcome the change in the style of Chinese diplomacy which has been in evidence of late and we hope that it will also lead to a change in substance.[5]

Much to New Delhi's surprise, China did not react immediately to the 9 August treaty between India and Soviet Union but instead invited an Indian ping-pong team to visit Peking in October-November. The silence did not mean any change in the Chinese assessment of Soviet aims in the subcontinent. Chou En-lai told a visiting Yugoslav editor late in August that the subcontinent and the Indian Ocean were under the control of the two super powers and China would keep doing everything for liberating the area.[6] The first reaction to the treaty was from a low-level source and not before 3 September when a spokesman of the trade delegation visiting Guyana said: "China certainly does not regard the signing of the Indo-Soviet treaty as a friendly act so far as it is concerned." Han Suyin was told in Peking that the military clauses of the treaty "actually put India in a position of inferiority".[7]

On 20 November came the most authoritative Chinese reaction to the treaty, in the course of Chou's interview to Neville Maxwell. Chou said the draft of the treaty "had lain for two years in a drawer" of the Soviet foreign office. Soviet Union had "hastily concluded this treaty" after Nixon's visit to China was announced. "Its aim is to realise Brezhnev's Asian collective security system", which is directed against the countries to which Russia is hostile. But this aim is probably difficult to realise. There is no response from any other country. It expressed its readiness to sign similar treaties with other countries, but was rejected by them".[8]

China was convinced now that the treaty was directed against it to the extent it was part of the Soviet design to secure through bilateral treaties what it could not achieve through a collective plan. Chinese reaction to the Brezhnev plan had never been secret. Chou thought the treaty would not achieve the objectives of the Brezhnev plan. Discussing Bangladesh he said:

> If India should brazenly provoke a war, can it benefit from it and can the problems be solved? Once a war breaks out both sides, not just one, will incur losses. You know what our attitude will be if a war breaks between India and Pakistan.

We firmly support Pakistan against India's subversive and

aggressive activities. India would in the end taste the bitter fruit of its own making. And from then on there would be no tranquillity on the subcontinent.[9]

A forthright Chinese denunciation of the treaty as a "military alliance" with which Soviet "social imperialists" had encouraged "the Indian reactionaries to engage in subversive activities" in East Pakistan came on 27 November from Chiao Kuanhua, leader of the Chinese delegation to United Nations. It marked a basic change in China's attitude to India and the Bangladesh issue.

Soviet Attitude

Between the signing of the treaty on 9 August and the outbreak of the Indo-Pakistan war on 3 December, the Bangladesh crisis moved to inexorable logic. The change in the Chinese attitude followed a shift in the Soviet position, from one of equivocation on the secessionist demand and opposition to war. Soviet policy moved into focus with India's late in October after the treaty had been invoked to discuss Pakistan's military threat to India. These developments perhaps prompted the Chinese to assess the treaty anew.

The refugee influx had assumed forbidding proportions and India's hope of reversing it lay in what it called a political settlement of the Bangladesh issue to the satisfaction of its elected representatives. Indira Gandhi visited Moscow from 27 to 29 September and her communique with Alexei Kosygin called for a "political solution of the problems which had arisen there paying regard to the wishes, the inalienable rights, and lawful interests of the people of East Bengal as well as the speediest and safe return of the refugees to their homeland in conditions safeguarding their honour and dignity". Impressive as this identity of Indian and Soviet views on the nature of the solution contemplated was, the communique covered up serious differences between the two. The Russian text consistently referred to "East Pakistan" while the English text mentioned "East Bengal". An Indian commentator cited four pieces of evidence to establish that avoidance of war was the first and foremost Soviet objective.

First, the Soviet side had only noted and *not endorsed* Indira Gandhi's statement that India was "fully determined to take all steps to stop the inflow of refugees from East Bengal to India and to ensure that those refugees who are already in India return to their homes without delay". Second, Kosygin had told Indian correspondents before Indira Gandhi's departure that Soviet Union was opposed to India going to war with Pakistan even after all efforts to find a satisfactory solution through peaceful means had failed: Kosygin in fact had suggested that what was happening was Pakistan's internal affair brooking no interference from outside. Third, Podgorny, on a visit to New Delhi stressed on 1 October the need to prevent a further sliding towards a "military conflict" in the subcontinent and offered Soviet help towards an "equitable political settlement" in East Bengal. He also denounced "imperialist forces of aggression" responsible for "the flames of war and hostilities" all over the world. Fourth, Soviet Foreign Minister Gromyko agreed with his United States counterpart William Rogers on 20 September on the need to prevent further escalation of tension in the subcontinent.[10]

Indira Gandhi went round six Western capitals including Washington (24 October-13 November) to enlist support for India's stand on Bangladesh. Soviet Deputy Foreign Minister Firyubin visited New Delhi late in October for talks. His joint statement with the Indian side amounted to Soviet endorsement of the Indian threat perception and measures to meet it. Admittedly, the talks were held "in connection with the present tense situation in the Indian subcontinent which threatens the cause of peace in the region. The two sides were in full agreement in their assessment of the situation".[11]

The disclosure that the talks were held under Article IX of the treaty vested the statement with special significance. This Article is meant to be invoked only when either side faced external aggression.[12] India and Pakistan were drifting towards a confrontation. Overt Soviet support to India, in the context of the treaty obligation, added a new element to the situation.

By the end of October, Pakistan and Indian forces were confronting each other on the western borders and Pakistani forces were dangerously overstretched on the eastern borders and the Bangladesh guerillas were operating behind their lines, making an impact on the military situation there.

A high-level politico-military Pakistani delegation led by Z. A. Bhutto visited Peking from 5 to 8 November. Acting Foreign Minister Chi Peng-fei who received the delegation urged consultations between India and Pakistan to reduce tensions in the subcontinent and backed what he termed "the reasonable proposal" of Yahya Khan for the pull back of troops to a reasonable distance from the border. Chen wanted a non-military solution when he said the dispute should be settled "through consultations and not by resorting to forces". Chen also backed Pakistan on the Bangladesh crisis when he referred to the "struggle of the Pakistani people" against domestic secessionists. He however emphasised that a "reasonable settlement should be sought by the Pakistani people themselves". In what could be interpreted as a reference to Soviet Union he said, "Certain persons are truculently exerting pressure on Pakistan by exploiting tensions in the subcontinent in a wild attempt to achieve their ulterior motives." Chen pledged support to Pakistan against any aggression.[13]

But this could not have meant promise of direct Chinese intervention in an Indo-Pakistan war. The phrase used ("the Chinese Government and the people will resolutely support the Pakistan Government and people") was identical to the pledge China had repeatedly given North Vietnam, where there was no direct Chinese involvement in the fighting. Even Bhutto appeared to rule this out when he told newsmen in Peking that "any decision would be our own effort".[14]

HARDENED ATTITUDE

China's attitude to Bangladesh crisis became clearer on 20 November when delegate Fu Hao spoke in the Third Committee of the United Nations. Without mentioning India direct, he charged a "certain country" with intervention in Pakistan's internal affairs and carrying on subversive activities against it. He blamed India for the refugee influx, and compared the situation to that in 1959 when there was a revolt in Tibet. What was happening in East Pakistan was Pakistan's internal affair and should be settled only by the people of Pakistan. No other country had the right to interfere in it "under any pretext". "The so-called question of refugees from Pakistan came into being and developed into the present state due to a certain country's intervention in Pakistan's internal affairs, which has resulted in the present tension in the subcontinent. We hold that in order to attain reasonable settlement of the question of refugees from East Pakistan, the interference in Pakistan's internal affairs must be stopped first of all."[15] Fu seemed to imply that if the refugees were the main cause of the tension (as India tried to make out) India could discuss it with Pakistan but support to the secessionist demand must stop. India was no longer maintaining that it was not supporting the Bangladesh guerillas who had stepped up their activities from Indian sanctuaries. Following skirmishes between Pakistan and Indian troops on the eastern border Yahya Khan proclaimed a state of emergency on 23 November. It was full-scale war on 3 December. But in the Chinese reckoning the war had begun on 21 November when India was alleged to have committed aggression in the eastern wing.

A *People's Daily* article on 3 December set the pace for the Chinese stand later at the United Nations.

> The Indian government, backed and abetted by social imperialism, is plotting to create a 'Bangladesh' in East Pakistan in an attempt to divide Pakistan and realise its expansionist ambitions to annex East Pakistan....
>
> In fact the so-called 'Bangladesh' is entirely a sinister means of the Indian government to interfere in the internal affairs of Pakistan, to divide and subvert Pakistan....
>
> The Chinese people are quite familiar with such Indian government insiduous tricks as creating a 'Bangladesh', ... It is precisely the Indian Government which engineered a rebellion in China's Tibet region, ... created the so-called 'Tibetan refugee' issue and energetically antagonised China.[16]

On 4 December, United States requested an urgent session of the Security Council which voted 11 to 2 for an immediate cease-fire and withdrawal of foreign forces. The resolution was sponsored by United States, and China voted for it with reservations: the draft had failed to condemn "armed aggression on Pakistan committed by the Indian government with the support of Soviet Union and has failed to voice support for Pakistan's just struggle against aggression", and China was against the practice of despatching United Nations observers.[17]

Soviet Union vetoed this and a second resolution soon later. On the same day China voted against a Soviet resolution which called for a political settlement in East Bengal which would automatically bring a cessation of hostilities. Soviet Union and Poland voted for the resolution, 12 others including United States abstained, and China was the only member to oppose it. China tabled its own draft to condemn India's role in the conflict but before it could be taken up, the matter went to the General Assembly which on 7 December voted for an immediate cease-fire and withdrawal of foreign forces. The vote was overwhelmingly against India: 104 to 11 with 10 abstentions. Only Soviet Union, its East European allies, Cuba, India and Bhutan opposed it. Most of the small and medium countries voted against India. The matter went back to the Security Council where Soviet Union blocked international action until the military operations in East Pakistan were completed on 16 December. After the surrender of Dacca, India offered a unilateral ceasefire in the western sector with effect from 17 December, which Pakistan accepted.

The Security Council demanded on 22 December (Poland and Soviet Union abstaining) a durable cease-fire, cessation of hostilities and withdrawal of troops by India and Pakistan. India had recognised Bangladesh on 6 December and with the surrender of Dacca on 16 December, Bangladesh had become a reality. The issues between India and Pakistan no longer included Bangladesh.

A strong anti-Soviet line was clear in the Chinese pronouncements on Bangladesh. Chinese spokesmen repeatedly suggested in United Nations that Soviet support had made Indian action on Bangladesh possible, and brought in the question of China's own security. Ambassador Huang Hua had seen a threat to Tibet in India's stand on the refugees. "According to the logic of the Indian government, are they going to use them (Tibetan refugees in India) as a basis for committing invasion against China?"[18] A *People's Daily* commentary assailed Soviet support to India's stand but this reflected apprehensions on a threat from Soviet Union to China:

> *Tass* declared with ulterior motives that the Soviet Union cannot remain indifferent to the developments, considering also the circumstance that they are taking place in direct proximity of USSR's borders and, therefore, involve the interests of its security.... It is clear that you, the super power, in collusion with the Indian expansionists, have been bullying Pakistan. How could it be said to the contrary that the security of the Soviet Union is threatened. You occupied by armed force your neighbour Czechoslovakia defending 'security'. Now by making a special mention about 'indirect proximity of the USSR borders', are you going to take action? This is barefaced blackmail and intimidation.[19]

In the wake of Huang's poser to Soviet delegate Jacob Malik two days earlier, there was little doubt that the commentary was reflecting China's fears of a Soviet invasion of Sinkiang.[20] Huang had said:

> We would like to ask the distinguished representative of Soviet Union: The Soviet government engineered a counter revolutionary rebellion in China's Sinkiang province, carrying out subversion and splittist activities against China. The several tens of thousands of civilians who were forcibly taken away by you under coercion still remain in your hands, and you have used some of them for anti-China scheming activities. According to Mr. Malik's logic, with regard to Pakistani refugees, are you going to take it as a pretext for launching armed aggression against China?[21]

The most vocal Chinese support to Pakistan against "external" aggression came in the form of an official statement on 16 December, after Dacca had fallen. On the same day China handed a note to the Indian embassy in Peking protesting against some alleged border intrusions on 10 December. The statement called India a "brazen aggressor" which had refused to comply with the General Assembly resolution of 7 December, had interfered in Pakistan's internal affairs, and established a "puppet regime". It also said India's treaty with Soviet Union was a military alliance and India had been encouraged by massive Soviet military aid.

Throughout the final phase of the Bangladesh crisis India had been assuring itself that China would not intervene in the event of a war with Pakistan. Right in the middle of the war, an official spokesman, asked about any Chinese troop movements on the border, quipped, "Well, both sides are praying for the snow!" leading to speculation that India might have secured some assurance (possibly through a third country) from China that it would not intervene in a conflict. When the passes are under snow, China would have an alibi for not intervening because it cannot move troops across the Indian borders. India had diverted some of its mountain divisions on the China border for the operations in the war with Pakistan on the assumption that China would not intervene. Indira Gandhi said on 31 December at a press conference that the Chinese response to the whole situation was neither more nor less than she had expected.

According to American columnist Jack Anderson, however, the Soviets had promised India a diversionary front against China in Sinkiang if the Chinese intervened in the war. Quoting secret White House documents, Anderson claimed that United States and China had come close to getting involved in a land and sea war with Soviet Union at the height of the Indo-Pakistan conflict.

To go by these documents, on 11 December White House received reports that five Soviet naval vessels had entered the Bay of Bengal, and were located 180 miles south-west of Ceylon. Admiral John McCain, United States Pacific Fleet Commander, who reported this, asked Washington whether he could send planes (presumably from the aircraft carrier *Enterprise*) to shadow the Soviet ships. Washington authorised the "appropriate screening surveillance flights" if the United States naval task force (then steaming down the Straits of Malacca from the Tonkin Gulf) was directed to transit the Straits. The task force is said to have entered the Bay of Bengal on 13 December and unofficial sources in New Delhi reported its movement towards Chittagong in East Bengal to bail out the Pakistan army from the eastern theatre. However, no source accurately traced its movement and position until it turned back on 18 December.

According to Anderson as three naval movements were taking place in the Bay of Bengal, the CIA, quoting a "reliable clandestine source", reported that Yahya Khan had claimed that the Chinese ambassador in Islamabad had assured him of Chinese troop movement towards the border in 72 hours. But the CIA could not confirm the report. The United States Military Attache in Kathmandu reported to Washington that the Soviet attache had told his Chinese counterpart that China should not be too serious about intervention because the Soviet Union would react, using missiles, etc. The CIA also reported from Kathmandu that since 8 December the Chinese had been gathering weather data along the Himalayan area, presumably to determine whether the passes into India were fordable through the snows. From New Delhi, the CIA reported: "According to a reliable clandestine source, Mrs Gandhi told a leader of the Congress party that she had indications that the Chinese had intended to intervene and that this action might come in the Ladakh area." But Soviet Ambassador Nikolai Pegov is said to have promised the Indian government on 13 December that they would open a diversionary front against China in Sinkiang and would not allow the Seventh Fleet task force to intervene from the Bay of Bengal.[22]

INDO-PAKISTAN RELATIONS

It was a decisive war in the eastern wing, India achieving its military objective of forcing Pakistan to surrender so that the exiled Awami League leadership could return to Dacca, and with it the ten million refugees. As soon as Dacca surrendered, India offered a unilateral cease-fire which Pakistan accepted. According to Jack Anderson there was impatience among the Soviet officials with the slow progress of Indian military operations in the eastern wing which they had expected to be over in ten days. Soviet Minister Kuznetsev is reported to have pointed out to India that Soviet opposition to a cease-fire would become untenable the longer the war lasted in the eastern wing. The General Assembly had already voted for a cease-fire and withdrawal of troops on 7 December despite Soviet and Indian opposition.

Over 90,000 Pakistanis, including over 60,000 military personnel were taken war prisoners in the eastern wing. According to India these prisoners had surrendered to a joint command of the Indian forces and the Bangladesh liberation forces (the Mukti Bahini). In the months to come, the prisoners of war became an issue between India and Pakistan, India insisting that it was a trilateral issue involving Bangladesh also. Bangladesh insisted that Pakistan should recognise it first before the two could talk.

In the western wing, the overall balance was in India's favour. The 1948 cease-fire line in Jammu and Kashmir, supervised by U.N. Military Observers Group, no longer existed and the new line of actual control resulting from the war was to India's advantage. India had occupied over 5,000 square miles of territory across the international border, displacing a million of truncated Pakistan's 56 million people. Against this Pakistan was in occupation of a small area of Indian territory. Either side had taken war prisoners in the operations in the western wing but Pakistan had none in the eastern wing against over 90,000 Pakistanis who had surrendered there.

After the cease-fire, India's leverage with a defeated Pakistan lay in the relatively large area it had occupied in the western wing and the large number of prisoners in joint Indo-Bangladesh custody. But the Kashmir issue, which was basic to the conflict between India and Pakistan since 1947, remained. India tried to secure a package deal including a final settlement of the Kashmir question within a framework of durable peace. In the past, Pakistan had insisted on a package solution and opposed a step-by-step approach but the roles were reversed now. India opposed a step-by-step approach and insisted on a package deal through bilateral negotiations (which meant elimination of third party intervention, including that of the United Nations) and renunciation of use of force to settle any of the issues.

Before India and Pakistan could begin a dialogue, China tried to queer the pitch for India through the Nixon-Chou communique from Shanghai on 27 February 1972. China maintained that India and Pakistan, in accordance with United Nations resolutions, should immediately withdraw their forces to their respective territories and to their sides of the cease-fire line in Jammu and Kashmir. China also "firmly" supported the Pakistan government and people "in their struggle to preserve their independence and sovereignty and the people of Jammu and Kashmir in their struggle for the right of self-determination". This was not the first time China was talking of self determination for the people of Jammu and Kashmir. But in the context of Bangladesh's secession from Pakistan, the reference to Jammu and Kashmir in the Shanghai communique had an ominous ring for New Delhi.

India and Pakistan had a summit meet at Simla in June-July and agreed to withdraw troops to their respective territories except in Jammu and Kashmir where they agreed to observe the actual line of control that obtained on 17 December 1971 (when the cease-fire took effect) pending a settlement of the Kashmir question without prejudice to each other's position on it. In effect, the two countries agreed to a step-by-step approach to normalisation of relations. The repatriation of prisoners who had surrendered in the eastern wing was not discussed and by implication Pakistan agreed that it was a trilateral issue concerning Bangladesh and therefore would have to await its recognition of Bangladesh. The agreement provided for meetings between representatives of the two sides before the next summit. India failed in its objective at Simla to the extent it could not pull off a package deal. The accord on withdrawal of troops was a tangible gain for Pakistan because it meant the return of territory.

The prisoners of war issue got linked with the question of Pakistani recognition of Bangladesh because Sheikh Mujibur Rehman had made such recognition the precondition for any talks with Pakistan. Over 80 countries had recognised Bangladesh when it sought admission to United Nations in August and Pakistan opposed the move. China vetoed Bangladesh entry to the world body on 25 August. China punctuated it—its first veto since its entry into the world body in October 1971—with a vituperative attack on Soviet Union and India, in that order. Ambassador Huang Hua said "Soviet social imperialism" was playing the "most insiduous role in South Asia" and that India, when it concluded "an aggressive military alliance" with Soviet Union, had "stripped off its own cloak of non-alignment.... The sole purpose of Soviet social imperialism is to further control India and Bangladesh, to expand the spheres of her influence and bully Pakistan at will."[23]

SINO-SOVIET HOSTILITY

Three days later, Vice-Foreign Minister Chio Kuan-hua, leading a delegation to Pakistan, said "a big power is encouraging its stooge to create trouble for China and Pakistan.... It is doing so because it possesses atomic weapons but it cannot frighten us." [24]

These two statements taken together identified China's principal target. It was neither India nor Bangladesh. It was Soviet Union whose treaty with India was a hostile military alliance in Peking's view. India, through its treaty with Bangladesh, linked Bangladesh and Soviet Union. This created a subsystem in the Indian peninsula.

Soviet diplomatic, economic and military support to India has long been an issue in Sino-Soviet ideological dispute. China had seen the convergence of super power interests on India as part of the Soviet-United States plan for an Asian confrontation against it. When United States sought normal relations with China it was admitting its failure to quarantine it through military pacts and alliances. The SEATO was disintegrating. China now saw the danger of a new collective security system for Asia aimed against it. (As late as 20 March, Soviet party chief Brezhnev revived his three-year-old collective security plan in so many words when he sought a new role for Soviet Union in Asia on the ground that nearly two thirds of Soviet territory was in the Asian continent.[25]

After the Ussuri clashes in March 1969, even as talks on the border dispute with Soviet Union went on, China foresaw a wide-ranging and indefinite conflict with Soviet Union and a threat from a dynamic Japan projecting itself militarily and politically in Asia. China's immediate foreign policy goals were: to secure United States withdrawal from Asia; reduce Soviet influence in Asia and the Third World in general; and to prevent the emergence of Japan as a military power and a super power. Tactically, China needed greater flexibility within the framework of its foreign policy aims to deal with the immediate threat it visualised from Soviet Union. China wanted to ensure that a United States-Soviet detente in Europe, when translated into an entente would not reduce its position into one of subordination to the super powers.

China's response to United States' overtures leading to Nixon's visit to Peking in February 1972 was a tactical manoeuvre within its foreign policy aims to counter the Soviet drive for influence in Asia. When Nixon's visit materialised, Soviet Union had signed a treaty with India, pulled off the four-power agreement on Berlin, and had backed the emergence of Bangladesh. China's achievements were more impressive. Making use of the fractured consensus in United States policy, it had gained entry into United Nations on a landslide vote (76 for, 35 against and 17 abstentions) on 27 October, got Taiwan expelled from the world body, and was rallying the small and medium countries of the Third World against the super powers. United States tried to develop a triangular relationship by seeking normal relations with China on one hand and continuing the process of detente with Soviet Union. Nixon visited Moscow in May and signed a series of agreements including one on strategic arms limitation. China was to pull off a bigger diplomatic coup at the end of September when Japan's Prime Minister Tanaka visited Peking to seek normal relations with China and recognised Taiwan as a part of China. A new relationship had emerged in Asia and the Pacific. Asia's most powerful military nation and Asia's most economically powerful nation were on the road to a detente much to the discomfiture of Soviet

Union, which has been seeking normal relations with Japan.

The Brezhnev plan in 1969, which aimed at enlisting India and Japan among others in a front against China, was the Soviet answer to the Chinese war against "social imperialism" declared at the ninth party congress in April 1969. A treaty with India was the Soviet response to United States overtures to China for a detente.

The assumption that China would be forced to mend its fences with India because the latter had a treaty relationship with Soviet Union has been belied by events. The treaty in fact reacted on China and hardened its attitude to the Bangladesh issue. China's attitude to India is the outcome of a more complex policy and largely the function of the Sino-Soviet ideological dispute which had now taken the form of open hostility at the state level. United States and Soviet Union have no border or territorial dispute between them and their forces have never clashed anywhere anytime. But China and Soviet Union have a complicated border dispute and their forces have clashed on the border.

The course of Sino-Indian relations will be determined by the outcome of the Sino-Soviet hostility unless China is convinced of India's ability to play an independent role outside the influence of the super powers. China is a factor in the normalisation of the situation in the subcontinent restructured with the emergence of Bangladesh.

Notes

[1] R.K. Nehru, "Lead for Detente," *Weekly Round Table*, 25 June 1962.
[2] *Ibid*.
[3] Article in *Foreign Affairs* quarterly, reported by Press Trust of India, 20 September 1972.
[4] "Ram and the Dragon," *Far Eastern Economic Review*, 7 August 1971.
[5] Lok Sabha, 20 July 1972.
[6] *The Mail*, 28 August 1971.
[7] *The Indian Express*, New Delhi, 20 October 1971.
[8] *Sunday Times*, 5 December 1971.

[9] *Ibid.*
[10] Girilal Jain, "Indo-Soviet Discussions," *The Times of India*, 6 October 1971.
[11] *The Times of India*, 27 October 1971.
[12] Article IX reads: "Each high contracting party undertakes to abstain from providing any assistance to any third party that engages in armed conflict with the other party. In the event of either party being subjeted to an attack or a threat thereof, the high contracting parties shall immediately enter into mutual consultations in order to remove such threat and to take appropriate effective measures to ensure peace and the security of their countries."
[13] *The Hindu*, 8 November 1971.
[14] *Ibid.*
[15] *The Indian Express*, Madras, 21 November 1971.
[16] NCNA, 3 December 1971.
[17] *Ibid.*, 6 December 1971.
[18] *Ibid.*
[19] NCNA, 7 November 1971.
[20] G.P. Deshpande, "China's Stand on Bangla Desh in UN," *China Report*, November-December 1972.
[21] NCNA, 7 December 1971.
[22] "U.S. and China were close to war with Russia," *The Hindu*, 11 January 1972.
[23] *The Times of India*, 27 August 1972.
[24] *Ibid.*, 29 August 1972.
[25] *The Hindu*, 21 March 1972.

Bibliography

The principal sources on which this study is based are given in the notes to the text. Therefore, what follows is essentially a selective recapitulation of those notes.

Though this study does not claim to be a complete history of Sino-Indian relations or an analysis of the Tibet question or of the merits of the border dispute, certain background reading can be listed here for the benefit of those who feel the need for it.

On Sino-Indian relations, the best chronological listing of the events up to 1962 can be found in *Leading Events in Indo-China Relations 1947-62*, Ministry of External Affairs, Government of India, New Delhi, 1963. K.M. Panikkar's *In Two Chinas: Memoirs of a Diplomat*, Allen and Unwin, London, 1961, provides an interesting insight into India's China policy during a transitionary period. Of the same genre are the memoirs of another Indian diplomat, K.P.S. Menon's *Flying Troika*, Oxford University Press, London, 1963.

On the conflict of Sino-Indian interests in Tibet and China's policy to the Himalayan border states there has been a torrent of studies, which incidentally are relevant to the merits of the Sino-Indian border dispute. Some of them are: Margaret W. Fisher, Leo E. Rose, and Robert A. Huttenback, *Himalayan Battleground: Sino-Indian Rivalry in Ladakh*, Praeger, New York, 1963; George N. Patterson, *Peking Versus Delhi*, Praeger, 1964; Alstair Lamb, *Britain and Chinese Central Asia: The Road to Lhasa*, London, Routledge and Kegan Paul, 1960; Dorothy Woodman, *Himalayan Frontiers*, Barne and Rockliff London, 1969. The Chinese case is documented in the official Peking publication, *The Question of Tibet*, Foreign Languages Press, Peking, 1959. The most authoritative Indian pronouncement on the question of Tibet and related matters are to be found in *Prime Minister on Sino-Indian Relations*, Government of India, New Delhi, published in two volumes, 1961 and 1963. Among the numerous articles, these might be useful here: George N. Patterson, "Recent Chinese policies in Tibet and Towards the Himalayan Border States," *China Quarterly*, no. 12, October-December 1962; R.A. Huttenback, "A Historical Note on the Sino-Indian Dispute over Aksai-chin," *China Quarterly*, no. 18, April-June 1964; Alfred P. Rubin, "The Sino-Indian Border Dispute," *The International and Comparative Law Quarterly*, vol. 9, January 1960, and L.C. Green, "Legal Aspects of the Sino-Indian Border Dispute," *China Quarterly*, no. 3, July-September 1960.

The course of the dispute itself is well documented by both the sides. Useful here are: *Documents on the Sino-Indian Boundary Question*, Foreign Languages Press, Peking, 1960; *The Sino-Indian Boundary Question* (Enlarged Edition), Foreign Languages Press, Peking, 1962; *Notes, Memoranda and Letters Exchanged and Agreements Signed Between the Governments of India, and China*, White Paper, Ministry of External Affairs, Government of India, New Delhi, 1959 onwards (cited as "White Paper" in the notes), a continuing publication; Report of the *Officials of the Government of India and the People's Republic of China on the Boundary Question*, Government of India, New Delhi, 1961 (cited as "Report" in the notes).

As for studies on the dispute, W.F. Wan Eckelen, *India's Foreign Policy and Border Dispute With China*, Martinirs Nijhoff, The Hague, 1964; J.A. Rowland, *History of Sino-Indian Relations*, Van Nostrand, Princeton, 1967; Neville Maxwell, *India's China War*, Jaico, Bombay, 1970, together provide a good wrap-up.

India as a factor in the Sino-Soviet ideological conflict is the focus of this study of Sino-Indian relations. And there is no dearth of material. To list a few: Howard L. Boorman and others, *Moscow-Peking Axis, Strengths and Strains*, Harper, New York, 1957; Donald S. Zagoria, *The Sino-Soviet Conflict 1956-61*, Princeton, 1962; Edward Crankshaw, *The New Cold War: Moscow vs. Peking*, Penguin, Harmondsworth, 1963; Geoffrey Hudson, Richard Lowenthal, and Roderick MacFarquhar, *The Sino-Soviet Dispute*, Praeger, New York, 1961; and Willlam E. Griffith, *The Sino-Soviet Rift*, Allen and Unwin, London, 1963.

This study has relied on the Communist Party of India's documents and official statements of the Communist Party of Soviet Union and the Communist Party of China for its interpretation of the border dispute in terms of the larger ideological conflict. The Sino-Soviet polemics are extremely useful but there is some very good documentation in David Floyd, *Mao Against Khrushchev*, Pall Mall London, 1964.

On Indo-Soviet relations, Allen Stein, *India and Soviet Union*, Chicago and London, 1969, is by far the best study. J.A. Naik, *Soviet Policy Towards India*, Vikas, New Delhi, 1970, and Devendra Kaushik, *Soviet Relations with India and Pakistan*, Vikas, New Delhi, 1971, are unihibitedly pro-Soviet.

Indo-Pakistan and Sino-Pakistan relations are relevant to this study. Z.A. Bhutto, *The Myth of Independence*, Oxford University Press, London, 1968, and B.N. Goswami, *China and Pakistan*, Allied Bombay, 1971, are useful references.

On the Sino-Soviet border dispute, Dennis J. Doolin, *Territorial Claims in the Sino-Soviet Conflict*, Hoover Institution on War, Revolution and Peace, Stanford, 1965, and W.A. Douglas Jackson, *Russo-Chinese Borderland: Zone of Peace Contact or Potential Conflict*, Von Nostrand, Princeton, 1962, provide a great deal of insight.

Overall, books found useful for this study included William C. Hinton, *Communist China in World Politics*, Hughton Mifflin, Boston, 1966; Michael Brecher, *India and World Politics: Krishna Menon's View of the World*, Oxford University Press, London, 1968; B.N. Mullik, *The Chinese Betrayal*, Allied, Bombay, 1971; Kuldip Nayar, *Between the Lines*, Allied, Bombay, 1969; and Lorne J. Kavics, *India's Quest for Security: Defence Policies 1957-1965*, University of California, Berkeley, 1967.

Index

Afro-Asian Conference in Bandung, 1955, 7, 20, 41-47, 51, 61, 126
Air Umbrella Plan, 151-54
Aksai-Chin area, dispute over, 1-5, 96-101, 106, 213, 214
Algiers Afro-Asian Conference, 10
Asia, United States' attempt to dominate, 20, 26, 35, 50
Asian Conference in New Delhi, 153
Aswan Dam Project, 42, 89

Baghdad Pact, 26, 27, 36
Bandarnaike, Sirimao, 6, 17, 143-47
Bandung Conference, see Afro-Asian Conference,
Bangladesh, 205-08, 215; China's attitude to, 15, 16, 216-19; emergence of, 2; recognised by 80 countries, 229-30; Soviet attitude to, 219-22; United Nations' attitude to, 222,227; U.N. resolution on, 224; withdrawal of Indian troops from, 17
Basu, Jyoti, 183
Bell Mission, 169
Bhoothalingam, 5, 152, 155
Bhutto, Z.A., 16, 222
Blitz, 137
Bongor (Indonesia), Five Prime Ministers' meeting at, 41
Brezhnev, Leonid, 13, 165, 197, 230
Brezhnev Plan, see Collective Security Plan
Bulganin, N.A., 51, 52, 54
Burma, 11, 24, 37, 51, 63, 142, 184, 185, 200, 202

Camp David Summit, 71, 77, 84, 89
Cariappa, K.M., 31, 32

Chagla, M.C., 186, 187, 189
Chavan, Y.B., 155
Chen Lu Chih, 187
CENTO, 26, 36, 39, 148, 159, 191
Chiang Kai-shek, 27, 70
Chen Yi, 113, 115, 118, 164
Chi Peng-fei, 222
Chiao Kuan hua, 220
China, Republic of, admission to the United Nations, 27; Soviet Union role in, 27; attitude towards Bangladesh issue, 15-16; China and the Korean war, 27; emergence of, 6, 20-21; foreign policy of, 6-12, 200-06; Cultural Revolution, 11, 177, 185; industrialisation, 20; Lin Piao's Thesis, 10-11, 177-78; Nehru's visit to, 54; and the *Panch Shila*, 36-38; peace offensive during the Bandung Phase, 7; Soviet military aid for United action in Vietnam, 9-10; Third World and, 8-9, 14-18; and Vietnam war, 10
Chou En-lai, 6, 17, 32, 36-39, 44-47, 60-63, 68-70, 77, 83, 85, 112, 119, 124, 142, 144, 160, 163, 165, 183, 200, 214, 216
CIA, 227
Coalition Ministries, in Kerala and West Bengal, 178, 179
Collective Security Plan, 199-200, 219, 230, 231
Colombo Conference, 1962, 41, 142-45; and its proposals, 142-48; India's conditions for formulating the cease-fire, 146; Nehru's Statement in the Lok Sabha, 145; Parliament's support for, 152

COMECON, 200
Commonwealth Prime Minister's Conference, 56
Communist Party of China, 73, 132
Communist Party of India, 23, 51-56, 77-80, 90, 131, 153-54; formulation of, 154; split in, 22, 54, 155-59
Communist Party of India (Marxist), 158, 178-81; Maoist line for, 181-85
Communist Party of Indonesia, support to the Government's foreign policy, 51
Congress Party, 178-79, 203; split in, 13-14

Dalai Lama, 65, 72
Dange, S.A., 128, 129, 132, 133, 180
Desai, Morarji, 190
Devaluation of the Indian rupee, 172, 173
Dhar, D.P., 194, 209, 214
Dinesh Singh, 199-200
Dulles, John F., 25, 36
Dullesian Doctrine, 12, 38, 199
Dutt, R. Palme, 24, 54

Eighty-one Parties Conference in 1960, 128
Eisenhower, General Dwight, 18, 26, 71, 77, 84, 90
Elections, Fourth General, CPM's assessment of election results, 178-80
European Party Congresses in 1962-63, 129, 133

Five Principles, *see Panch Shila*
Five Year Plans, 12
Foreign policy of India, 12, 52, 53, 95, 126, 173-74; features of, 33; CPI support to, 54; non-alignment, 21, 25, 122, 151, 163; Panch Shila, 36-38; *Pravda's* praise for, 54-55; opposition of SEATO, 38; Indo-Bangladesh Treaty, 17; and Indo-China, 25; and the Korean war, 24-25, 33; relations with Pakistan, 5, 6, 227-32, Simla Agreement, 3, 6, 17-18, 229-30; Sino-Indian relations, 16, 28, 34, 40; *see also* Sino-Indian border dispute; relations with Soviet Union, 13, 21, 51-52, 173-74, economic aid, 8, 12, 52, 88, 91, Indo-Soviet Treaty, 13, 15-16, 26-27, 191-93, 208-11, 215, 219, 221; relations with United States, 91-92, 150-51, 169-74; PL-480 foodgrains, 92, 169, technical cooperation problem, 25, arms aid, 91; relations with Vietnam, 170-71, 173, 174; relations with Yugoslavia, 164

Galbrith, J.K., 49, 122, 123
Gandhi, Indira, 5, 13, 16, 66, 71, 170-74, 190-94, 199-200, 205-09, 213, 214, 220, 226
Geneva Conference, 36, 39, 40, 41, 44
Ghosh, Ajoy, 53-56, 65, 73, 75-78, 84
Goa liberation, 120; Chinese support to, 110; US role in, 110; Soviet attitude to, 52
Grechkov, Marshal, 194
Gromyko, Andrei, 197, 209, 221
Guam doctrine, 197, 198

Harriman, Averell, 123, 149
Ho Chi minh, 39
Hsinhua, New China News Agency, 6, 66
Huang Hua, 225, 230
Humphery, Hubert, 159, 171, 173
Husain, Dr Zakir, 192,193

Indo-China, China's six-point plan, 37; India's role, 25
Indonesia, 11, 24, 37, 51, 142, 184, 200

Jagjivan Ram, 204
Jana Sangh, 73, 111
Jha, L.K., 209
Johnson, 163, 169, 170

Kashmir issue, 1-5, 148-51, 155, 160, 162-64,
Kaul, Lt. Gen. B.M., 117
Khan, Ayub, 148-50, 167, 191
Khan, Yahya, 192, 205, 215, 216, 222, 223, 227
Khrushchev, N.S., 8, 51, 52, 54, 57, 71, 76, 77, 84, 88, 89, 95, 109, 124, 133, 148, 160, 163
Kissinger, Henry, 11, 14, 15, 207, 214
Korean war, 6, 24-27, 30, 33, 35
Kosygin, Alexei, 174, 191, 192, 195, 220, 221
Kripalani, J.B., 111
Krishnamachari, T.T., 151, 155
Krishna Menon, V.K., 44, 45, 70, 117, 119, 131
Kutch dispute, 163, 164

Ladakh Sector, 1, 60, 64, 85, 90, 108, 142, 143, 155, 177
Lin Piao, 101, 201, 202

Macmillan, Harold, 124, 149, 151
Manila (SEATO) Treaty, 41
Mao Tse-tung, 89, 202; *New Democracy*, 23
Marxism-Leninism, 23, 127, 184
MEDO (Middle East Defence Organization), 160
MiG project, 153, 154
Military aid, British and US arms mission to India, 123-24, 141, 149, 151-55; Soviet aid, 130, 133, 135-36, 154-55
Molotov, V.M., 42, 51
Moscow Conference of Communist Parties, 1960, 72, 78
Mountbatten Award, 22; Moscow's assessment of, 22-23
Mountbatten, Lord, 155
Mujibur Rehman, Sheikh, 205, 207, 229

Naga and Mizo, Peking support to, 180
Namboodripad, E.M.S., 158
Nasser, 42, 46, 173
NATO, 35, 110
Naxalbari movement, 182-84, 187
NEFA Sector, 1, 5, 60, 61, 64, 69, 70, 83, 85, 86, 93, 142
Nehru-Chou declaration in 1954, 37
Nehru, Jawaharlal, 1, 5, 20, 21, 24-39, 42, 43, 46, 50, 51, 54, 56, 59-66, 70-72, 80, 83, 85, 87, 89, 91, 93, 104, 110, 114-16, 119, 121, 125, 141, 145, 152, 160, 162, 188
Nehru, R.K., 113, 214
Neutral Nations Repatriation Commission for Korean War Prisoners, 133
New Age, 89
Ne Win, 145, 184
New York Times, 172
Nixon, Richard, 14, 17, 25, 23
Nkrumah, 145
Non-aligned Conference at Belgrade, 1961, 151; 1964, 148
Nuclear test ban treaty, 109, 156, 158

Operation Shiksha, 54,
Organiser, 34

Pakistan, foreign policy during Ayub regime, 160-61; entry into the Middle East Defence Organization (MEDO), 160; member of Baghdad Pact, 26-27, 36, CENTO, 26-27, 36, 39, 92, 159-60, 191, and SEATO, 26-27, 36, 39, 44, 52, 131, 159, 160; relations with China, 4, 12, 159-64, Soviet Union, 12-13, 161, 190-95; US

defence pact in 1954, 23, 25-27, 36, 41, 23; and Turkey, 26, 36
P'an Tzu-li, 67, 113
Panch Shila, 7, 20, 43, 51, 61, 67, 126; principles of, 33-39; Nehru-Chou doctrine of, 44 45; Soviet response to, 51
Panikkar, K.M., 27, 28, 31, 32, 60
Parthasarathy, G., 94, 204, 214
Patel, Sardar, 24
Peking Review, 179
People's Daily, 40, 43, 68, 72, 80, 131, 132, 135, 145, 163, 165, 167, 168, 180, 184, 216, 223, 225
Ping-pong diplomacy, 14; *see also* Sino-US *detente*
Podgorny, Nikolai, 221, 216
Portugal, member of NATO, 110
Praja Socialist Party, 34, 111
Pravda, 51, 54, 55, 74, 124, 125, 128, 129, 136, 164, 195, 196
Prince Nordom Sihanouk, 43,

Radhakrishnan, Dr. S., 155, 186
Red Flag, 76, 95, 132, 185
Rusk, Dean, 150, 152, 159

Sabry, 146
Sandys, Duncan, 123, 149, 150
Sanjivayya, D., 210
Shastri, Lal Bahadur, 148, 163, 166-68, 173
Sikkim-Tibet boundary, 93, 189
Sino-Burmese border treaty, 95
Sino-Ceylon Communique, 6, 17
Sino-Indian border dispute, Longju clash, 69-74, 77, 83, 89, 108; Chen Yi remarks in his Geneva interview about Chinese refusal to withdraw, 113, 116; China proposes talks, 92-96; Chou's letter to Nehru November proposals, 86-87; CPI delegation to Peking for negotiations, 84-85; demand for breaking diplomatic relations with China, 114; failure of Chou-Nehru talks, 108; ideological dimension of, 2, 6-12; Indian approaches to, 5-6 87-92; Indian Government's assessment of the Chinese 2 January 1960 note, 93; India's forward policy, 109-10, 112; India's protest against the Chinese maps, 62; McMahon Line, 1, 5, 60-64, 112, 124-25, 130; maps, 60-61; Nehru's press conference, 93-94; Nehru's letter to Chou En-lai, 62; Nehru's three suggestions, 85; shift in Nehru's stand, 63; six rounds of talks with the Soviet ambassador in Peking, 94-95; Soviet support to, 21, 88; US response to, 21
Sino-Nepalese agreement on border, 95
Sino-Soviet border dispute, 11, 71, 101-06, 133
Sino-Soviet ideological differences, 2, 8, 13, 50, 51, 56, 58, 74-76, 88, 89, 136, 137, 155, 189, 230-32
Sino-US *detente*, 11, 14, 15, 70, 214, 215, 229, 231
SEATO, 6, 26, 27, 36, 38-40, 44, 46, 51, 68, 131, 159, 230
Soviet-Japanese relations, 10
Soviet-United States *detente*, 77
Stalin, 25,
Suez crisis, 56
Swaran Singh, 205, 207, 213
Swatantra Party, 73, 92, 111

Taiwan issue, 6, 27, 33, 36, 41-43, 45, 76, 77, 77, 134, 160, 204, 231
Tass, 74, 75, 89, 136, 225
Third World, 7, 11, 15, 16, 18, 58, 177, 178, 231
Tibet, revolt in, 1, 8, 27-33, 38, 63 65-70, 160; Sino-Indian agreement on, 30, 31-35, 41, 60, 65, 111, 113

Titoite theory, 23
Tito, Marshal, 54, 133,
Togliatti, Palmiro, 133
Truman, 27
Truman's Four Point Programme, 25
Turkey-Pakistan military alliance, 42, 43

Ulbricht, Walter, 129
Unna, Warren, 112
U Nu, 38

Zhdanov's two-camp theory, 23-24, 53

1V02M1802 30:00